A SOLDIER'S
VIEW OF EMPIRE

A SOLDIER'S
VIEW OF EMPIRE

The Reminiscences of James Bodell,

1831–92

Edited by Keith Sinclair

THE BODLEY HEAD
LONDON   SYDNEY
TORONTO

British Library Cataloguing
in Publication Data
Bodell, James
A soldier's view of Empire.
1. Great Britain—Army—Military life—History
2. Soldiers—Commonwealth of Nations—History
I. Title II. Sinclair, Keith
355.1'092'4   0767
ISBN 0–370–30224–9

© Andrew Newton 1982
Printed in Great Britain for
The Bodley Head Ltd
9 Bow Street, London WC2E 7AL
by Redwood Burn Ltd, Trowbridge
set in Linotron plantin
by Western Printing Services Ltd.
First published 1982

CONTENTS

ILLUSTRATIONS

Thanks are due to the following for permission to reproduce copyright photographs: Blackburn Museum and Art Gallery, Blackburn, Lancashire, 1 a & b; BBC Hulton Picture Library, 2; The Archives Office of Tasmania, 3; The State Library of Victoria, 4 and 5; The Auckland Institute and Museum, 6; Alexander Turnbull Library, Wellington, 7, 8, 9 and 10; Tauranga City Council, 11. Other photographs are in the possession of Mr Andrew Newton, Leicester.

Introduction

James Bodell was born near Nottingham, England, in 1831. His parents were poor people, his father a stocking-knitter. He had three years at school, worked at various jobs, and enlisted in the army at the age of sixteen—pretending to be seventeen, which was neither his first nor his last untruth. He was sent to join his regiment, the 59th, the 'Lilywhites', in Ireland during the rebellion of Smith O'Brien and his men in 1848. This was the year of European revolution. Later the regiment went to Hong Kong where most of them died of malaria and other diseases, or were invalided home. He bought himself out of the army and went to Van Diemen's Land (renamed Tasmania in 1855), where he kept a hotel. He found the population of Hobart a very rough lot—and, as an ex-soldier, he knew a great deal about rough and tough people. Many of them were 'ticket of leave' men or women, or 'pass-holders'. He became 'disgusted' with the atmosphere of a recent convict settlement—transportation had been abolished as recently as 1853. In 1856 he moved to Victoria where the great gold rush had begun in 1851 and acquired other hotels on the gold fields at Maryborough and in the vicinity. He left Tasmania with £1200 in gold in a money-belt. In Victoria he made much more, and lost it again, from unwise speculations made in a period of excessive drinking, as he later frankly confessed. In 1863 he volunteered to serve in the Waikato Militia in New Zealand, during the Anglo-Maori wars, indeed, just as the British invasion of the Waikato district was beginning. This was a great come-down in the world, of which he was bitterly aware. He was made a sergeant, but he continued drinking too much and was reduced to the ranks after a court martial.

Bodell missed the major actions but was under fire in a skirmish or two. In 1866 he was discharged in the tiny settlement and armed camp of Tauranga. As a 'military settler' he was given a town lot and fifty acres for a farm. At first times were hard but, as we shall

(9)

see, he was an outstanding 'pioneer' and eventually he made a great deal of money. He also became Mayor of the town. He made two return trips to visit his family in Leicester.

In about 1881 Bodell began to write his reminiscences.[1] Since he had had only three years at school and was never a bookish man, this was an unusual and ambitious undertaking. However, by the late eighties he had succeeded in writing 241 pages and a further seventy-two recounting events during a trip to England in 1883. Portions of this manuscript, abbreviated and rewritten, possibly by a journalist but perhaps by Bodell, or, alternatively, of an earlier and briefer draft version, were published under the initials 'J. B.' in the Tauranga newspaper, the *Bay of Plenty Times*, in 1888.[2] A further twenty-four pages were written in 1891.

The handwritten manuscript was sent to England, presumably after Bodell's death in 1892, and remained in the possession of successive members of his family. In 1978, on the death of his mother, it came into the possession of Mr Andrew Newton of Leicester, James Bodell's great-great-nephew, who offered it to the Bodley Head for publication.

Bodell's reminiscences are extraordinarily accurate. The dates of battles in the Anglo-Maori wars could have been looked up, but frequently he recalls the exact date of events which he could not have checked in books—for instance the date of a fire in Hong Kong, or of his arrival in New Zealand. The accuracy of his recollections is confirmed by official documents, such as birth, marriage and death certificates, in every country in which he lived, the official records of his regiment, lists of Australian hotel licences and ratepayers, New Zealand army records, and so on. It might be thought that he kept a diary over many years, but this seems unlikely. It is hard to believe that a soldier in the Transport Corps of the 1st Waikato Militia, living a very hard life, carried diaries with him. Bodell records that he lost his box of civilian clothing, boots and papers which he had left for sake-keeping in the barracks at Otahuhu, just south of Auckland. On the other hand, if Bodell

---

[1] James Bodell/Annie, 2 January 1882, letter in the possession of Mr Andrew Newton. By this date Bodell's manuscript reminiscences had reached 1863, when he came to New Zealand.

[2] 16 January, 27 January, 5 March, 12 March, 31 March, 3 April, 16 April, 23 April 1888. A microfilm is held in the Tauranga Public Library.

relied on his memory, it was remarkable, although he did make a few mistakes.

Editing James Bodell's reminiscences has posed a few problems which should be mentioned. He could not spell, and most pages of his manuscript contain various spelling errors, as well as mistakes in grammar and syntax. Nor did he know how to punctuate sentences or to use inverted commas or brackets. After much thought, I decided that there was no point in publishing Bodell's memoirs exactly as he wrote them; in demonstrating that a common soldier was not very literate.[3] A photograph (Plate 15) of a page in his handwriting demonstrates this well enough. Moreover, his manuscript is not always easy to follow because it is, at times, not immediately clear where sentences begin and end. Consequently his sentences have been given initial capitals and end stops and his spelling has been corrected. Sometimes that involved much research, for his spelling of place names, in particular, in the various countries he visited, was very uncertain. However, he had a good ear, and generally his spelling approximates to the usual pronunciation. Bodell used capital letters indiscriminately and inconsistently for nouns, verbs, adjectives or prepositions. These have been retained only for nouns. Finally, there are a very few places where, because of faulty syntax or lapses of concentration, his meaning is unclear. Apart from spelling corrections these passages have been published as he wrote them.

Bodell concluded his manuscript by writing that his reminiscences, 'if properly compiled and arranged should make a good-sized book'. He wrote that in September 1891. Now, in 1982, they do. Moreover, in the opinion of those who have read it, it makes a fascinating and very rare kind of book. For one thing, it has a quality of real autobiography: it is extremely frank. There are aspects of Bodell's life which he almost ignores, notably his domestic and sex life, but he is uninhibited in relating the life of the common soldiery, whether drinking or looting or drilling. Bodell's reminiscences reveal a man's world. He leaves his Irish lover in Ireland. His first wife, married in Hong Kong, vanishes in Australia. We do not read—and do not know—where or when she died,

---

[3] About forty per cent of the regular army were illiterate or could read but not write. The infantry was the least literate arm of the service. See A. R. Skelley, *The Victorian Army at Home*, Montreal, 1977, pp. 85 ff.

though he is registered as a widower when he marries Jane Munro in New Zealand in 1866. When he travels to England in 1883, and again in 1891, he does not take his wife or any of his four step-children. He expresses little or no sympathy or understanding of women—but is very upset indeed when his servant, William Marston, is accidentally killed in Tasmania and he has to pay for him to be, first, admitted to hospital and then buried. Convicts were admitted and buried free, but not free men, which shocked Bodell. 'I was so disgusted with the whole affair, I was determined to sell out and leave such a country.'

James Bodell's reminiscences give us a very clear picture of the qualities that made a successful soldier—he rose to sergeant in Hong Kong as well as falling to private in New Zealand—and settler. He was rough and tough, unsentimental, unscrupulous. He was extremely determined: as a new recruit he refuses an order to clean some officers' boots and cutlery. He was very strong: five feet ten and eighteen stone as a grown man. In the gold fields he captures a villain who tries to garrotte him. One quality he had which was presumably not very common in the ranks of the British Army: he had a keen desire to make money and a natural business instinct which enabled him to achieve it. He began making money when he was a soldier in Hong Kong by weaving horse nets. He wrote, 'I must say all through my career in the Service or out of it I have always been anxious to make money and never begrudged working hard for it.' In New Zealand, he wrote, he used to work fourteen to sixteen hours a day.

He possessed another quality which made him an outstanding example of a pioneering settler: he was extremely resourceful: he could turn his hand to anything. In the course of his life in Australasia he worked at an astonishing number of occupations: gold prospector, brewer, publican, photographer, and many other jobs. The early settlers had to be good at do-it-yourself.

There cannot be many accounts of life in the British Army and the Empire written by a common soldier. His uninhibited prose often has some of the qualities of oral history—we can hear the common people speaking. He takes part in many important events, which have been recorded in the histories of the various colonies, but rarely seen from his point of view. He shows us the Empire as seen from below.

There has been a prolific scholarly literature since the early

1950s on whether the early and mid-Victorian age was marked by anti-imperialism (the anti-imperialism of free trade) or imperialism. In Bodell's world there were no doubts: his was a robust and unquestioning imperialism. He meant to get on and he saw that the Empire provided opportunities not to be found at home. In a letter to one of his sisters he wrote, in 1873, 'As long as you can do well in England never leave it, the colonies is very well if people can't get on at home.'[4] At that time he was not prospering.

The bare outline of Bodell's life presented at the beginning of this introduction gives little idea of the scope of his life or the variety of his adventures. He experienced or observed some of the main processes of nineteenth-century imperialism. He begins his imperial career in Ireland, a quasi-colony, occupied by the English centuries earlier. There he saw the results of the potato blight which caused enormous numbers of Irish to migrate in the 1840s. He sees something of the Empire in Asia, in an area dominated by the Royal Navy rather than the army. Then he becomes a settler himself, taking part in a remarkable phenomenon, the 'British diaspora', by which English became the most widely spread language on earth. (Before the British went to America, languages related to Maori were the most widely spread.)

In Van Diemen's Land he saw something of another sort of colony, part of an empire founded on crime. New South Wales had been occupied by the British in 1788 as a convict settlement. Early in the nineteenth century parts of Van Diemen's Land were occupied as a further convict settlement. It had become a separate colony in 1825. In Victoria and later in New Zealand Bodell experienced the imperialism of gold, which led to a series of gold rushes and scattered tens of thousands of diggers to California, British Columbia, Victoria and New Zealand in the mid-nineteenth century. Bodell did not become a digger, although he went on a prospecting expedition near Tauranga, but he made a living on the Victorian gold fields by selling beer to the diggers.

The economy of Australasia was based on gold and grass. One of the most striking of imperial phenomena was the spread of European farmers on to the grasslands of North and South America, South Africa, Australia and New Zealand. In the two latter col-

---

[4] James Bodell/My Dear Sister [Annie], 14 March 1873, in the possession of Mr Newton.

onies the pastoral industry consisted of running sheep, because, in the days before refrigeration, their wool could be exported across the ten or twelve thousand miles to Europe. Before Bodell died refrigerated vessels were transporting mutton and beef and butter and cheese as well to Great Britain.

Bodell lived in farming communities but he never attempted to farm—indeed that was one of the few local occupations he did not try. He did, however, take part in one rural activity, by starting a timber mill. Thus he assisted one of the colony's main 'extractive industries'.

Finally, of course, in New Zealand Bodell took part in one of the most important of all imperial processes, a war of conquest. He gives us a vivid and, it is believed, unique account of the Anglo-Maori war as seen by a private soldier. After the war he stayed in Tauranga as a 'military settler', while small military actions continued in the vicinity. At this time he became 'respectable'. He remarried, joined a temperance lodge, became a regular church-goer—and made money.

James Bodell's manuscript was divided into three sections, his general reminiscences, his much shorter account of his return voyage to England in 1883, and a brief concluding section of reminiscences of the years 1883–91. I have divided it, for the convenience of the reader, into eight sections or chapters. With one exception, each is preceded by a brief introduction giving necessary background information about the situation at the time in Ireland, Hong Kong and so on. Bodell wrote almost nothing about the last years of his life, and does not even mention his mayoralty, partly, presumably, because he was very busy in business and local politics. But it is also clear that he became disillusioned with the latter. In any case the quality of his memoirs declined—the diary of another trip home in 1890 is uninteresting.[5] Some sections of his memoirs from 1883–92 have been deleted, for instance an account copied from the Press of the eruption of Mount Tarawera in 1886. Also he is repetitive about his earlier life in Tauranga. These deletions are identified in footnotes.

In the course of editing these interesting reminiscences I have incurred several debts. Mr Andrew Newton, of Leicester, was very helpful in checking English army, birth and other records for me.

[5] In the possession of Mr Newton.

Mrs Freda Christie's work in typing a very difficult manuscript went well beyond the call of duty and involved her in research into place names in various countries and other scholarly problems. Dr Evelyn Stokes and Mrs Barbara Oram, both of whom have studied Tauranga history, provided many details of Bodell's life in Tauranga. Ms Elizabeth Macfarlan was a source of much information about the Victorian army. Mrs Trudie McNaughton kindly assisted with my research. Associate Professor W. H. Pearson helped with the interpretation of some nineteenth-century expressions. Mr Trenear DuBourg assisted me with research in Maryborough, Victoria.

I

England and Ireland,
1831–49

James Bodell's reminiscences form an imperial document; he does not say much about England, which he left at the age of sixteen. Yet even here, as so often, what he does mention illustrates significant historical trends and conditions. This is worth saying because, at least in the past, history has tended to be written about rulers, the elite, the educated. The lives of the ruled, the illiterate or barely literate poor, have been recorded in birth, marriage and death certificates. If known, their lives would often be as revealing as those of their social betters. James Bodell's reminiscences reveal aspects of the past which might generally be available in statistics rather than in personal terms.

His father was an illiterate frame-work knitter[1] in Arnold, just outside Nottingham. The knitters made stockings on frames, generally rented from the manufacturer. Often they worked in their own homes.[2] James Bodell was baptised on 3 July 1831.[3] Not long afterwards the family shifted to Leicester. It is recorded that Nottingham manufacturers were at that time moving to Leicester, to escape from high rents.[4] James Bodell describes his father as 'a rank Chartist'. Chartism was very strong in Nottingham.[5]

James Bodell says little of his life in Leicester, where he went to school for three years, or of his first jobs. He relates how, on 8 November 1847, he enlisted in the 59th or 2nd Nottingham Regiment, the 'Lily-whites'. By a strange coincidence this is confirmed in one of the three lists

---

[1] 'William Bodel' signed his name with a cross in the marriage register when he married Maria Margrom, also illiterate, on 19 July 1828. Register PR 2615, p. 155, Nottingham County Records Office.

[2] Roy A. Church, *Economic and Social Change in a Midland Town. Victorian Nottingham 1815–1900*, London, 1966, p. 3.

[3] Register 2200, p. 275, Nottingham C.R.O. When another son was born the father's name was written as 'Bodle'.

[4] Roy A. Church, p. 3.

[5] *Ibid.*, chapter VI.

of company strengths which have survived from the period 1820–80:[6]

No.	Name	Date of Enlistment	Age	Height	Religion
2219	Joseph Bowdell	8th Nov. 1847	17	5' 7"	P

He was, in fact, only sixteen. He had falsified his age. Volunteers for the infantry had to be eighteen, so he must have joined as what was termed a 'growing lad' — and he did, indeed, grow three inches in the army.

Almost at once he was sent to join his regiment in Ireland where rebellion seemed imminent. Bodell had known poverty in Leicester, but nothing comparable to what he found in Ireland. In 1845 the potato blight had devastated the potato crop in many parts of Ireland. There followed a great famine which lasted for several years. 'Soup kitchens' were set up, and £8,000,000 was spent on famine relief between 1845–8. In 1847 there were some 3,000,000 living on charity. There were severe outbreaks of scurvy, cholera, typhus and other diseases. It is believed that half a million people died during the Great Famine. Over two million emigrated within a decade.[7]

1848 was the year of revolutions in Europe. The French monarchy fell. There were revolutions in Italy, Germany, Austria-Hungary. In England there was fear of a Chartist uprising. In Ireland there was Smith O'Brien's rebellion. William Smith O'Brien was a leader of the Young Ireland movement, a national movement which stressed the importance of Irish culture and some of whose leaders spoke of armed revolution. Smith O'Brien and two others were prosecuted for sedition. O'Brien was found not guilty, but John Mitchel was transported to Van Diemen's Land (Tasmania)—Bodell mentions him as a prisoner in Cape Town. O'Brien and his men roamed the country, urging the people to rise in the cause of Ireland. There followed a tragi-comedy, called 'the battle of Widow McCormack's cabbage patch', when O'Brien and some half-armed youths fought a small force of constabulary. O'Brien was sentenced to death, but the sentence was commuted and he was transported to Van Diemen's Land too. It seems that starvation and

---

[6] Fulwood ref. no. 312, Fulwood Barracks, Preston. This reference, and those to the register of births and deaths, were kindly found for me by Mr Andrew Newton.

[7] The book I found most useful on Ireland at this time was R. D. Edwards and T. D. Williams (eds.), *The Great Famine. Studies in Irish History 1845–52*, New York, 1956.

fever did not provide a fertile atmosphere for revolution. The population was demoralised, not revolutionary.

—————

After many years of thoughtful consideration I have taken upon myself the onerous task to put into writing the experiences, incidents, and adventures of my Travels, during a Period of 38 years from the Year of Grace 1847 to the present Year 1885. During the year first mentioned, I was a youth, ignorant and inexperienced of the difficulties and hardships a young man of my small attainments who had taken upon himself to face the troubles of this world. I hope my readers will forgive any short comings they may detect in the Compilation of this Narrative.

I am the offspring of honest and humble Parents, born in the Village of Arnold near the Town of Nottingham England. Before I was two years old my Parents with your humble servant and an elder Brother about two years my senior removed to the Town of Leicester. The first impression I have of Leicester was when 3 years old being run over by one of Pickford's waggons or trolleys in Red Cross Street. The next shortly after, was I was throwing a brick end into the Canal near the Old Mill, West Bridge. Giving the brick too much force I fell over it head first into the water, and by good luck the Miller seen me go in, and rescued me. For this I had a good dressing down on my arrival home. Before I was 7 years old I was sent to school to [illegible] three years. I must have been fairly good—I only played the truant once—and on that occasion, my Aunt had seen me during the afternoon looking at the Pictures in the Market Place. I knew nothing of this till after breakfast next morning when my Aunt asked me as a favour to hand a letter she gave me to the School Master. I was glad of this as I thought this letter might be the Cause of him to look over my absence from School the previous afternoon. I entered the School with the usual Morning Salute, and boldly marched up to the Master and handed him the letter. I had scarcely got to my Class before I noticed him pick up that dreaded Cane, and make straight for me. In a twinkling he had me by the waist of back of my trousers so as to tighten the trousers on my Posterior and he commenced to belabour me unmerciful. I commenced to kick and plunge, and he gave it all the heavier, till he completely exhausted himself and made me so sore I could not sit down for a week. I made a determination when I got big I certainly would punch his head.

My term of three years expired in 1841 and having received a Bible and Prayer Book for good conduct, I left School. The next three years, I worked at various Factories, Harrises, Kellys and Whitmores. By this time I began to have a wish to see other Places, and in 1845 myself and a companion started for Liverpool, with the intention of going to Sea. However this was not to be, as we found employment at Birkenhead, remained here till September, and returned to Leicester in time for the Leicester Races. I recollect at this time reading the account of the fight between Bendigo and Ben Caunt,[8] at Newport Pagnell.

I could not remain in Leicester long. I was soon off again, to Birkenhead and up to Septr 1847 I passed my time between Leicester, Liverpool, Birkenhead and North Wales. Birkenhead docks commenced in 1845, and the SS *Great Britain* was exhibited. From the time I left School the Midland Towns of England suffered very much from depression of trade and other Causes, and many thousands of People was half starved, what with the Chartists, Whigs & Tories, and then the Famine in Ireland the Working Class in England suffered very much.

In November 1847 I had been in Leicester a few Weeks and one Monday Evening 8th Nov. 1847 after tea a few young chaps had collected together and the time passed rather heavy. As three of us was walking down High Street I suggested we should go and enlist in Her Majesty's Service, and if they did not take the three of us, none of us should enlist. I was determined to be a Horse Soldier or Artillery man, or even a Marine, but when we got to Cole Hill neither Artillerymen or Marines could we find, and we were too short for the Cavalry. We got down to the Horse & Jockey in Humberstone gate. Here we met several Soldiers flying the ribbons, and one of them belonged to the 59th or Second Nottinghamshire Regt. of foot. Why, was not I a Nottinghamshire Man and to be in a Nottinghamshire Regiment was all I wanted, but before I would enlist, I must have half a Crown. I considered myself too good to take one Shilling. The three of us were put under the

---

[8] According to *The Ring Boxing Encyclopedia Record Book* 1975 edn., the fight was at Stony Stratford, five miles or so from Newport Pagnell, on 9 September 1845.

Standard. One was too short and I could see there was some Consideration about the other. However they enlisted two of us. My mate took one shilling but I got half a Crown. I shouted half gallon of ale and two screws of Tobacco. My mate done the Same, and all we had left was 1/6. During the drinking of the ale, the recruiting Soldier donned the Colours on our Caps, with the understanding if we lost or soiled them we should have to pay 2/6 for them. Off we went and on passing the old Amphitheatre, it was open and I invited my two Companions into the Gallery. This took the remainder of my half Crown. When we were in our Seats all eyes were on us the ribbons denoting we were new fledged recruits. I could not stand this so I took my ribbons off and put them into my Pocket. After the Performance was over we made for home.

After leaving my Companions on top of the Market Place, and when by myself, I began to reflect on what I had done, knowing my Father was very much against anything connected with a Soldier, he being a rank Chartist. However I had done it and I made up my mind to go through and face it. A few Yards from home I donned the ribbons again and on entering the house my mother called out and on finding it was me she told me my supper was in the oven, and asked if I had seen Father. I was glad to hear Father was not at home. Supper I wanted none so upstairs I went colours flying, and on entering my Parents Bedroom, my mother begged of me to take those dreadful ribbons off. I had time to declare I had enlisted for a Soldier, in a Nottinghamshire Regiment, when who should come into the House but Father. I was off into my room like a Shot and into Bed in a jiffy. Father comes upstairs and I heard Mother tell him about me enlisting and in a few Minutes, he makes tracks for me. I was buried over head in the blankets in a Second and pretended being asleep. He came and sat on the Chair alongside and called me twice and I threw the Blankets off me and sat up in bed, and said Yes Father. He commenced, is this true that your mother tells me about you enlisting for a soldier. I said Yes Father it is true, and if you buy me off I will enlist again, because I am determined to see foreign Countries. He sat there several Seconds and said foolish boy. I had made up my mind to start you in business. I said it is no use Father I certainly intend to see other Parts of the World, and Leicester is about the poorest Place I have been in. I said I cannot earn above 10/- to 12/- per week. At Birkenhead, and other Places I can earn 21/- per week. When I looked at Father again, I saw the tears on his Cheek and recollect no more.

I woke early next Morning and was off as I did not want to see either Father or Mother, and I did not intend returning until I have been sworn in and then it would take £20 to buy me off. At 10 o'clock myself and several other recruits attended the Doctor and recruiting officer for medical examination and we all passed and got our day's Pay. Next day we attended at the business Place of Mr John Biggs the Mayor in Belvoir Street and was sworn in, and got beside our day's Pay 10/- each. Part, as I ascertained, [of] the bounty Money of £4. The balance was reserved until we joined Headquarters of the Regiment stationed at Templemore, County of Tipperary, Ireland.

After leaving Mr Biggs we had plenty of money so we thought, and after calling at several Public Houses the Soldier took us to his house between Barkby Lane and Wharf Street. Here he was living as a Married Man, and induced us to purchase myself a button Stick for 2/6. On joining the Regt. I got the same article new for one Penny. He also induced us to go to the Police Office in Town Hall Lane and apply for tickets to be billeted on some Public House as he said the Landlord would not keep us but give so much money and pay us off. The others were paid off all right but my ticket was on the Nottingham Arms, Belgrave Gate and the Landlord to my great Surprise knew me and said he could find me accommodation. This was a disappointment, and Mr Soldier as far as I was concerned, nonplussed.

About Friday 12th Novr. all our extra Cash was spent and on this afternoon Mr Soldier induced me to go home and get all the Clothing I could and bring them to him as he said they were no use to me. I did so and the Villain sold them for a few Shillings and by Saturday Night this was gone. On Saturday morning we were told we should leave for Coventry on Tuesday Morning. Since Tuesday Morning I had not been Home, and I knew my Mother would be fretting about me. In the afternoon I went into Charles Street and visited a Mr Fowler, Solicitor and his Lady, they being friends of our Family. Mrs Fowler always made a great Pet of me and on this Visit Mr & Mrs Fowler made me several Presents. During the Evening I was at my Billet, the Nottingham Arms, about 7.30 o.c. who should walk in but my Father. He said he had been on the look out for me and had some bother to find me. When I told him I was leaving on Tuesday next, he looked very serious. When he came into the Parlour where I was sitting I had a Pint of Ale in front of me and smoking a long Pipe. On his approach I put the Pipe down as I dare not smoke in his Presence. He made no remark, but asked me into another Room. Here was another of his acquaintances and they commenced to talk seriously to me. However it was no use, I was determined to go for a Soldier. At last he persuaded me to go home with him so as to go to Church next day. This I did do.

Next Morning my poor mother was nearly broken hearted about me going for a Soldier, and losing poor Jim. I was glad when Night came. Before going to bed my Father asked me as a favour if I would tomorrow go to our Garden up Brick Kiln Lane and dig some Carrots and Potatoes. My Brother Ted being away I was the only one in the Family strong enough to do this work. I promised to do this if he would let me smoke. He remarked what would my neighbours think of me if I allowed you to smoke. Now I had been smoking for $2\frac{1}{2}$ years and many times had stolen his tobacco. He kept his Tobacco under the Chest of Drawers in the front room and many times early in the week when a fresh supply would be there, [I had] taken some out and loosened the remainder so as to make the bulk appear the same. On this my last day at Home he would not give his Consent for me to smoke. For two Years when at home my mother allowed me quarter ounce of Tobacco per day. This day Monday 15 Nov. 1847 I got up, had Breakfast, took a Sandwich and repaired to the Garden, and I certainly worked my best, digging Potatoes, Carrots and other Vegetables. After filling a Wheelbarrow put remainder into a Pit with Straw. About 3.30 o'clock my Father came. If he had appeared a few minutes earlier He would have caught me having a comfortable Smoke. My back had been aching for some time, and I was glad when he did come for I was getting tired. In a short time we started with the Barrow load for Home and on arrival there was mother and my eldest Sister Elizabeth. Both dreaded the Morrow. I intended giving them the slip. After Tea I cleared [off] not intending to return and from that Night about 7 p.m. I did not see my Father or Sister for 35 and a half years. I slept at the Nottingham Arms the last Night in Leicester as I could not bear to be near my Mother. I liked her so much, when she fretted it hurt my feelings, so I considered we were better apart. Afterwards I often would have given my very life to be with her again. When I got to be a Man with sense I often regretted leaving my Mother and Sister the way I did. I felt for them more than I did for Father. When in China I often thought of Monday Night in Leicester 8 Novr. 1847.

Next Morning we mustered about 9.30 o.c. at the recruiting officer's quarters opposite Trinity Church, top of Wellington Street after getting our Pay and having our Names taken down again. I was waiting outside when who should come up but my Mother. A scene ensued for a few Minutes, and ten Minutes later we parted and did not see my dear Mother again for 35 and a half Years, when I visited Leicester from New Zealand in 1883.

At last off we started along the Hinckley Road. On the way I called at my aunt's for a small Present. My Cousin a buxom girl of 18 years was at home with her Mother and we parted, never to see Aunt again but in 1883 I found the Cousin at Liverpool with a large Family, some of them married, herself I did not know her, an old grey headed woman wearing Spectacles. To tell me this was my Cousin, the buxom girl I used to know, I could not believe it until we had a Chat over our youthful days. Yes, it was the same or remnant of the former Miss M. Marlow. I did not consider the Alterations of myself. She did not know me, as I left a Stripling of a boy about 9½ Stone and [was] now a big man of 18 Stone, and to read a book by Candle light I also had to use Spectacles. I stopped with my Cousin till the following day.

When about 3 Miles from Leicester on the Hinckley Road I believe it was on the Shoulder of Mutton Hill I turned round to have the final look at the tall chimneys and Church Steeples of Leicester and on we tramped. On reaching Hinckley we stopped at an Inn. Next Morning on the road for Coventry. This we reached early in the afternoon, had a look at Peeping Tom, and then to the Barracks. In a short time, we were taken to a large Building to be examined by two Doctors. This was a very strict examination, and several recruits were rejected, my Mate was one of them. So here I was the only one left out of the three, who started to enlist. Next day about 8 of us was put into the train for Liverpool and arrived there that afternoon. On arrival we were marched to a Rendezvous, a rough Place, and next Morning we were taken to the recruiting officer for the Liverpool District to get our Pay. Here we mustered about 20 in all.

On getting my Pay I was returning through the Yard when a Servant Girl called me on one Side she asking me to follow her. On entering under a back Verandah near the Kitchen she pointed out to me a long row of dirty Boots I should say about 20 Pairs and also a quantity of dirty knives & forks, saying, 'Master says you have to clean these'. I looked at her and the boots etc. and said did your Master say I was to clean these. She said Yes of course he did. I did not know what to do for a Minute I felt so hurt. In a Moment my metal was up and I said you can tell your Master whoever he is, I did not enlist to turn Shoe black, and that I refused to clean the Boots etc. She looked at me in Astonishment saying do you know my Master is your officer, and if you refuse he can punish you. He can punish away I shall not clean them and you can go and tell him so. In a few Seconds he arrived. He commenced, what is this I hear. Do you refuse to clean those things and do you know Sir the first duty of a Soldier is Obedience. I looked at him, and for a Moment I was rather confused but next moment I said cleaning Boots Knives Spoons and forks is not Soldier's duty and I refuse to do it, expecting to be made a Prisoner but no he left me and I saw the two Servant Girls smiling at each other. I remained a few minutes and no one came so I turned to the right about and left expecting every minute to be made Prisoner. On my return to quarters I related to my Companions what had detained me. One of them who had been several days in Liverpool said he had a spell of cleaning boots one morning. During my three days' stay in Liverpool each Morning on going for my Pay not one word was said about my refusal, but got my Pay without any remark.

At last we embarked on board a Steamer bound for Cork and I took a Pork Pie about 4 lbs. for aboard ship. Went up the Mersey smoking. We had scarcely got to Sea, before the Vessel commenced to toss about and during the two days and Nights it took us to reach the Cove of Cork, I did not look at the Pipe or see the Pork Pie. The miserable hole we had to sleep in would not hold half of us and a number of deck Passengers were on board and we had a very rough Passage, the Sea coming over us in Tons. Two Boilers, one each side of Deck was crammed full of poor People, dozens of them rolling in their Vomit, next moment the Sea coming over and clearing the Decks, and so it was through the Passage about the roughest trip I have experienced during my travels.

At last early one Morning we arrived at the Cove of Cork and on going on Shore I turned quite giddy. I managed to get with others to a Public House, here I got a Glass of Whisky, the first I had tasted. I thought it would burn a hole in my throat, it being so sore from retching so much. However it appeared to do me good. By Breakfast time we were in Cork Barracks. These were the first large Soldiers' Barracks I had ever seen, and during the time I remained in Cork, I took some Pleasure of walking about them. To get to them it was a tiresome Walk from the Town, being erected on a large Hill. The entrance and sail through the Cove of Cork was very grand.

We remained in Cork Barracks two days and then started for Headquarters at Templemore. Out of about 20 recruits who left Liverpool 12 remained in Cork, and 8 proceeded on our March. On leaving Leicester I brought with me several Presents that had been given to me, amongst them my Bible and Prayer Book I received on leaving School in 1841. These things combined made a tidy parcel for me to carry, amongst them that half crown button Stick. The first day we stopped at the Village called Watergrasshill. This day some Lord got married, living near this Village. Next day we got to Fermoy. Here were two large Barracks the old and new. The third day we made Mitchelstown, next day Cahir, a few Soldiers were stationed here. Fifth day Cashel.

I enjoyed these short Marches very much, and the People living along the Road were very kind and obliging to us. As we arrived in Cashel early, I went on to the celebrated Rock, a very interesting spot and could plainly see the Mount called the Devil's Bit. I was told the story about the Devil taking a mouthful out of the Devil's Bit and dropping it at Cashel and forming the present Rock. A kind of a Castle on a small scale stood on top of the Rock, and from this spot we had a fine view of the surrounding country. Next morning we were off to Thurles, so celebrated the following year, for the Cabbage Garden exploit of Smith O'Brien and the Police.

The 7th and last day we arrived at Templemore Barracks, the Headquarters of the 59th or 2nd Nottinghamshire Regiment of Foot commonly called the 59th 'Lilywhites'.[1] Here also was stationed the 55th Regt. Next day marched to Hospital and another Doctor's inspection. This over marched to the Orderly Room to be inspected by the Adjutant and Sergeant Major. This over the Quarter Master Sergt. marched us off to the Military Stores. Here

[9] In 1881 the 59th Regiment amalgamated with the 30th Foot to form the East Lancashire Regiment.

we were served out with our first suit of Regimentals, or commonly called our Kit, and then told off to our Companies. I was sent to the third or Captain Gordon's Company, this Company being on Detachment. I was attached to the Light Company. That afternoon we attended Drill for the first time, and put into such positions that did not feel very comfortable at first. We had two hours at being put into the proper Position for a Soldier and learn the first rudiments of balance step. We had four hours each day at this drill. I felt very awkward with the wide leather Stock under my Chin, and elbows in the hollow of your Sides, Palms of hands to the front with your toes separated 45 degrees, Chest and head up.

The greatest hardship I experienced was the three Meals each day, and two of these was not much of a Meal. In the Morning we each got 1½ lbs. Bread, for Breakfast a Pint of bad Coffee. Tea, Pint of indifferent Tea. Dinner about half Pound rough Meat and 1 lb. Potatoes, with some Soup. During my Drill I had such an Appetite, I often visited the Canteen about Tea time for a Penny Roll, sometimes again before 8 o'clock. In time I got used to the three Meals per day and found the Rations sufficient.

Things went on very well till Christmas Eve. On this evening I was invited out to have a little Jollification, and we repaired to a Shebeen in the Township, and we got drinking a most delicious drink called Skaltcheen, a compound of Whisky, fresh butter, carraway seeds, Sugar, etc.[10] It was a very nice refreshing drink. About 8.15 we had to make for the Barracks. On reaching the open air I found myself getting quite tipsy and was making my way towards the Barracks, as fast as I could. I missed my Companions and on turning round to see where they were, my right foot got into a hole and when I turned round I hurt my foot and fell down. Next Minute I could not get up, and as the last Post was sounding my Companions left me, and here I remained until the Police removed me to the Police Station. In about half an hour the Picket called and seeing my Leg was so badly hurt they sent for a Stretcher and from the Police Station I was carried to the Barracks and put into the

---

[10] Later in the century a *scaillin* or *scailtin* (pronounced somewhat as Bodell spelt it), was a mixture of boiled whisky, butter, sugar and hot milk, taken to cure a cold on the chest. Sometimes rum was substituted. In Scotland a similar mixture was given to people, including children, with 'a spot on the lung'. For the identification of *scailtin* I am indebted to Mrs Elizabeth O'Higgins.

Guard Room. By this time my ankle was very painful. However the Skaltcheen sent me to sleep and next morning I was in a miserable State.

About 9 o'clock on Christmas Morning I was carried from the Guard Room in a turf crate[11] to the Regimental Hospital suffering great agony. I was deposited in the examining Room and the Doctor gave me great Pain on examining my foot. He said he thought my ankle was broken. I was carried upstairs into a Ward where about a dozen other Soldiers were, some with loathsome diseases and various complaints. I was put on to a Cot with my right leg out of bed, with orders to rub a certain lotion into it and to keep a cold wet Cloth on it night and day. For three days I could not eat anything. The sights I seen every morning as the Doctor visited each Patient were so disgusting, it certainly took all inclination away to eat. One of the men in a very bad Condition was a Leicester Man, by name Thompson, who had been a Soldier about 12 Months. Nearly opposite me was a fine tall man in the Prime of life, a Grenadier who had lost the roof of his mouth and when he swallowed anything he had to hold his head up like a fowl drinking. I was a miserable Creature for the first 3 or 4 days. I could not sleep at Nights with the Pain of my ankle and thinking about the Condition of my Companions and wondered how they got into that fearful Condition. I was certainly totally ignorant of the disease they were suffering from, never seen or heard of anything of the Kind before. After I was often chaffed about my Ignorance.[12]

About the fifth day my Appetite commenced to improve and by the end of the first week, I found my allowance of quarter diet was not nearly sufficient to allay my hunger. I used to lay on my Cot half famished. At last I could not bear it no longer, and something to eat I must have, by hook or by Crook, and I told my state to the Leicester Man. He soon told me I could get plenty if I had the money to buy it with. What little money I had on Christmas Eve. Next Morning I had not one farthing. I could not bear the Pangs of hunger no longer. I felt I could have eat the iron Cot I was lying on, and as my Parcel of Presents had not been touched I got a friend to

---

[11] The turf crates were used for carrying the turf, which was used as fuel, to each barrack room. *Bay of Plenty Times*, 16 Jan. 1888, article by James Bodell.

[12] They were, of course, suffering from venereal disease.

get me these. The first Article I could sell out of the lot was some of the Presents Mr Fowler the Solicitor and his Lady gave me. Of course I did not get one tenth of their Value, and by the end of the second Week I had nothing left saleable but my Bible and Prayer Book. The big Grenadier several times expressed himself that he would buy them, but I did not wish to part with them. However the Pangs of Hunger and the want of Tobacco carried the day and the Grenadier got my Bible and Prayer Book for a very small Sum, I believe one Shilling and four Pence.

During the third week I began to get better, and could stand a little on my right foot and on the 22nd day I pleaded so hard to the Doctor he let me out but for the first few days I had to attend the Hospital each morning at 9.30 o'clock, and out I went and very glad I was. Before I crossed the large Barrack Square, my ankle got very weak, and I had a difficult job to get to the Barrack Room. At last I did so and never left it all day, as I was afraid if I went to the Hospital limping next morning I should be kept in. The thought of this was enough to keep me quiet. I nursed my leg so well on the fourth day I was sent to my Drill, and the Drill instructor was very gentle with me for a few days. In about a week I felt all right and commenced drill in earnest. I was over a Month behind my Companions that joined with me, but I made up my mind to catch them [up] at Drill if possible. I done my best to pick up the Drill. The squad I joined after coming out of Hospital was some recruits who joined about two weeks after I did and a young officer was learning his drill in this squad, a thorough awkward young Gent he was. In about 10 days the Sergt. Major stood some distance off watching the various Squads at drill and he came up to the Corporal who was instructing us, and next minute he came up to me and ordered me to join the Squad that I commenced Drill in. I was very proud of this, and I certainly was very anxious to learn my Drill.

About this time February 1848, there was a General Parade of all the troops in Barracks, and recruits also and all Soldiers on Parade were marched into the Turf Yard. Three sides of a Square was formed and I noticed three sticks of Wood with Straps on them in the Centre. Presently some of the Guard arrived with fixed Bayonets and a Prisoner in the Centre. The Adjutant came forward and read a Paper and the Prisoner was ordered to strip. He was tied up to the Triangles and punished with 50 Lashes with the Cat of nine tails, it made his back nearly raw, this made a great impression on my Mind. I forget his Crime. After the Parade at our Drill, this Drill four times a day went on until some time in March, when I was picked out of a Squad of eighteen and sent to my duty. I was really astonished at this unexpected Proceedings, but certainly to my Satisfaction. I considered myself a Soldier in earnest now, to mount Guard and do Sentry go as well as the old Soldiers. At first I could not understand the favour the Sergt. Major conferred on me on several Occasions but I found out he was from Nottingham, and he was very partial to Nottingham Men who did their duty to his Satisfaction, and conducted themselves as good Soldiers should do.

About the second Morning after I was dismissed Drill I mounted my first Guard and each Soldier had to carry all his Kit in his Knapsack and 60 Rounds of Ammunition in his Pouch and the Big Coat rolled neatly on top of his Knapsack and the Canteen behind. I should say the whole weighed fully 70 lbs. including belts firelock bayonet and Scabbard and very often on parading for Guard, the Adjutant would have Kit inspection. By the time you got to the Guard Room to relieve the old Guard you have this load on you fully one hour and with a 4 inch leather Stock under your Chin, and the heavy Shako on your head, you felt very anxious to be relieved of this load, and if it come to your turn to go on Sentry in the first relief you had to carry this heavy load another two hours. This unfortunately came to my Duty, and when I got on Sentry near the Turf Yard and in full View of the officers quarters and the whole Barracks, I strutted up and down as much like a real Soldier as it lay in my Power particularly during the time when a squad of recruits came during their Drill near my Post, before one hour had expired. I found the Knapsack very heavy and was wishing my first two hours Sentry go was up by hitching the Knapsack up now and again. I eased the breast strap across my breast and gave relief to my arms. At last I was relieved, and on arrival in the Guard room, I was glad to get the Knapsack off my back. Up to this time I considered Soldiering was not such a nice life as I expected but in a few weeks, I took to it a little more agreeably, because I had more time on my hands to go out of Barracks.

I believe it was in May when the Soldier that enlisted me joined Headquarters. I was passing in front of the Orderly Room, when who should come out but this individual. I stood looking at him, scarcely believing myself it was him. Since I had joined the Regiment that half a Crown for the button Stick and the way he enticed me to sell my Clothes, for next to nothing, often troubled my mind and I had made up my mind if ever I came across Isaac Parsons (that was the Soldier's Name) I was bound to have an explanation of the half a Crown for a Penny button stick, and about other little Matters between us: I went straight up to him, and accused him about the button stick and other matters, and instead of replying to me, he laughed at me. This was more than I could stand. I lost my temper and I there and then struck him right and left. He tried to defend himself, but I was too sharp for him, and at last he made for the Orderly Room and as he got to the entrance he met the adjutant and Sergt. Major. He said something to them when I was made a Prisoner. Whilst he was talking to the Adjutant I made for the Sergt. Major, my escort after me. I related the Circumstances of the button stick, and clothes etc. and next moment the Colonel came out of the orderly Room. By this time I was on the way to the Guard room, when the Colonel called to the escort to halt. The Colonel adjutant and Sergt. Major came up. I could see the adjutant telling the Colonel something very earnestly on they coming up. The Colonel say, what's this you young scamp have you been doing. I explained the Matter as well as I could, but before I had said many words he said Sergt. Major let this Young Man go to his Barrack room I'll see about this matter tomorrow. I was released about twenty minutes after. I was crossing the Barrack Square, when who should hail me but the Sergt. Major. I had time to explain matters to him, but he said I had done wrong by striking Parsons, and cautioned me from striking any Soldier again as I should not get off so easy another time. He also said Parsons had claimed his discharge having two good Conduct Marks and 14 Years' service, having got married during his stay in Leicester whilst on recruiting Service. I never seen Mr Parsons afterwards.

It was early in June No. 3 Company returned to headquarters, and I had to leave the Light Company and join it. I was not many days with my Company, and in the Room I lived in amongst about 20 Soldiers, one surly Brute by name Brown was amongst them. This man had insulted me and others several times and would make free with my blacking and other little requisites a Soldier requires. One day I had been playing Skittles at the Canteen Yard, and had several drinks of Ale. I had occasion to go to my Barrack room. The only occupant was this Brown and the Wife of the

Corporal of the Room. I almost forget how the row began, but I know Brown had said something to Mrs Rogers, and on me speaking to him, he struck me. I let him have it [and] a regular fight commenced. Mrs Rogers commenced to scream. Me and Brown were upsetting all the Beds, up and down all over the room. When he got holt of me I could do little but by keeping from him I could hit him where I liked. He got holt of me several times and gave me Pepper. At last some Soldiers came and separated us. Next day by the intercession of Corporal Rogers, Brown was shifted to another room. After we were separated I went to the Canteen, and although I had a few slight marks on my face, I felt about my body as if some one had been giving me a good kicking. Next Morning I felt worse, and felt great Pain, and with the greatest difficulty I attended Parade, and felt very sore for several days. About 10 days after I was alright, but as for Brown I left his face pretty well marked as he was confined to Barracks. The Sergt. Major got to hear about it but when Corporal Rogers explained matters to him, he was satisfied, but shook his head at me. I heard he had insulted Mrs Rogers on several occasions. You will hear more about the said pretty little Mrs Rogers during our stay in China.

Shortly after this word came that Smith O'Brien and his rebellious Comrades were in the Vicinity of Nenagh, and that 500 of the 59th Regt. had to march at once. Next day 500 paraded myself being amongst them we paraded about 9 o'clock and off we went with all our worldly Possessions on our back. We had 18 Irish Miles to go. Before we got 4 Miles I thought the breast strap across my Chest and the Knapsack straps under my Arms between them I certainly expected I should be cut in two, or compelled to fall out, but on I trudged. I think it was Borrisokane and about half way between Nenagh and Templemore. Here we halted for one hour. Directly the arms were piled I was down on the Ground requesting a mate to take my Knapsack off. When off it was a great relief. Took belts, Stock and all off, but I could eat nothing. Just before the hour was up I got a small bottle of Porter and managed to drink that. In a few Minutes, we were on the March again. During this day a good many Soldiers fell out knocked up and the Knapsacks were carried on the Baggage Waggons, and some of them were there also. I was determined not to give in as I considered it a disgrace to do so. About four Miles from Nenagh the Drum & fife Band of the 34th Regimental Depot stationed at Nenagh came to meet us accompanied by some 200 of the Nenaghites mostly women. Many of these carried various Kinds of fruit and other eatables. These things they distributed very freely and about one Mile before entering the Town we fixed Bayonets sloped Arms and marched to attention from the time the Band commenced to play till we halted in the field outside of the small Barracks. I scarcely felt Knapsack, but directly we halted in Column of Companies waiting to be told off to our tents the Knapsack felt heavy again and down I went on the Ground and managed to get the end resting on my Ammunition Pouch. This took the weight off my Chest and Shoulders. During the few Minutes I lay in this position who should come up but the Colonel, and said to me, well my boy do you feel tired. I turned my head and on seeing it was the Colonel, I said No Sir not very. He went away smiling as much as to say I was telling him a fib. Directly after we were told off in Squads of 15 for each tent. (This I recollect was Saturday afternoon in the month of June 1848.)

Guards were mounted and Double Sentries posted, all round the Camp, each Sentry firelock was loaded and capped with Ball Cartridges. Picket of 50 Men also told off for any emergency. These I escaped, but all hands off duty had plenty to do fixing Tents making water drains Cook Houses etc. Before dark we were all right had Tea, and ready for Stroll to see the Town of Nenagh. In one hour after taking the Knapsack off I felt all right, and went into the town. Here we found a troop of the 4th Royal Irish Dragoons stationed in some old Buildings, and a Company of the Irish Constabulary, besides the 34th depot in the Barracks next to the fine grass field we were encamped in. I suppose all told 1000 Troops could take the field to oppose Smith O'Brien and his men who we were told were in the Ranges close by. At 8.30 p.m. we had to be in Camp. After Tattoo [at] 9 p.m. all Sentries had a number and Countersign and all Guards had a Parole in addition. Any one out of Camp and on approaching a Sentry, could not give the Number was made Prisoner. Visiting Rounds during the Night had to give the Countersign, and the grand rounds the Parole, all Sentries being doubled with Arms loaded and capped. Each Sentry walked on their Post outwards and inwards that is from and to each other.

About Midnight a very heavy Storm came on, and after the fatigue of the day I slept very sound. Sometime early in the

1 Soldiers of the 59th Regiment of Foot — the 'Lilywhites' — in (left) the standard uniform and (right) tropical kit that James Bodell would have worn when he was in Ireland and Hong Kong.

2 Hong Kong seen from Kowloon, c. 1840.

3 The 'Crown and Anchor', Hobart. The palings used for shillelaghs are clearly visible.

4 Life in the Australian gold fields. 'Possum Jack's Claim', Maryborough, *Illustrated Australian News*, 12 June 1876, p. 85.

Morning, our tent came down on top of us. This woke me. About 12 Stands of Arms and accoutrements came down on us as the tent Pole had broken. I got from under and tried to get room in other tents that was still standing, but many tents had suffered like our own. Each tent I visited was crammed and I returned to my tent like a drowned rat, and crept underneath it and managed to get three firelocks piled under the tent and so raised the tent and got some wet Blankets and a Knapsack for a Pillow I lay down and was soon fast asleep. About 4 o.c. I was awakened by the water surrounding me. I was lying in about 3 inches of Water. As day light was breaking, and the Storm had ceased, I got a great Coat and made for one of the Mud Bank Cookhouses. Here I found several trying to make a fire. Two men appeared with the Material for making a good fire from the 34th Barracks and more followed and the morning Sun commenced to shine, it was a bright fine Summer's Morning and Sunday Morning to boot. By 6 a.m. we had hot coffee and the hot Sun soon made things comfortable, but to look around the Camp, the Storm had made sad havoc. I may say 200 Men had been in the same predicament as myself. My first experience as a Soldier under Canvas in the field is still most vividly impressed upon my Memory.

Although it was Sunday the Colonel on inspecting the Camp about 9 a.m. gave orders for no church Parade, but all hands to repair tents and make drains to carry all water out of Camp if another Storm should come, and to clean and dry our bedding and clothes also Arms and Accoutrements. By dinner time the Camp looked all right again. Adjoining our Camping field each side we had fields of Wheat Potatoes etc. the latter suffered much the first week. After dinner some of us walked down Town and at 6 p.m. I had to mount Guard. About 10 p.m. word was brought into Camp that Smith O'Brien and his rebels were amongst the Hills in the Vicinity of Nenagh, and an expedition of 150 Rank & file was ordered. This Contingent left the Camp about 11 p.m. being joined by a detachment of the 34th and Irish Constabulary. During the Night this expedition were out of camp, the Guard and Sentries were very much on the alert, strict orders being given to each Sentry. Also each Sentry was visited every hour by the Visiting Rounds and twice during the night by the Grand Rounds. During my seven Years soldiering in Ireland and China I never experienced such strict Disciplining as we had during our Stay in

Camp at Nenagh. The expedition returned to Camp about 7 a.m. next morning not having seen anything of Smith O'Brien and his men.

During our Stay in Camp we had very pleasant times of it, duty easy Drill twice each day. About one Month after being in Camp word came that Smith O'Brien and some of his principal men had been taken Prisoners at Thurles 7 Miles from Templemore. About one Week from this News arriving we quitted Nenagh, and in place of returning to Templemore we received orders to march to Limerick. I was pleased with this News, as I wanted to see as much of Ireland as I could. On our way to Limerick we march[ed] by way of the Silver Mines and O'Brien Bridge. On arrival in Limerick we were sent to the new Barracks, here the 64th Regt. was stationed, and I was surprised to meet the Leicester Man who had enlisted with me in Leicester, in this Regt. He told me he was determined to be a Soldier and so enlisted again into the 64th Regt. and passed the Doctor all right. I ascertained the reason we were sent to Limerick was Viscount Hardinge the Commander in Chief of the Troops in Ireland[13] intended as Smith O'Brien was Prisoner to hold a Field day in Limerick of all Troops who had been on expedition in his Command during the Rebellion of Smith O'Brien (in the Limerick District).

The first Guard I mounted in Limerick to my great Surprise I was picked out as Orderly to Viscount Hardinge and a very easy time I had of it. About two hours on duty and his Secretary told me I could consider myself off duty, for that day. We remained in Limerick about 10 days. The Muster of all Troops in the District for a Field day was a grand Sight. The Horse Artillery to me was the most interesting. I was sorry I had not enlisted into them. How I longed to be on Horse back galloping about with the Field Guns, like they did on that day, a poor line Soldier, carrying a Swag on his back, enough to break it. Here I met the 42nd Highlanders commanded by Colonel Cameron[14] the same as had the command of the troops during the War in New Zealand.

At last we received orders to go to Templemore, and we went by Railway via Tipperary. On Arrival at Headquarters, the 55th Regt. had took their departure and the 43rd Light Infantry took the[ir]

[13] Sir Henry Hardinge, first Viscount Hardinge.
[14] Lieutenant Colonel Duncan Cameron.

Place at Templemore. We had not arrived many days before the 59th Regt. left Templemore for Birr[15] or 'Parsonstown' [w]here we found a large Barracks. During my stay in Templemore many times I had been on the Devil's Bit at Ball Practice. This was where I first learnt how to use old Brown Bess and the round Balls. On one occasion three Companies were having Ball Practice, each Company had its own target. On this occasion a dog ran in front of the three Targets and during his Progress about 50 Shots were fired at Mr Doggy but our Sharp Shooters could not hit him, and when he was clear a loud Shout went up cheering the dog.

A few days after our arrival in Birr, three Companies were sent on detachment to Gort, myself amongst them. We passed through Portumna and Loughrea. This was the 30th October 1848, and at the Place I was billeted with three others. (One Man had his Wife with him.) Several young ladies belonging to the house in the evening amused themselves by casting hot lead into cold water, to ascertain what kind of Husbands they would get. I had never seen this Process before, which caused much Amusement. When bed-time arrived we were in a little fix as far as the Wife of one of the Soldiers was concerned. Only two double Beds were for our use (four and 1 woman) [and] of course three must be in one bed. This was settled satisfactorily by myself agreeing to sleep in the same bed as the married Couple, as I was the youngest man amongst them. I suggested that the Woman should lie in the middle. This the Husband would not agree to. When the three of us got into bed we had to lie very close as the bed was not a very wide one. I was glad when morning arrived. At Breakfast a large dish of Stirrabout with plenty of Milk and plenty of Potatoes. I could always make a good meal out of Stirrabout and milk. This I did ample Justice to and we had a good Breakfast.

By 9 a.m. we were on the march for the town of Gort. On our way I noticed several strange young Girls in Company. I ascertained that these lasses had been captivated by the Soldiers, and had consented to share their Joys and troubles. Before we arrived in Gort one of these Girls was overtaken by a relative and taken back home. It is wonderful how young Girls get captivated with

[15] The Registers of Service of the 59th, held at Fulwood Barracks, Preston, Lancashire, record that the regiment marched from Templemore to Birr on 19 October 1848.

Soldiers, but such is the Case. As hereafter as I proceed, I shall have to relate an adventure about myself in this line.

Early in the afternoon we arrived at Gort a modern size Town for this part of Ireland. The Barracks were for one troop of Cavalry only being small, and stationed in the Barracks was one Troop of the 4th Royal Irish Dragoons. We took Possession of empty Houses in various Parts of the Town, one as Guard room next the Barrack Gate. I found Gort a very nice place and every Saturday a Market was held of all kinds of Farmers' Produce and cattle. I considered Gort held a Market the best I had seen in Ireland. You must remember Ireland was still suffering from the Famine, and Poverty was plentiful and Labour scarce. A strong able bodied man getting from 9 Pence to 1/– per day and to keep a large Family out of this. One Market day I was on Guard and the Vegetable Part of the Market come very near the Guard Room, and my attention was directed to two old women and on the approach of three young Urchins at short intervals these old hags would disappear down a narrow Street opposite the Guard Room. In a short time I found these young lads were stealing Potatoes, Carrots, Turnips etc. and delivering them over to these old Women.

Six nights in each Week several Places for dancing was opened and the Red Coats and young Girls was the principal in attendance and some very enjoyable nights were passed. Near the Part of the Town I was stopping in a field was a Potato Pit I should say several Tons and the first week we helped ourselves pretty freely until the owner caused a noise to be made about losing his Potatoes.

Two Companies of the 59th one Troop of 4th Dragoons and about 100 Constabulary formed an Expedition to a Village on the Bay of Galway, Kinvara I believe. On reaching this Place we were billeted on Farm Houses in the Vicinity, the Village being too small. Myself and three others were billeted on a Farm House near the Village. During the Evening myself and another Soldier named Haggerty, one young woman and the Master of the Farm played Cards, the Game known as twenty fives, for half Pints of Whisky. It did not matter if we lost the Whisky appeared and we had to pay nothing. I may state in this Part of Ireland all talking is done in Irish, and my Partner Haggerty could talk the Irish Language as well as any of them, only for this we would not have been able to play, as I knew no Irish and the residents knew no English. By the aid of Haggerty we got on very well. After several Whiskies Haggerty began to make strong love to the young Girl. Of course I could not understand their Conversation and Haggerty I supposed saw I was listening to their talk, and he thought I may surmise what he was doing. On my going into another room he followed me and begged of me not to let on he was a married man (his Wife was at Birr). The other two Soldiers had not been idle they had been doing a little Courtship with other Girls of the Family or maybe Servants. We had spent a most enjoyable Evening and about 11.30 p.m. we began to prepare for Bed. Two of us were told off, for one room, and when I was partly undressed I noticed in the Corner a Gun with a long barrel, and on trying the ramrod in the barrel I found a four inch charge in it. The Whisky made me as I did not care about going to bed so I got a worm and tried to draw the Cartridges. Our Ramrods were too Short, and I was bothering at this for some time. I extracted Part of the Charge and I went into the Yard and fired off the Gun and it kicked unmerciful and slightly hurt my Shoulder. Our Arm and accoutrements was alongside our bed, as we heard the People in this part of Ireland were very anxious to have plenty for fire Arms and Ammunition.

Next morning we got up early and breakfasted. By nine o'clock we all mustered in the Village, and off we went along the Bay of Galway. The Police led the way, we in the centre and the Dragoons in rear. During the day we visited several Farm Houses. I understood that these expeditions were looking for Arms, and the Military were supporting the Police. It was a rough stony country, and the Peasantry ran away at our approach. They could not speak English. A wild desolate Place. After a hard day's march we returned to Kinvara, and went to the same Billets. I notice[d] the Farmer and his Family did not appear so friendly as on the previous Night. However cards and Whisky as usual, and more love making.

Next day we went in another direction. This morning I saw 6 large fresh Herrings sold for one Penny. This day the Police collected several lots of Arms. Another fatiguing day's work. At Night went to the Billets, cards and Whisky as usual. The Whisky I thought was manufactured on the Premises, as it did not take long to fetch it. As our rations cost nothing we could save money. During the time I was knocking about Ireland, I always found the country inhabitants very kind and generous. Particular so in those parts where no English was spoken and the inhabitants appeared

(37)

poor. The following day we march[ed] to Gort, on our way we passed a strong Irish Lass carrying 1 cwt of Potatoes on her back, 9 miles into Gort, enough for a donkey. Twice each week when weather permitted we had a marching out Parade. On these occasions we march[ed] to near Lord Gort['s] Place, and passed the Place of Saint Katherines Well and the Devil's Punch Bowl.

After a few Weeks residence in Gort we cleared out for Birr, through Loughrea and Portumna. We had not been long at Birr, before the cholera broke out in the district. At this time I had made acquaintance of a Farmers Daughter living on a Farm, near Lord Ross's Place of Great Telescope Fame. Two or 3 Night[s] each week when off duty I used to meet my dear beloved at the House of a Friend of her Family, where she was residing in Town of Birr, the Barracks being at Parsonstown about 1½ miles away. Often I have done the distance in a very few minutes, to be in Barracks before Last Post had sounded. At last we were confined to Barracks the cholera getting so bad. I was very much put about for this Confinement. One day word came to me I was wanted at the Gate. I went and who should be there but Winifred (this was her name). She said she had been so lonely she wanted to see me. In a few minutes we had to part. However in a few days we were allowed out of Barracks, and on Sunday I got a Pass and went to see Winny's Parents. Before I got to the house she had seen me coming and out she ran to meet me. Her Parents received me very pleasantly and during the fore part of the day left us together walking about the fields. About 4 p.m. Tea was ready, and after this her Parents would not let me leave them, but talked seriously to me about their Daughter, about my Prospects etc. All my Prospects were I was a Private Soldier on four Pence half Penny per diem, and had to pay for washing, Barrack damages, and keep my Kit in good condition out of this. Not much left to commence House Keeping with. At this time I had no intention of doing so, but the following week she came to me, and said she could not live only with me. During this time she had got acquainted with a young girl from Roscrea who had just got married to a Private named Burke a recruit in fact. Burke was married when he enlisted. He had joined about two months, and belonged to my Company. It is astonishing what delight some women take in Match Making. This Mrs Burke assisted Winny and advised her, also, I supposed because she was in a fix having a Husband with about 3½ Pence per day she liked to see others in the same Predicament. However the upshot of it was, I consented to try to get a ready furnished Room. My first attempt at this was a failure as the Landlady wanted to see my Marriage lines. Of course I had none. On reporting this to Mr & Mrs Burke and Winny, Burke suggested using his Marriage lines or going to the Priest and get married at once. This kind of Marriage, I could not relish, so Burke advised altering his Marriage lines John Burke to James Bodell. On a little consideration this appeared the easiest course, and they was altered accordingly and I went to the old Lady who wanted to see them and they passed Muster, and we were finally installed in our Lodgings. Before I did this I talked seriously to Winny, but it was no use, and here I was as a married man on about $3\frac{1}{2}$ Pence per diem and not five shillings to start with of my own and very little in Possession of Winny. However, I determined to drag through some how, if possible.

A few days after on my arrival at the Lodgings, to my great surprise Winny was missing. Mrs Burke told me her mother and Brother had been and taken her home. On hearing this, I did not feel the least sorry, but this was not to be for many days, as about 4 days after Winny came back, and next day her mother came to see me, and I suppose she saw it was no use, as her Daughter would not stop at home. She talked very serious to me, to take care of her Daughter etc. Three times per Week after this we had plenty of Eggs, Butter etc. sent us and we got along very well. For myself I had my rations in Barracks and had to sleep there also.

About March 1849 we received the route for Fermoy. Here was a go we did not expect. The day before we left Birr Barracks I impressed on Winny the folly of going with me and persuaded her to go home. The next day a bleak and cold day, we left Birr. On the March for Roscrea, we had not got above 5 miles on our way but who should come alongside of me but Winny. This very much surprised me. I got Permission to fall out and she told me she had not been home, but stopped at her relative in Birr, and that morning watched us leaving the Barracks. So I could see it was no use, and I got her on top of one of the Baggage Carts, and so proceeded on our March. At this time it was snowing rather heavy. During the afternoon we reached Roscrea and I was billeted with 3 others on a Inn, or Shebeen house. While on the March each Soldier received one Shilling and four Pence per day for his Pay. When we got to our Billets I suggested I should buy the Provisions for our Supper and breakfast, and each one to pay his Share, after. This was agreed to, and we myself and Winny, went shopping, and on returning Winny cooked and prepared our Supper. For this I only paid same share as others. I recollect it was a bitter cold Night.

Next Morning off to Templemore and on arrival at the Railway Station (we went to Tipperary by Rail) here a difficulty arose I did not expect, as no Women were allowed in the Train but Married Women on the strength of the Regt. I certainly expected we should have to leave Winny behind here. On our parading in line in front of the Carriages each Company were to occupy, it occurred to me to ascertain the fare to Tipperary [which] was 3/6d. One man told me not to pay it but on the bugle sounding the advance, we would open out and let Winny pass and shove her into the Carriage first and tell her to lie down under the Seat. This was done and on leaving the Railway Station, fully 30 Women in this train got a cheap trip. Of course the officers and non-commissioned officers shut their eyes to all this. At last we got to Tipperary, and march[ed] to Cater and billeted as before. Next day Mitchelstown and then Fermoy. My Company was told off to the new Barracks. Here on being dismissed, directly the accoutrements were off I was out of Barracks to look for a furnished room. This I got at 1/3d a week. During the March I had saved a few Shillings. I also got Winny to wash my shirts etc. By this I saved 1/3d per Month. In a Week or so I was cleared out of every Penny, and I had been put down for a new Shell Jacket.[16] This cost 8/6d. What to do I did not know. I wrote a letter full of lies to a Friend and represented I had broken my firelock and if I did not pay £5 for a new one I should be tried by Court Martial. This had the desired effect. The Morning I received this £5 I recollect crossing the Bridge that crosses the Black water river, returning from the Post office with Winny at my side I considered myself the biggest man in Fermoy. This money was a blessing. I paid this £5 back in 1855 when I was in business in Tasmania, then 'Van Diemen's Land'.

A few days after this, six Companies each 100 Rank & file were picked out for foreign Service. I was amongst them and was transferred to the Light Company. I got round the Colour Sergt. to get me off Rations so as I could have my meals with Winny. This was done, and several Nights I could stop out of Barracks, and the

[16] An undress tight-fitting military jacket.

men gave Winny their clothes to wash, and some sewing also. Years after I often thought of this. I certainly got more Privileges than I deserved. I must have been a bit of a Favourite. I passed very pleasant times in Fermoy.

At last the Six Companies for foreign Service got the route for Cork, and off we went, the Band playing us out of Fermoy. Going through Watergrasshill a house on the Road Side wanted to charge us half Penny each for a drink of Water but the men took the bucket and got several buckets of water, and paid nothing. It certainly looked one time as if some damage would be done. This trying to extort vexed the men. Only for the officers I believe they would have wrecked the house. All the Women and Children rode on the Baggage Waggons. I was surprised at seeing so many Women on the Carts belonging to the Regt. On our arrival in Cork as usual like many others, I was off to look for lodgings. Winny had procured these as she learnt by Fermoy the last in the field have to put up with the worst rooms. Here we stopped about three Weeks, when it was read out in Regimental Orders we should embark on Steamer, by Companies, lying at the quay in Cork to be conveyed on board HM Troopship *Apollo* at anchor in the Cove of Cork. Many were the inquiries about our destination, but no one knew. Some said the West Indies etc. The last night in Cork and the next day, I shall never forget. One good thing all Women left behind had their Passage paid home, whether in Ireland, England or Scotland, and our Colour Sergt. was good enough to put Winny['s] name down. I was up all night, Winny would not leave me, and on parading next morning in column of Companies, and the Speech of our Colonel, about going on Foreign Service and if we met an enemy of our Country, that we should show ourselves as British Soldiers. Our Colonel was a fine specimen of a Soldier, six feet two inches in his Vamps,[17] and stout broad shouldered in proportion weighing I should say 15 to 16 stone. I thought he looked grand that morning with the Waterloo Medal on his Breast. (He proved otherwise.) At last off we went the Band playing The Girl I Left Behind Me.

When we arrived at the quay, and as we were told off in Companies to go on board of the Steamer, I shall never forget that day. I could not keep Winny off my neck. I was so bothered I forgot to

[17] Socks.

(41)

unfix my bayonet. The Colonel was standing one Side of the gangway, and through Winny clinging to me, my bayonet went straight to the Colonel's Chest. He let [out] a roar (and he could roar) brought me to my senses, and Winny was gently requested to return to the Shore. This was the last time I touched Winny. After getting on Board, we stopped at the quay about 20 minutes, and the sight was something awful. Women and children screaming, young Girls fainting, others half mad in a frenzied Condition. I assure you Women with 3, 4 & 6 children each was left behind. Poor things it was a sad Sight to see them. Some of them expected shortly to bring another into the World. This was the 8th day of June 1849. At last off we went, and on getting on Board we were shown our living or I should say sleeping Place. 500 of us was told off for the lower deck and no Ventilation but the Hatches and round Scuttle holes, and one hammock for two men. All our Meals we had to take on upper deck with the Sky or clouds for a ceiling. We remained at anchor till June the 12th, even now we did not know our destination. The four days we lay at anchor was even worse than leaving the quay in Cork. All day long boats crowded with Women and Children, Winny amongst them, pulling around the Ship. Those four days were really miserable ones. At last we commenced our Voyage. I forgot to mention several men deserted and one man shot himself in Cork Barracks before they would leave their Wives and families.

II

Voyage to China,
1849–50

This Voyage was the longest and I should think the most miserable any British Troops endured. We did not get to our destination until the 31 January 1850, occupying 235 days. The second day at Sea we were all mustered on deck and our destination was read out to us, which was Hong Kong China. If many of us had knew this, many more desertions would have been recorded, myself amongst them. China was reckoned a bad station and so it turned out to be. During this Voyage half of the men were on duty Watch and Watch with the Sailors, this is how one Hammock did for two men. Our Mess table was the upper deck.

The third day out several men took ill and the Doctor, O'Leary, announced the illness to be Cholera. When the men knew this consternation was depicted on each face. Next day 2 men died and with very little ceremony [were] thrown overboard and so it went on each day, one or two went over. On the eleventh day we made Madeira, entered the pretty Harbour with the yellow flag at our Mast Head. We were ordered out, not letting us have one Barrel of Water, and we were getting short of this article. About this time a man of our Company (the Light) named James Scott, took the Cholera as he was lying in his hammock, very severely in the abdomen. He called out and the next moment he rolled himself out of his hammock, on to the deck. I and others immediately went to him. The Doctor came and ordered him to the Hospital. Next day he was all right, but very pale and weak. He attributed the fall from the hammock to have saved his life. Another poor fellow took a very severe attack, and he lay in a square canvas Cot near the main hatch. The Pains of the Cholera was so bad that it drew his Mouth on one side and his eyes were so wide and unnatural the poor fellow looked fearful. He died in a few hours.

About this time a Marine belonging to the Ship, was tried by Court Martial for stealing two Shillings. He was found guilty, and sentenced to receive four dozen lashes on the bare back with the

Cat of nine tails. On the morning he received his Punishment, two bodies was committed to the deep. On the 7th or 8th lash the Marine commenced to yell for his Mother, and about the 24th lash his back bled freely. The flogging on board a Man of War was much more severe than that amongst Soldiers on Shore.

After leaving Madeira we made for Tenerife, the cholera raging all the time. I recollect the Peak of Tenerife being pointed out to me by a Boatswain. He said it was 70 miles distant. On approaching the Harbour we had the yellow flag flying as usual. A boat came off and ordered us away. Some palavering took Place, and as we required water, we were allowed to cast Anchor well outside of the Harbour. In a short time several boats put off from the Shore towing large Barrels full of fresh water. These were left about one mile from Shore for our boats to pick up and tow to the *Apollo*. In this way we took in a large quantity of these large Water Casks.

As the last one was being hoisted on board, it being nearly dusk, I was standing alongside of the long boat near the main hatch, when Colour Sergt. Nolan of the 8th Company came and asked me if I had seen an Hammock about. I pointed to some thing like one near the main hatch on the spare booms alongside of the long boat, and he was just leaning over the boom as the last Barrel of Water was being hoisted up to the main Yard. Before it descended to the main hatch it being the last Barrel, the men at the rope run it up quick and let it descend very quick. Just as Sergt. Nolan was in the act of reaching for the Hammock the huge barrel of Water descended out of the line for the hatch, and caught Sergt. Nolan in the Back and completely smashed his body. Myself being quite close, I saw the blood shoot from his mouth, and his body rebounded as the Cask got clear and fell on his back on the deck. I immediately walked forward as the sight of poor Nolan was awful. I again returned when his body was carried to the Poop, and the Doctor pronounced him dead. The body was left on the Poop and the Union Jack covered it. So much for the unexpected death of Poor Nolan. His Wife and two Children were on board, and word was passed not to let Mrs Nolan know about the accident if possible, but in a short time, she knew something unusual was the matter, and she went aft and found out the awful truth. She poor Woman went nearly mad. All night she was pleading to see her Husband but was not allowed, as the Sight of the body in the fearful Condition it was would have made her worse. It was committed to the deep early in the morning. After the last barrel of water was taken on board, we set Sail for Rio de Janeiro in South America. After leaving Tenerife the Cholera was not so bad, not so many Deaths, but still the fearful Epidemic was on board, and the discipline was something amounting to be unbearable, tyrannical in the extreme. None were allowed to sit upon the deck, and not allowed below during the day. Everything was done to make us miserable. A Soldier's Rations on board Ship in these days was Six ups four, that is 6 Soldiers had to live on 4 Sailors rations, and sometimes it was 10 Soldiers on 4 Sailors Rations, and mouldy weevily crumbs of Biscuits, stinking Bully Beef, and half rotten rations served out. If ever there was an Hell upon the Ocean, HM Ship *Apollo* was, during this trip to China in 1849. Men [were] flogged for petty offences and some morning[s] other[s] thrown over board from the Cholera.

It was on the 22nd July 1849 when we crossed the line, and early in Augt.[1] we entered the fine Roadstead after ascending the Sugar loaf into Rio de Janeiro Harbour, on our right a three tier Battery and as we entered this fine Harbour a three tier Battery was on our left, also. We anchored miles from the usual anchorage until the Authorities we[re] communicated with. We had the yellow flag at the Mast Head, and as usual was ordered away. This was too much. We remained here a few days, and Captain Massey of the HM Frigate *Cleopatra* was here also bound for China. It was a Sight to see the black slaves the Skins nearly black through such a powerful hot Sun, working bare headed in the boats. Every other stroke the rowers would rise upon their feet and fall on to the seats with the oars, as regular as clockwork. We were fully 6 miles away from the usual anchorage. At last it was decided if the Captain of the *Apollo* wished, he had Permission to go about 150 miles down the coast, to a place called Ilha Grande. It was decided to go there and send all hands on Shore and fumigate the Ship, and get a good supply of Water, before starting on our Voyage.

Next day off we went and early the following day we made the Ilha Grande, and a fine Harbour it was, fully one mile by two. On one Side we could see a few small Buildings. We no soon[er] cast anchor than all Sails were taken off the Yards, the Top Masts taken

---

[1] The 59th's Register of Service records that the date was 7 August and they reached Ilha Grande on 11 August. Bodell spells it 'Hella Grande'. Its full name is Baia da Ilha Grande.

down. In fact the ship was completely dismantled. The second morning all available boats were crowded, each company in turn for the shore, and each company received so many ship sails as could be spared, to make tents with. Sails or no sails we did not care so as we got on Shore. By Night we had made ourselves as comfortable as possible. We landed at the spot where three little huts were. These were taken Possession of by the Doctor for an Hospital. The owners fled at our approach.

I was in my glory. Plenty of fine Oranges and lemons, Bananas, Plantains fish etc. coffee growing in abundance, in fact all kinds of Tropical fruit in plenty. Just the Place we wanted. The first week we buried about twelve men. After that the Cholera thank God left us, and we felt ourselves free from that Scourge. During this time myself had enjoyed the best of Health, only I could not get enough to eat. A few days after our arrival a Brazilian Man of War came into the Harbour bringing us some wild Bullocks and a few Sheep also a detachment of Soldiers. These Soldiers were sent on Shore each morning and Sentries placed around the Orange Groves to keep us from them, that is the Groves at a distance, they not coming near us. Where the men was buried we made and fenced in a Grave Yard and erected rough stakes at the head of each Grave, with name date and ship roughly cut on each slab. A Sentry was also placed Night and day over this spot. Every night Sentries were placed all round the Camp to keep us from the Orange Groves, but it would have taken several Regiments of British Soldiers and all the Brazilian Army to keep us from the Fruit. This is how we did it. If myself or any of my Comrades were on Sentry by night, a Party off Guard would be made up say 6 men. These men if I or others was on Sentry would be allowed to pass say at 10.30 p.m. This Sentry would be relieved at 12 Midnight and come on Sentry again at 4 a.m. So any Party going out between 10 and 12 p.m. would always return between 4 & 6 a.m. as the same Sentry would be on the same Post. If the Party went out before Ten they would return by 4 a.m. and as the Party returned, the Sentry would always get lots of oranges etc. Each Sentry kept a large fire burning on his post to keep wild Animals away. In a short time we found out the Brazilian Soldiers always returned to their Ship after sun set each evening. So at Night we could go to the orange Groves, without any fear.

One Sunday afternoon four of us got outside our Sentries and was well amongst the fruit when two Brazilian Sentries seen us and fired at us, the bullets whizzing over our heads. On this occasion we met one of the Sailors and a young Woman amongst the fruit. We also came across a runaway black Slave who seemed to be very bad[ly] off. We gave him some tobacco. Wild Animals were also plentiful. One black Gentleman about as large as a sheep came close to me, and stared at me with eyes large and glistening, and I was afraid he was going to spring on me. However he went to the right about, and turned tail. I believe he was a Panther, or Hyena.

After being on Shore about two Weeks the Cholera left us completely, and the Ship had been thoroughly fumigated several times. Each day 50 of a Fatigue Party went on board to assist the Sailors to fumigate the Ship. The old troop ship *Apollo*, with mast down and all Yards off looked like a coal hulk, anchored about one mile from Shore. On our approach, the fishermen left the huts and we did not see them again during our Stay.

We had been using a root as a Potato for Dinner that grew in rows like Potatoes, a good Substitute for that article. It was known as the Cassava Root, and on dividing it a silver looking thread was found in the Centre. We had been using these roots daily, and after a time our bellies began to swell. On Several applying to the doctor, it puzzled him for some time. At last he gave orders for anyone using this Cassava Root, be sure and not eat the silver string. This turned out to be the Cause of the swelled bellies. After this if any Woman appeared in the family way, it became a joke to ask her if she had eaten any Cassava Roots.

One morning myself and another man named Walsh were sitting on some rock near to our Tent talking, when to my great surprise a large Boa Constrictor emerged from under a Crevice in the Rock and came between my legs. Of course on first seeing it in that Position, I was horror struck, and for a second did not know what to do. Before I could speak to Walsh he had seen the Serpent and gave a yell and bounded off. About 8 feet of the reptile was through my legs, when I sprang up the rock and dislodged a boulder about 12 Pounds. I let fly at it. The stone frightened him and he commenced to go along at a good Pace. When I followed and with another stone about 20 lb I nearly cut him in two. By this time Walsh [had] returned with several men and the reptile was killed. On skinning it I [found I] had badly injured the Skin, by the Stone I thrown on it. On being measured it was 11 feet. The Doctor asked for the Skin, and he got it. I saw Part of it on a walking stick when in China some years after.

On some wild Cattle being landed for our use some of them got away into the bush, and our adjutant Lieut. Lloyd, asked for Volunteers to go and capture these Cattle. I volunteered and three others, and off we went accoutred with Side Arms 10 Rounds of Ball, Cartridges and firelock. On this trip I had the Satisfaction of seeing some of the finest, smallest, prettiest, plumaged Birds I ever had seen or read about. After going two or three miles we overtook a few Head and turned them towards Camp, and after some trouble we got them into Camp. On them approaching one of the Sentries one wild Bullock charged the Sentry. He came to the charge with Bayonet fixed like a man and stood his ground. The Bullock nothing daunted charged straight at him and the Bayonet caught the Bullock in Centre of the forehead. The next moment the Sentry was hurled some yards away and the Bayonet bent to half moon shape. It was a brave action for the Sentry to do, and I am glad to say he was not hurt. After this the Bullock was much worse and he charged every one he came across and finally got clear away and was left to go where he liked.

We also caught some very fine fish during our Stay here. I often made one of a Party to go to the Orange Groves at Night. On one of these occasions we came across a hut and on the Clearing in front there were several Tons of raw Coffee and in rows adjoining the Coffee trees were very numerous. In this Hut we ascertained it was the day Residence of the officer in charge of the Brazilian Soldiers who come on Shore to guard the Fruit, and in this Hut we found a quantity of Cape Smoke, a kind of Gin, but very nauseous to one's Palate not use[d] to it. However we reduced the stock pretty considerable and in another Building there were some Machinery for crushing the Sugar Cane, and I believe for making the Cape Smoke. Several times after this I visited this Hut, but no Cape Smoke could we find.

After one day a Fatigue Party from our Company (the Light) went on Board the *Apollo*, and during the day they had to remove some Casks of Wine on Board and four of the Party was caught taking some of this Wine. They were tried by Court Martial, and each one was sentenced to receive 50 lashes with the Cat o nine tails. The following day all hand[s] on Parade to hear the Sentence read out and the Punishment inflicted. After the reading and

Sentence, the Colonel stepped into the Square, and made a Speech caution[ing] every one against pilfering etc. and the two youngest Soldiers was forgiven. The other two received their Punishment. I may here remark it was a noted fact all the men who received the Cat during this Voyage died within two years after landing in Hong Kong. It appeared to destroy their self respect and [they] never appeared in a joyous mood or I may say in so lively a spirit afterwards. I can assure the reader of these lines.

Our Colonel (Arthur H. Trevor K.H. with the Waterloo Medal on his breast) was a martinet and many times inflicted severe Punishment when not needed. In fact the Commander of the *Apollo* could do just what he liked with the Soldiers of the 59th Regt. Our Colonel proved a thorough Coward after landing in China, as all bombastic, bullying Martinets are. I never seen such men staunch when danger come, but generally Cowards.

At last after four weeks on Shore, it was in orders to embark tomorrow. That Night I made one of a Party for the orange Groves and it was a fine moonlight night. We got some fine Lemons, as also some of the finest oranges I ever seen. You could pluck them off the tree and eat them, Skins and all. The Skins were not as thick as a Sixpence. The day we embarked I can answer for our Company, nearly every Knapsack and haversack were crammed with oranges & Lemons. During our stay here, nearly every morning our Breakfast would be fried Bananas, or Plantains, being fine mellow fruit and fried brown in Beef Suet. They made a delicious meal, better than Biscuit and Cocoa nearly all rough Grounds. I left Ilha Grande very reluctantly for I detested the *Apollo*. Before leaving we trimmed the Grave Yard. Next day we were out at Sea making for the Cape of Good Hope.

After about two weeks at Sea all hands (Soldiers) were put upon short rations. Biscuit, water, meat and all rations getting short. Surely our gallant Commander, or our quarter Master had made a great mistake by putting to Sea with so many mouths on Board, to be getting short of the necessities of life in 14 days when by a good wind it would take us a Month to get to the Cape of Good Hope, when they could have got plenty of Biscuits, Beef & Water, at Ilha Grande as twice each week a Steamer came into the Bay with anything we required, and plenty of fine pure water at Ilha Grande. For the next three weeks the *Apollo* was a famine stricken Ship. Each morning we got ¼ lb of mouldy, weevily, biscuit dust. ¼ lb salt

Pork and a small quantity of thin Pea Soup, for dinner one day. Next day 2 oz preserved Potatoes and stinking Bully Beef. Many times this Beef stank so bad the Doctor ordered it over board. We got so weak on this short rations that our 12 o'clock three water Grog made us tipsy & sleepy. One day I was so weak I had to sit on the deck after getting the Grog. I was reported for it and was sentenced to have three days Grog stopped just for sitting down on the deck. Many a time during these three weeks myself and a Comrade named John Bradley sat on the upper deck Guns, and we have been that hungry we could have eaten our boots and every night when it come to my turn to turn into the Hammock, your Mind would be continually thinking about all the nice eatables you have seen in Cook Shops and confectioners' Windows, till sleep was out of the question. For drinking Purposes each man was allowed two drinks each day of half Pint of red water. Two Sentries night and day over the water tank with drawn cutlasses. I can assure the reader I often wished the Ship to sink. From 6 to 8 each night we were allowed to smoke. Plenty of tobacco to be got but the smoking made you ill, your Stomach was so weak.

We caught a large Shark from the forecastle. This was devoured in a few minutes. Another day three Porpoises was caught, these also was eaten in a few minutes. I took a piece to the Galley and the Cook as a favour allowed me to put it on the fire for a minute and it eat fine. Another day it rained. Anything we could get we spread out to catch water. Every Contrivance was done to get a little water, but unfortunately very little we got as all the available tarpaulins and spare Sails were spread out to catch a Supply for the tanks below, for all hands.

During this time I had made acquaintance with the Master at Arms. During the Voyage, at 8 a.m. each morning the Master at Arms used to muster all the boy sailors in the Ship on the quarter deck, cane in hand and at a given Signal all the boys would make for the port main rigging and a regular race would take Place, who should be up the Port rigging to the cross trees first and down the starboard rigging. Any boy showing any laziness would get a sharp stroke of the cane. By me making the acquaintance of this important Personage as the Master at Arms holds on Board of a Man of War, I often succeeded in getting a little extra food. Every fine Evening four Glee Singers of our Company would go aft on the quarter deck and give some Glee and they would get a Glass of Grog each from one or two officers belonging to the Regt. Some of the officers were very kind, but the Colonel was a brute. I must say some of the officers behaved very kindly. The only Punishment I received during my seven years Service was the three days Grog stopped for sitting on the deck when I was too weak to stand.

At last on the 10th October 1849 we made Simons Bay. Here was the *Neptune* Ship bound for Van Diemens Land with Mr John Mitchel[2] the Irish exile, one of Smith O'Brien's comrades in the rebellion of 1848, and HM Frigate *Castor* of 30 Guns at anchor not far off. It was a great relief to get here. In a few hours we had full rations, and caught Cape Salmons 60–80 & 100 lb in weight [which] took four strong men to haul them on Board a small boat. No yellow flag at Mast head this time (thank God). We had plenty of rations. I heard some talk about the inhabitants refusing supplies, and they objected for Mr Mitchel to land. After being at anchor a few day Sir Harry Smith the Governor ordered us to land as the Kaffir War was breaking out. We landed and camped in Bell Tents on a level Piece of Land.

We were ordered on Board again to proceed on our Voyage, after remaining here in clover three weeks. On the 1st Novr we set Sail towards China. Up to this date we had been 141 days on our Voyage and not half way to China. The miserable life on Board the *Apollo* commenced again. I should have mentioned before the Scenes on Deck during Dinner time between 12 & 1 o'clock. At Breakfast time this Part was easily got over as each man got his Pint of thick Cocoa. The remainder of his Breakfast each man carried in a small calico or canvas bag. This was his days rations of small broken biscuit. The Biscuit we got at Rio de Janeiro was made of Rice. It was that hard you had to soak it to get your teeth into it. The Supply of Biscuit received at the Cape was better. At 11.30 o'clock the Grog bugle sounded, all hand[s] Parade, and your three water Grog served out. This Grog was looked upon as the great feast of the day, and made you feel happy for a short time. At 12 noon the Dinner bugle sounded. The orderly man and his assistant for each mess of 15 men, spread the tin Plates out on the deck. The meat & Soup came from the Galley and the orderly man for the day commenced to divide the Meat and serve out the Pea Soup, the Grog being taken about 30 minutes previous. The effects were dying out

[2] See above p. 17.

but gave you a keen Appetite, and the orderly and his assistant were watched with keen interest, each one spotting the Plate that he fancied best. When the word dinner was given a regular rush took Place for his favourite dish and many was the upset occurred and fight took Place. The fights would be of short duration, to be finished when we got on Shore. Several of these short fights myself took Part [in], as I came to the conclusion if you did not be in the melee I should often go short. At this time only in my 20th year I could take my Part with any on Board.

After leaving the Simons Bay at the Cape we commenced to cross the Indian Ocean. About three Weeks from leaving the Cape we passed St Pauls Island[3] and about the second week in Decr. we were off the Coast of New Guinea and the Island of Timor, the entrance to Timor Straits. Here orders were given no one was to sit down on deck under Penalty of being severely punished. What caused this was every night and morning a dense fog enveloped the Ship, and the dreaded Cholera was to be feared. I recollect sailing through the Straits of Timor with about a four knot breeze.

One fine afternoon, myself and Bradley were longing to be on Shore, and during the afternoon we agreed if a favourable opportunity occurred when rounding any of the headlands ahead, as it appeared the Ship would get rather close to them about dusk, if so we agreed to slip overboard from the bows and swim on Shore. We put two Pair of trousers each on and a Shirt extra, and we waited our opportunity. In a few minutes a Sergt. came and ordered us aft on to the deck, and eyed us as much as to say, not this time. We were disappointed and perhaps it was the best for us [for] after getting ahead of the Point of land the distance appeared fully two miles, but when the land was close on our beam it did not look above half a mile. If we had attempted to swim on Shore we should either [have] got drowned, or a boat would have been sent for us, and then we should have been tried by Court Martial, for attempting to desert. However it was not to be.

On the 21 Decr. 1849 we entered the fine Harbour of Buru an Island between Timor Straits and China Sea, and near the large Island of Borneo. Here we remained for some days to get water etc.

[3] Bodell rarely makes a factual error, but he saw St Paul's Island after leaving Brazil, not South Africa.

It was [a] very hot Place. About the third day here 24th Decr. I was one of a watering Fatigue Party sent on Shore to fill water Barrels. We had filled a good number. As the boat did not return when the Barrels were all filled, I went into the bush to look for Coco Nut Trees. These and other fruit were very plentiful and I had not gone far before I was amongst plenty of fine tall trees, and plenty of nuts to be seen, on top. The Notches the Native had made to climb the trees for the fruit was [seen] plainly enough. I tackled one fine looking tree, the nuts appeared to be fine large ones. Up I went and I found it pretty hard work to swarm such a distance fully 60 feet. When I got to the top I rested a few minutes and then commenced to knock off the nuts. About the fourth I over reached myself and all the time I had to stick close to the tree. However on trying to knock off the fourth nut, I must have relaxed my hold of the tree, for next moment I found myself descending the tree at a rapid Pace and I was hugging the tree with all my Power. The next thing I recollect was lying on the Ground with two of my mates and two natives alongside of me. I felt as if every bone in my body was broken. I was told I come down the tree at a rapid rate and on reaching the bottom my body come with such force that I bounded from the tree to where I was lying and they thought I was killed. No doubt by me clinging tight to the trunk of the tree it saved my life, but I paid dearly for it in another way. The trunk of a coco nut tree is ribbed from the Ground to the top and no branch till you get to the top. It is like a huge Umbrella. The roughness of the tree and there was I stuck to it. When I got round to look at myself I was a fearful spectacle, the inside of both arms, thighs and calves of my legs was all raw flesh, my left heel rubbed off, part of my Chin and my Chest was raw also. I was a Sight, but after a good rest I could walk, so no bones were broken.

When we were going toward the boats in a small River a Crocodile was visible. We also got some Pineapples. Towards evening we went on Board and my condition was reported to the doctor and I was sent for. He dressed my body in Parts required, my heel was the worst. I begged on the Doctor not to put me on the sick list as I wanted to go on Shore again. Next day I did not feel inclined to go on Shore, this being Christmas day, it was observed as a Sunday. I thought of Christmas eve 1847 when I sprained my ankle in Templemore, Ireland and here I was laid up again with loss of heel and sundry Pieces of flesh. I only managed to get on Shore once more and that was a favour, not as on Fatigue. I supposed I begged so hard with the Doctor that I was permitted to go on Shore.

During this time a Whale ship come into the Harbour and the Crew had mutinied. Four of their Sailors come on board and two of our Sailors volunteered to go on Board of the Whaler. On New Years eve I had got into the good Graces of the Master at Arms, he gave me some plum cake and about half Pint of Cape Smoke. This Cape Smoke made me quite tipsy. However at this time I often got tit bits from him, that tree affair and other little matters I had been conspicuous in had got several officers in my favour, and times passed much better with me, and I often gave my chum Bradley little extras.

About 2nd January 1850 we left Buru and in a few days the Philippine Islands were in sight and to our disgust remained in sight for 14 days. I don't believe we made 30 miles in 14 days. At last we got a breeze and in ten days we finished this long protracted Voyage. A few days before we reached Hong Kong, several large Chinese Junks crossed our Stern and on each Junk two Chinese Sailors would go to the Mast Head and come so close they could see all along our decks. The second day this was done all hands were sent down below. We heard these were Pirate Junks but they did not tackle us. Many is the ship they did tackle and [in] several instances murdered the Crews.

Just for the information of the Reader I'll give our life for one day on Board of the *Apollo*. As I said before we had one hammock between two men, that half the Soldiers had watch and Watch with the Sailors, that is half the Soldiers belong[ed] to the starboard watch and the other half belonged to the port watch. Those belonging to the port watch had their meals on port Side and those belonging to starboard watch on starboard Side. At meal times it was impossible to move about as each man was busy consuming his small rations and so many men on deck, 540 Soldiers (one company went by another Ship), with say since leaving Rio we were about 480 strong having [lost] about 60 with the Cholera. All these men getting their dinner on a Space from main hatch to forecastle, about 80 feet, & 12 feet wide and four big guns in that space each Side, besides under the forecastle the Crew had their quarters. At 6 a.m. those on Watch had to holystone decks. At 7 a.m. hammocks piped up. Those last in hammock (each numbered) had to fold them up and carry it on deck to be inspected, and placed in hammock nettings. Eight a.m. Breakfast, 10 a.m. Parade inspection and mounting Guard, 11.30 Grog, 12 Noon dinner, 1 to 2 smoking, 4 p.m. Grog, 4.30 Tea, 6 to 8 Smoko, then Hammocks below, turn out at 12 Midnight and your mate turn in to your Place, the hammock being quite warm.

III

Hong Kong,
1850–54

Of James Bodell's years in the army in Hong Kong not much needs to be said by way of explanation or background information. He himself says most of what seems relevant, commenting on many aspects of life in the colony, including some of the chief points noted in modern history books.

European traders in the large city of Canton had found relations with the Chinese officials, who regarded them as barbarians, very difficult. The traders were largely engaged in bringing in opium from India. Opium smoking was illegal in China—but there was a big demand. The Chinese government was powerless to stop trafficking in the drug, but they confiscated the merchants' stock. The merchants now wanted an off-shore island, where they could trade unimpeded by Chinese officials. There followed the 'Opium War', when the British navy blockaded Canton and occupied Hong Kong, a small island nearby, which the Chinese ceded to Great Britain in 1842.

The port, Victoria, did not grow rapidly as had Singapore. It acquired a reputation as a 'shack town' with its sheds made of bamboo and mats. But by the mid-1840s there were some substantial buildings on the waterfront, as well as Government House. The port acquired a very unsavoury reputation for vice and crime: it was said in 1845 that there were twenty-five respectable Chinese families and twenty-six brothels.[1]

Hong Kong was also notorious for the constant attacks by pirates on junks and other small trading vessels. But worst of all, among the European settlers, and especially the British regiments, it had a very bad name indeed because of its epidemics of fever, notably malaria and cholera. In 1843 one regiment lost a hundred men. In 1848, the death rate among the troops was over twenty per cent! When Bodell was stationed there two years later, as he vividly relates, the 59th Regiment was decimated. No wonder that the Colonial Treasurer, R. M. Martin, believed that the colony had no future. But it slowly grew. The Chinese

[1] N. Cameron, *Hong Kong the Cultured Pearl*, Hong Kong, 1978, p. 47.

*population rose from 20,000 in 1848 to 120,000 in 1865—by which
time the British had also leased from China Kowloon, an area on the
mainland nearby. Even so, when Bodell left for Australia in 1854 there
was little to hint that a great city would stand on the site in the century to
come.*[2]

On the 31st January 1850 we came to Anchor in the fine Harbour of
Hong Kong,[3] this extraordinary Voyage occupying 235 days.
Hong Kong was not much to be looked at in these days, the most
conspicuous [building] was the Barracks. Early on February 1st
Preparation for disembarking. We were to relieve the 95th Regt. A
strange coincidence, the number reversed to our[s], the '5 & 9'. By
afternoon we were all on Shore parading in Column of Companies
and the 95th marched out of Barracks and we marched in. The men
of the 95th was very pleased on leaving this the worst of Stations
for a British Soldier. The Company that came out in another Ship
had been here over three months and had left Cork three weeks
after us. We had been two-thirds round the Globe to go to China.
We crossed the line twice, not far from Buru the second time.

The Barracks of Hong Kong were the old and new. The old
Barracks were close to the sea, the new Barracks was opposite
across the Victoria Road and comprised three large stone Buildings
three storeys high with a 10 feet Venetian Verandah back & front.
The lower or basement Storey was for Guard, tailor and Shoemakers, Shops, the Bandroom, orderly Room etc & at each end large
wash houses and Bath rooms, with a good Supply of Water. The
old Barracks were built of wood with the Venetian Verandahs and
formed a T two storeys high. The 59th occupied both Barracks.
Adjacent was the Artillery Barracks and near the General Hospital

[2] Most of this information comes from the standard history, G. B.
Endacott, *A History of Hong Kong*, 2nd edition, Hong Kong, 1974. I have
also consulted various official reports and E. J. Eitel, *Europe in China*,
Hong Kong, 1895.

[3] The 59th's Register of Service records that they were in Cape Town on 30
October to 2 November, and reached Hong Kong on 11 February 1850, so
they were at anchor for eleven days before going ashore, giving the 95th
Regiment time to prepare to embark. Bodell's reminiscences are so accurate on such points that he may have kept a diary.

about half Mile towards Happy Valley was the quarters of the Sappers & miners, and on the Hill above the Cathedral was the Barracks where three Companies of the Ceylon Rifles were quartered. In addition of two companies of Royal Artillery was two companies of Lascar Artillery. I should say the total Strength of troops in Hong Kong would be about 1200.

After being so long on board ship each man had several Pounds to get balance of Pay. For the first two weeks we had lively times, Wine red and white, Sixpence per bottle, and each day an orderly Corporal of each Company would take names of Men for Wine at 12 Noon. Each man was allowed one third of a bottle or one Bottle between three men. This midday wine was only charged fourpence half Penny per bottle or three half Pence each. Any man requiring Wine, no tick but cash at once. Many a time I used other names beside my own and got a full bottle.

Each morning at 5 a.m. a Chinese Servant would enter the Barrack Room with a bucket of hot coffee and at 6 a.m. a Chinese Barber would come round to shave or cut your hair. Each man had to provide himself with six suits of white clothing, pith hats and 6 Hat covers in addition to the usual Soldier's Kit and all this to be paid out of Sixpence per diem. Before 8 months unfortunately these white and red clothing became cheap. The first six months our Colonel thought of nothing but Drill, heavy marching order Parades each day and four hours drill. Knapsacks on Sentry the same as at Home the leather stock under your chin. After being on Shore a few weeks I got a sore eye. This tormented me for several weeks. All this time nothing but Guards and Drill. About June the Hospital became pretty full, and the Doctor had these heavy drill[s] discontinued, and black neck ties substituted for the leather stocks, the ordinary soldiers' clothes put on one Side and white clothing instead. Each man had a large Box at end of his iron cot to hold these surplus clothing. The Regimentals would still be in the old Place, the Knapsack.

During July Augt & September, we buried about 300 men. I never seen or heard anything like the Epidemic that got amongst the men and every one, native and European has this Sickness. A man would appear in excellent Health today and in a few hours become raving mad with as the Doctors called it, Remittent Fever[4]

4 Malaria.

and in his Grave the next day. My sore eye compelled me to go into the Hospital early in March, and I was tortured for several months until by bad treatment I became blind with my right eye. 107 days on Spoon diet the Doctor (Powell, not our Regimental Doctor) said Starvation was the best cure for sore eyes. The Epidemic got into the sore eye ward and carried several strong men off. Every day at this time July & Augt three dead bodies put into the Hearse at once and four men of a Fatigue Party with Side Arms, at quick march, off to the Happy Valley (Grave Yard named). The Coolies every morning would come to the Hospital and nearly all the rations issued the previous day would be carried away, as refuse. This was a fearful time for the 59th Regt. The new Barracks was reported unhealthy and all the men and officers were removed out of it and crushed into the old Treasury and other Places. Several Doctors arrived from England and these appeared to cope with the Fever much more successfully than the old Doctors. A Dr Dickson took me in hand and instead of starving me he ordered one half fowl and half Bottle of Porter each day and allowed me to exercise myself along the Banks of the Harbour. In five weeks I left the Hospital but my eye affected me for years. I went under several operations under the hands of Doctor Powell, he nearly blinded me, but Dr Dickson treated me splendid. Poor Dr Powell succumbed to the scourge, and died. I had an attack. The General Doctor brought me round in a few days. If you had an attack and did not rally in 48 hours it was a case and you would surely die. A John Preston from near Leicester occupied next bed to me. One night about 8 o'clock the poor fellow commenced to eat Bread and told me he had seen the good Place and the bad Place, and gave three loud cheers, and fell back in bed and expired. Another man doubled a spoon up. He snapped madly at the spoon [with which] I was by the Doctor's orders giving him a little Brandy.

No one seeing the operation of this Epidemic can conceive its fatal and strange Death. What with this Remittent Fever and Dysentery the 59th Regt in 8 months after landing in Hong Kong, could not furnish sufficient men to mount Guard.[5] These duties

[5] It was recorded in 1844 that out of a hundred soldiers there were sometimes only five or six fit for duty. In 1843 there was one death out of every three and a half soldiers. R. M. Martin report, 1844, in *British Parliamentary Papers, China 24, Correspondence Relating to the Affairs of*

had to be performed principally by the Ceylon Rifles and Lascar
Artillery. I can safely say for three months I did not see 30 men
muster on one Parade which were principally Roll Call Parades. All
men on Guard and all Sentries were supplied with a Gill of Rum
and barks[6] at 8 p.m. and 5 a.m. as well as hot coffee. Each morning
a Coolie would go round each Sentry all round the Garrison with
the Rum & bark accompanied by a Corporal. About October 1850
our gallant Colonel who gave us such a Lecture on the duties of a
British Soldier in Cork Barracks on the ever memorable morning
8th June 1849, turned tail and ran away from us, and left his gallant
Lily Whites to fight it out. On his arrival Home he exchanged into
the 4th of Foot. At this time October 1850 the remnants of the 59th
were about 250 and 150 of these were either in Hospital on Shore or
on board the *Minden* Hospital Ship across the Harbour, so many
men dying. Their Kits, that is Regimentals and six suits of white
Clothing did not fetch above 5/- for the lot, Box included. These
Kits costing the poor fellow who had died about 5 to 6 Pounds.
Shakos & Coatees got amongst the Chinese, and you would see
Dozens of them parading about in full Soldier dress, many of the
Shakos became footballs for the Chinese and other Pedestrians.

At this time many large ships from America, and other Places
come into Hong Kong Harbour, and we lost many men by Desertion. I met several of these Deserters in the Australian Colonies

Hong Kong, 1846–60, Irish University Press, 1971, p. 113. The engraving
on a memorial for the dead of the 59th Regiment recorded that:
'Dead between 11th June, 1849 & 18th November 1858
Officers Regt. Col. J. L. Boughey, Capt. H. E. Stanhope, Lt.
R. Hackett, Lt. R. Cockell, Lt. T. E. Boughey, C. W. Powell, Surgeon
T. Cambell, Assistant Surgeon Downing, 2nd Lt. W. Macdonald,
Sergeants 21
Corporals 14
Drummers 4
Privates 446
Women 46
Children 170
Erected by the officers, NCOs and men of the LIX Regt.'
Lilywhite Gazette 1888, Fulwood Barracks, Preston, Lancashire.
[6] This was an infusion of the bark of the cinchona tree, which contained
quinine, a palliative for malaria which had been known for years as a
febrifuge.

afterwards. Two years from the time we left Cork Barracks, there was a General Parade called of the Originals, that is of the men we come out in 1849, and out of the 650 men that left Cork Barracks in 1849 only 62 remained. They had either died deserted or been invalided out and your humble servant was one of the 62 left and excepting several attacks of the Intermittent Fever (Shakes and Ague) and the prickly heat and one time hundreds of small boils broke out all over my body, I enjoyed good health.

In 1851 I did my best to get invalided. I had the Shakes and Ague so severely for three weeks before I went sick. I was reduced in flesh very much and I tried all I could by drinking Vinegar etc. to make me look pale that I was sent to the Hospital Ship *Minden* and during my stay on Board a General Doctor's inspection was held on Board to pick out sickly men for invaliding. My turn came in due course and I went crawling up to the Doctor. (I had taken an extra dose of Vinegar that morning that made my belly ache.) I stripped and the old Doctor examined me. In a few Seconds he stepped back a pace and said my good man dress yourself. Your are one of the healthiest men in the Regiment. I retired crestfallen, my hopes of seeing Leicester vanished. I was soon on shore at my duty, scheming was no use. A short time after this I made up my mind to desert and a comrade and myself put on three pair of two white and one Regimental trousers, and three Shirts and we planted near where we intended to ship on small boat a small bundle of clothing. This also we were nonplussed in as the Ship got under way about half an hour too soon for us. At this time I should have mentioned I was Lance Corporal and was Stage Manager and belonged to the Regimental Theatrical Company and one of the principal Performers, likewise a fair cricketer and rower and a fine jumper. In fact a good all round Athlete and could play skittles or have a bout with the Boxing Gloves with any one.

To resume about our Colonel about six months after he left us a Colonel Mainwaring came out to take the Command with his Wife and Family. He stopped about three months when he got enough and returned to England. We were without a Colonel another six months. I believe no Colonel in the British Army could be got. At last Major Henry Hope Graham was made Colonel without Purchase (at present time 1884 General H. H. Graham). Colonel Graham commenced to improve the condition of the men. A Racket Court we always had behind the old Barracks, but Colonel

Graham had Cricket Clubs, football Clubs, Skittles alleys and each Company had three sets of Boxing Gloves and he also enlisted the Merchants of Hong Kong on our Side and in a few weeks these Merchants presented us with several good pulling boats and in place of so much Drill as we had under other Colonels, we had constant contests with either the Civilians or Sailors in Cricket, boat racing and theatricals, foot racing, jumping etc. etc. Our lives was made fit to live for, in place of moping about, on Guard or confined to the Barrack Room, watch[ing] the Coolies carrying the Sick in the doolies[7] to the Hospital. Several Detachment[s] from Home had arrived and we again made a good Show on Parade. We also planted many hundred of ornamental Trees along the Victoria and other Roads, and all round the Barracks. I am told by a Person recently from Hong Kong these trees are an Ornament and are the principal Promenade in Hong Kong.

In 1852 I was made full Corporal and four months after, on account of being a good drill I was promoted over 13 senior corporal[s] to be full Sergt. and had to don the Scarlet Jacket with the silver chain and Whistle. I certainly was surprised at this Promotion. How I was promoted was this. The Regt mustered at 2.30 for adjutant Parade, six companies the Grenadiers on the right and my company the Light on the left. We had been at drill about half an hour when the word was given from being in line, to change front to the rear. The Sergt in command of the Grenadiers had made several mistakes during Parade. I was doing duty as Covering Sergt. for the Light Company and this move of changing fronts to the rear from the Regt. being in line, the commander of the Grenadiers could not give the right word of command correctly and the adjutant called on me to take command of the Grenadiers, and I did so, and executed the various words of Command during the remainder of the Parade all right. The Colonel was in the Verandah of the officers' quarters watching the drill. About 4 p.m. we were dismissed and in two hours I was in Orders for the Rank of Sergt, jumping over the lance Sergt stripe. Of course this Promotion got the neddy up of the 13 senior Corporals. A Yorkshire man of our Company Corporal Smith was also promoted over 8 other Corporals. Two Promotions in one Company the same day was unusual. From this act my life and daily duty was much improved, I doing

7 Litters.

my best to fulfil the duties I had to perform. I became a great friend of the Sergt Major, a Leicestershire man named Shepherd who come out with a draft, and was promoted for his good soldierly and drilling qualities. Many a comfortable evening we passed in his quarters. By this time 1852 our Regt was enjoying good health and many drafts having arrived from the Depot, to an old hand the Regt appeared not like the old 59th but like a new Regiment.

About this time a fire broke out one night in the west or Chinese Part of the city of Victoria, the only Town in Hong Kong of any note.[8] Our Company with two others was sent on duty about 10.30 p.m. to take charge of any goods removed from the fire and prevent pilfering, also to stop the Progress of the fire. By the time we arrived the fire had done a great deal of damage, and was approaching the European Part of the Town, and it was doing great damage, and proceeding westerly demolishing the whole of the Chinese Part of the Town very rapidly. We placed Sentries around a large heap of Merchandise piled up in the Square at the Junction of the European & Chinese Part. We stopped the fire spreading to European Buildings and as the fire burnt itself out we placed Sentries on the ruins. As many of the Buildings were the business Places of Chinese Money Changers, many thousands of Pounds worth of Dollars and Chinese Money, also golden Sovereigns were inside the burnt Buildings. At one time going round relieving Sentries and going amongst the Ruins I was ankle deep in Dollars. Amongst the Buildings burnt were several Hotels kept by Yankees and other Europeans.

Early morning I visited this Part of Town, and such a Sight was to be seen here. At this time several English Men of War were in the Harbour, and of course plenty of Sailors from these Vessels, and Sailors from other Vessels were ashore, as well, and I can safely say that hundreds of these sailors were helping themselves to bottled Ale & Porter. They must have demolished many Casks, and of course the Soldiers had their Share. Towards morning the fire had burnt itself out. The Chinese Playhouse stood amongst the Buildings in the west end and this was destroyed, and dozens of

[8] The fire was in December 1851. It destroyed much of the Chinese part of the town. Several soldiers were killed fighting the fire and twenty Chinese died. See G. B. Endacott, *A History of Hong Kong*, 2nd edition, Hong Kong, 1974, pp. 85–6.

Joss Houses also. The Chinese must have been very heavy losers by this fire and several Europeans also. When daylight appeared this part of Hong Kong had a very desolate appearance. The Pile of goods in the Square composed of Dollars silks & Satins and other valuable goods I should say fully one hundred thousand Pounds worth were saved and I noticed plenty pillaging went on. I could not resist the temptation, and I took several Pieces of Silk. Of course we could not hide much. After this fire burnt dollars and other Silver coins, as well as Chinese Cash was very common in circulation.

During the night Capt Massey and some Sailors from HM Ship *Cleopatra* were on Shore, this Vessel you recollect we met at Rio de Janeiro in 1849. About 9 a.m. a fresh Guard arrived to relieve us, and we went to Barracks. About 8 a.m. the Governor and Suite arrived to see the destruction the fire had done. During the fire hundreds of cats and dogs were burnt. Several cats I seen myself fall into the fire as roofs of Dwellings fell in.

One day I was drowning a little terrier dog in the Harbour behind the old Barracks and when I considered the dog had been under water long enough to Drown. Five minutes after I seen a Chinaman who had been watching me drown the dog go into the Water and dive for the Animal and bring it out. He would take this home and skin it and roast it and make a good meal from it. On another occasion I was over at Kowloon and here I saw the Chinese roasting a cat, and in another Place roasting a young dog. Bunches of frogs were very common things offered for sale in the Market (dried).

On this Visit to Kowloon I visited the Chinese Soldiers stationed at a Battery of 6 Guns, at the entrance to the Village of Kowloon. The Town was walled in, the Guns by appearance had not been fired for 20 years, and I should say if any one attempted to discharge them with Shot, the Gunners would stand a good chance of being killed. These Guns were all honeycombed rusty old Pieces of Iron. What a difference to the Kowloon Battery and the Battery on the hill near the Treasury in Hong Kong, the Guns pointing down the Main Street. In this Battery I learnt Battery Drill both for big Guns and large Mortars. This Battery could demolish the City of Hong Kong in a short time.

Every Summer several Ships from America arrived with plenty of ice, and so sure when any of these Vessels appeared and they cleared out again we always lost plenty of men by desertion. After my disappointment I never tried it on again. After Colonel Graham got command of the 59th the condition and comfort of the men was all that could be desired, any one leading a fairly steady life could do very well, and not eat too much fruit. Certain Seasons of the Year delicious fruit such as Pineapples, Bananas, and other tropical fruit would be very cheap and so sure fruit became cheap dysentery become frequent. Men would not guard themselves from over indulgence in these fruit and many [a] fine soldier lost his life by it.

For myself, I could not lie about the Barrack Room every afternoon. The men were allowed to lie on their beds. As a Sergeant I had a Room to myself and a batman as my Servant, only one Parade each day except Bathing Parade before breakfast. From Dinner if you had not to mount Guard or Picket you could go out of Barracks. I had made several acquaintances amongst the Civil Population, and a particular friend of mine was a young Gent who had brought two Race Horses out for John Dent & Co. This Person was located in comfortable quarters adjacent to the Racing Stables of Dent & Co. I also was on visiting terms with several of the Firm and also other Europeans in good Positions, and any time I felt inclined (which was very often) to pay any of the Friends a Visit I was always welcome. As I said before I was a member of the Garrison Theatrical Company and Stage Manager for the same. This position brought me in contact with many leading Merchants and other Europeans, Residents of Hong Kong, and in consequence, my spare time was passed amongst them. In the hot weather at various friends' houses, they would keep Bottles [of] Ale Gin etc. in a basket down a Well to keep it cool. These drinks would be very soothing and acceptable.

On one occasion I was in charge of the Governor's (Sir John Bowring) Guard when he gave a grand Ball. Dozens of Sedan Chairs arrived with the leading Ladies & Gentlemen of the City, and of course as Commander of the Guard, I had to keep things square. About one o'clock a.m. I was going around to see if things were all right, when two Bottles of prime Madeira Wine was given me. I thought I had a Prize, but on opening one, I did not like it so well as good Port Wine, it was too sweet. However it was very acceptable that hour of the morning.

Every year we had the Races at the Happy Valley Course. On the main road running around the Race Course in Happy Valley opposite the Grand Stand was the burying Ground where so many of our Comrades lay buried. I attended several of these Races, but I always considered the Race Course was in the wrong Place, as the Sight of the Grave Yard generally dampened my Spirits and took all Pleasure away at these Races. The Mandarins and the Chinese Nobility turned out very strong. You would get more Chinese ladies in one day at the Races than you would in five years in the City of Victoria Hong Kong. How this Happy Valley looks now I know not as I have not seen it for 34 years.

On one occasion I was sent out of Barracks with 4 men with Side Arms, on Duty to bring into Barracks four men reported absent from Tattoo Roll Call. On this occasion I had to visit all the rough Places generally frequented by Soldiers. One of these men absent was married, and through bad conduct his Wife was not allowed to sleep in Barracks, and of course we made straight to her Lodgings, but he could not be found on our first Visit. On our second Visit we pulled him from underneath the bed. We also found two others.

I was acquainted with several very nice little Chinese Ladies. On one occasion I expressed a Wish to see their small feet bare flesh and bone, and one of these Ladies complied very readily, and took the numerous bandages off, and what a Sight. It appeared that the foot had been made to grow into the ankle, the toes being crushed into and partly under the foot. It must have been great torture to bring the foot into such small compass.

There is in Hong Kong, I should say more Houses of bad repute kept by Chinese Women, than any Place I have seen with the same Population. Chinese Women of the lower order are very much given to misconduct themselves with the opposite Sex. On one occasion the Cathedral was robbed and the thief was caught as he was leaving a side door. A Chinese Policeman caught him and the thief cut the Policeman very much with a Knife.

During my Stay in China, Piracy was carried on by large Chinese Junks. These Junks was generally well and numerously manned, and would tackle a large Ship. The SS Man of War *Reynard* was called the devil ship by the Chinese Pirates. The HM Ship *Reynard* was only about 200 Tons but she was a Screw Steamer and could take down her funnel and burn her own Smoke and could go along about 7 Miles per hour with no Sails set and no Smoke to be seen. This Vessel did great execution amongst these Pirates. This Vessel burnt & otherwise destroyed several hundreds of these Pests. On one occasion an English Ship was not far from Formosa and one of these piratical Junks boarded the Vessel and killed nearly all of the Crew, took the Captain's Wife and kept her Prisoner a few days, and fearfully abused the poor Lady. The Captain by good fortune, got on to some Island and was taken to Hong Kong. A Man of War was sent off in pursuit of these Junks, and captured two Junks with part of their Crews. I recollect six prisoners were brought to Hong Kong, when landing they were all tied together by their [pig] tails, and tried at the General Criminal Sessions and all were sentenced to be hanged. These Pirates were all hanged together at West Point, a Gallows hav[ing] been erected for the occasion, three facing each way being back to back.

On another occasion a Gang of Pirates were taken and several hung. One man took ill, and lost the use of his limbs, and this man had been carried out of his cell every fine afternoon for many months, and deposited on the large stone Slab, that covered the Grave of his Comrades. On one occasion on myself visiting the Gaol, I seen this man carried to the stone Slab. It was usual for Petty Larceny, after the Prisoner had been sentenced, to place a board on his back and march him about half mile to [the] centre of the Chinese part of the Town. Here a set of Triangles would be ready and the culprit's back would be bared and receive several Strokes with a split bamboo as Part of his Punishment. I recollect two French Missionaries dressed as Chinese [with pig] tails also. They had been to Stanley a small Chinese Town on the west Side of the Island, and on their way back, these Missionaries were attacked by some Chinese Highwaymen, and brutally beaten and cut very badly about the back and neck.

During the time I was Stage Manager to the Regimental Theatrical Company we gave several Performances at the City Theatres and on these occasions the Colonel always allowed the Regimental Band to form the Orchestra and generally we had a full House. Of course members of the Theatrical Company always stopped out of Barracks all night and we used to have a regular Jollification. Several times I was the other side of the Island, on a shooting expedition, but did not get much Game. During the time I remained in Hong Kong after Major H. H. Graham was made Colonel, we planted thousand[s] of Trees, along the principal roads, and I have been told that the roads are fine Promenades.

In 1853 the Rebels and Imperialists commenced fighting against each other, and we expected weekly to be called out. Several times some great Chinese General with a numerous body Guard would arrive to have an audience with Sir John Bowring the Governor. The previous Governor [Sir George] Bonham was knighted in the Treasury Buildings. The improvement in the Health of all Troops since 1851 was very marked and soldiering was a Pleasure to what it was during Colonels Trevor and Mainwaring. Early in 1854 our adjutant received Leave of Absence to visit England, and on his departure six Sergeants rowed him from Shore to alongside the Ship he sailed to England in. I was one of these Crew. After being in England some months, he exchanged into the 57 Reg^t and when I was a Volunteer during the War in New Zealand, a Captain Lloyd, belonging to the 57 Reg^t was taken by the Maoris, his body mutilated the head cut off and carried by the Maoris on a Pole from Village to Village. This was the same Gentleman who was with us in Brazil after the Bullocks a good officer and a fine Soldier. Lieu^t Edward Hackett of our Company was appointed acting Adjutant during Lieu^t Lloyds absence and in 1857 Lieu^t Hackett was surprised by a Party of Chinese Soldiers, and his Head was cut off near Canton. In 1852 a War broke out at Burma and the HM Line of Battle Ship *Hastings*, was sent to Rangoon to take part in the War, and I can assure my readers many of us was hoping to be sent also.

In 1853 a great Commotion was caused in the Reg^t. One day the Orderly Room was cleared out to be white washed, and on removing the coal box several hundreds of letters were found. These letters some of them had been there for 18 months, two I wrote many months before were amongst them. Now these letters had been foolishly put there and the Pennies purloined, and the orderly Room Serg^t was accused of the theft. This Serg^t had been orderly Room head clerk on and off for many years. He was one of those unfortunate men [who] in his Youth had received a good education, but turned out a regular Drunkard. He had been reduced from Corporal and Sergeant several times, and being a good Penman when he kept steady for a few months he would be put into the orderly Room. He was made Prisoner for taking the Pence belonging to these letters, and was tried by Garrison Court Martial found guilty and sentenced to be reduced to the Ranks, to receive 50 Lashes with the Cat and drummed out of the Reg^t and this

Sentence was faithfully carried out. Although this Serg^t Tuke a Yorkshire man had been a favourite with the Colonel, the Crime he committed, the Colonel could not do anything to have the sentence of the Court Martial mitigated, and Tuke was reduced and marched to the old Barracks and received 50 lashes. He felt the Punishment severely. After he had had his buttons cut off his coat and marched through the Ranks of the Reg^t the Band Playing the Rogue March, he was detained a Prisoner until the first Ship sailed for England. I believe it is against the Articles of War to drum a Soldier out and leave him in a foreign Country. The feeling against Serg^t Tuke was very severe as many of the men had been deprived of letters from their relatives and friends, and this was felt to be something in a Place like Hong Kong.

I must not forget to mention my industrious Habits the time before I was promoted to Serg^t in 1851 and Part of 1852. I had as a comrade a Yarmouth fisherman, or had been such before he became a Soldier. This man was an expert in making all kinds of Network. I had seen on several occasions Horses belonging to Merchants & others dressed off with fine net tassels dangling about from these nets, and it occurred to me to get my mate to learn me to make nets. I soon picked net making up, and as I was in the habit of earning money by painting the name number Reg^t and Company on the Boxes belonging to the men also the Same on the Knapsacks, and type cutting also, and Hair Cutting I had a little Cash in hand [and] I suggested to my mate to commence making Horse Nets. To this he agreed, he making the Needle and holder out of Bamboo cane. I proceeded down Town and purchased several Pounds weight of the required size cotton, and we commenced operations. We could generally make one per week. In a few months we had opened a regular business [and] made Horse Nets for the General and his Son besides numbers of Military officers and Merchants. We used to get from 5 to 6 Dollars for each net the material costing from 1½ to 2 Dollars.

We did very well at this business better than painting Boxes or Knapsacks, in fact I must say all through my career in the Service or out of it, I have always been anxious to make money, and never begrudged working hard for it. Since I have been in Tauranga New Zealand I can safely say 15 years ago 1870 I worked 14 to 16 hours per day as a Carpenter, Builder, undertaker, Barber, Cordial Manufacturer and made many hundreds of Dozen of Lemonade &

Soda Water, by hand without Machine, and then it went off Pop when opened. Anyone understanding this business will soon understand the difficulty I have to over come. I have carried 5 Gal. ginger beer 3 Miles on my Shoulder to a customer. If I had paid the Carriage it would have took all the Profits, to get a dray was uncertain.

A few more words about China. At the west end of the Harbour is what is called Jardines Village named after the Firm of Jardine Matheson & Co. large China and East Indian Merchants. This firm had been very kind to the 59th Regt in presenting boats etc to exercise ourselves on the Water. About one Mile nearer to the Barracks in the celebrated Happy Valley three sides of the Valley is surrounded with Hills, and in the centre is the Race Course. [On the] north west Side is the Road to Jardines Village and on the south Side is the Grave Yard, where many thousands of British Soldiers and other Europeans lay mouldering. The Epidemics that visited Hong Kong was a real Puzzle to Medical men. Some attributed [them] to the Water as this Water came from the Mountains at the back on south Side of the City of Victoria. Possibly the Water had something to do with it. About 1851 a road was made along the side of these Mountains by prison Labour (Chinese) and Dozens of Bodies in various Stages of decay, others nothing to be seen but Bones and [pig] Tails, were dug out of the Earth.

A Chinese Funeral is well worth describing. A Chinese coffin is made to stand on either end, and round, resembling a Part of the Trunk of a Tree about 2 feet diameter and about six feet long, with the bark taken off, each end is made wider than the Centre. From the Place where the body is taken from, to the Grave a Person goes ahead of the cortege distributing Pieces of Rice Paper with Chinese Characters (letters) stating the name age etc of the deceased. Then follows the Body and Mourners, playing Music a discord between the Sound of a big Drum and the squealing of a Pig, and following in the rear of all is generally two men with bamboo Poles across their Shoulders carrying large Baskets full of eatables for the Corpse to consume before he enters into another world. At a funeral of a Lascar quantities of Rice and other eatables are also left at the Grave. Generally the Burying Place is on the Side of a Hill.

Now I must describe the last few weeks of my military life. The last few months several Sergeants had claimed or bought their discharge, one of these Sergt had run away with another Sergt Wife and cleared off as was said to Australia. The Serg^t that lost his Wife was still in the Reg^t. Now this woman was the same Mrs Rogers that was the Wife (pretty one) of Corporal Rogers that occupied the Barrack room in Templemore Barracks in 1848 when I had a fight with Brown for insulting her, described early in these Reminiscences. When it was known she had cleared out with Serg^t Barrow, Serg^t Rogers applied for his discharge and in a few weeks left the Reg^t but did not leave Hong Kong, as we expected he would. At this time I was paying my addresses in the love line to a young Lady living in Hong Kong, and myself began to think I could do better out of the Service than in it. So in the first week in September 1854 as both her Mother and herself expressed themselves if I had any intention of marrying the Daughter they wished me to leave HM Service, and I attended the Orderly Room one Morning, and applied to the Colonel for my Discharge. The Colonel and all the officers seems astounded, and the Colonel could not answer me for a Minute. Then he said Serg^t Bodell are you in earnest. I am Sir says I. I shall have to refuse you your request, as I cannot part with You. I told him that many others had got their Discharge and why could I not get mine. He said he had received Authority not to let any more men leave as War was or going to be declared between England and Russia. He refused me point blank. I was so much hurt by this refusal that I went into a bath Room and had a good Cry. This made me more determined. Why should I be kept in the Army when I could better myself. On my coming out of the bath Room Serg^t Ross Master Tailor met me. He said hello whats up and I told him.

I went straight to my Rooms, and dressed myself as neat as I could and went out of Barracks and went straight to the Acting General Griffin's Quarters. On my arriving there I asked the Sentry if the General was in. Yes. I approached the Building when I met the Orderly. As told him I requested to see the General he looked at me and I said you will oblige me by telling the ADC that Serg^t J. Bodell of the 59 Reg^t wishes to speak to General Griffin. Now by the Rules of the Service I was liable to be made Prisoner for attempting to see the General without Permission from Colonel Graham. I had made several nets years before for the ADC and he knew me, and in a few minutes the Acting General appears, and I went up to him giving him a Salute, and asked him if he would allow me to say a few words to him, of very particular import. He nodded assent. The ADC went on one Side and I told him my Grievance. He looked at me very keenly. I was expecting every minute to be made Prisoner but he said in a very kindly way Serg^t Bodell I will see your Colonel today, and you will hear more about this matter tomorrow. I assure you I put it to the General in a way that touched his feelings. I saluted and retired. I must have appeared very excited or resolute, as the Orderly said as I passed him if anything was going wrong. I answered him No.

I went back to the Barracks and all that day I did not know what to do to pass time away. In the afternoon I went down Town, and told my intended the Colonel refused and my interview with the Acting General. It was a very anxious time till 10 o.c. next morning. After 10 o'clock Parade [in the] morning the orderly Room call sounded and I being orderly Serg^t I had not to attend, but in a short time I was called and informed my Presence was required at the orderly Room. I dressed and was there in a very short time. The Acting Assistant Ensign E. Hackett called me into the Orderly Room. On my appearing before the Colonel with the Customary Salute, he said I see you are determined to leave us Serg^t Bodell. I pleaded the same as I did to the General and added Colonel Graham in one sense I am sorry to leave the Reg^t but I've considered matters over and Colonel Graham I have come to the Conclusion I can do better out the Army than in it and pleaded very hard hoping he would let me go etc. He said you know the Colours [of] the Grenadiers will soon be vacant and I was going to make you Pay Serg^t of the Grenadiers and shortly you would get the Colours. I sincerely thanked him but that would not induce me to remain. Then he said you will have to Pay £18, turning to the Paymaster is that the Sum. He answered Yes, and [if] you stop another few weeks that will be reduced considerably then you will have seven Years Service. I told him I hope[d] he would let me go as a Commission would not induce me to stop. Then he made the remark he was lately losing some of his best Serg^{ts} but as I seemed determined he would let me go, but I should have to remain till end of the month. I thanked him and withdrew. I felt so elated I could have jumped the Barracks. The Adjutant followed me out and took me by the hand and wished me every success.

I went straight to my Room and made out a Pass for 7 days, an unusual time as three days was generally the time on Stations like Hong Kong. However I went straight to our Captain

W. W. Lodder (General Lodder for years, on half Pay at present) and he smiled but signed it. I took it to the Adjutant. He also nodded and smiled and in a few Seconds he appears with the Colonel's Signature on it, and I felt more elated than ever. I certainly was very fortunate. I was out of Barracks in a short time and that day I had a full suit of civilians clothes made, Belltopper and all, and I can assure you I was envied by many of the officers, besides many others. I enjoyed myself very well during these 7 days. At expiration of the term I appeared in the Barracks, and in a short time I was warned for Guard, done my Guard. Next day wrote another Pass for 7 days and got it, done another Guard after expiration of the second term and then applied for 3 days to end the Month and got it and attended the Orderly Room on the 30th September 1854 paid the £18 and got my Discharge from the Army. Whilst in the orderly Room every officer in the Reg[t] offered to do anything they could for me wishing me every Prosperity. I suggested perhaps a Character from them might do me good and in a short time I had over a Dozen, the only one I have at present (1885) is the Character I received from the Acting Adjutant Lieu[t] Edward Hackett who lost his life at Canton. On my Discharge the Character is very good. This I have at present. I had served in HM Service six Years ten Months and half, and had been a non-commissioned officer more than half the Period.

I went up to the Serg[ts] Mess and had a short Jollification, and then to my Room where I had a suit of civilian clothing [and] into these I jumped. My silver Bugle for the forage Cap I sent home to my Parents in England. The silver Chain & Whistle and other costly articles I sold, and gave many things to my batman, and cleared out of Barracks and took up quarters with a friend. The next consideration was my Marriage. This took place on the 3rd of October, and a grand turnout it was.[9] Sedans was the sort of Carriages we had carried by Chinamen, and a long string they were of these and as we passed the Barracks, the Reg[t] Band turned out and played Haste to the Wedding. A few days after I paid a Visit to the 59th Serg[ts] Mess and of course we had another spree there. The

[9] James Bodell married Sarah Mackinay on 3 October 1854. St John's Cathedral's Marriage Register, 1838–76. (P.R.O. HKMS 40). This reference was kindly obtained for me by Professor Leonard Young, University of Hong Kong.

Colonel met me in the entrance to the Barracks, and come up to me shook me by the hand wishing me every success and many more of the officers did likewise.

After about a week I felt anxious to leave China and wanted to get to the Australian Colonies. To get there I had to take Passage in a Spanish Brig *Tempo* and about the 14 October we sailed for Manilla. When we were well out at Sea several Chinese piratical Junks came pretty close, and we had two 12 lb. cannonades on Board. These the Captain loaded and gave each Passenger, eight I believe, a Revolver to protect themselves. We had a fine Breeze and they did not molest us. This Spanish Brig was a very comfortable Vessel. The Table was very good. 6 a.m. each morning hot coffee or Tea brought to your State Room, Breakfast at 10 a.m., Lunch at 2 p.m. Dinner at 7 p.m. This lasted till about 9 p.m. and after that you could drink as much cognac as you liked or Wines. I brought a case of Hollands Gin on Board [as] I preferred this. About the fifth day out a tall Sailor annoyed me very much, every morning during washing Decks this Sailor would stand at the port hole of my Cabin, trying to see anything going on. On several occasions I spoke to him about it but he still kept up the annoyance so I spoke to the Captain about it and he said let him do it again and if so tell me. Next morning he was at the port hole as usual and I told the Captain. About 10.30 that morning I was sent for to go forward to the Captain. When I got there the Captain had this tall Sailor tied down across a thick Spar, with his Posterior bare and the Boatswain slogging at him with a rope end. The Sailor roared out terrific, and struggled, but he got a severe Punishment. When the man was loosened the Capt turned to me and said are you satisfied. Of course I said Yes. I was sorry to see the man get such severe Punishment. The Captain said he is only a Shoemaker and no Sailor. The other morning I spoke to him about the port hole but he took no notice of me said the Captain. I think he will another time. I had peace from that quarter.

After about 12 o'clock Midnight I heard an unusual noise direct across the small Saloon. I may say two cabins were occupied by a Chinese Mandarin, his Wife and Servants, and as it was rather warm Weather each Cabin was covered at entrance by Curtains hanging in front. I peeped through the curtain to see the Cause of the Noise and there was the old Mandarin trying to take liberties with his Wife's Maid, and she was resisting him all she could. I called out to him and he went into his Cabin. Next morning at 9 o'clock the Maid was on the quarter deck, and seeing myself and Wife, she came to us and I left her to talk to my Wife. As I did so I turned to have a good look at her and she was about as pretty Specimen of a Chinese Woman [as] I had seen. But my eye caught a Sight of the butt of her [pig] tail and the back of her head was all alive with Vermin. When I caught my wife's eye I beckoned her to come away, and I told her. She said the Chinese Woman told her all about the old Mandarin's Conduct the Night before, and she wanted my Wife to take her into our Service on arrival at Manilla, but I considered this out of the question. In fact I knew the old Mandarin would have objected.

In 10 days from Hong Kong we arrived at Manilla, a fine large Bay and several large Ships at Anchor. We no sooner cast anchor than several Watermen's boats were alongside. Myself and a Gentleman who had just returned from England by the Overland route via Hong Kong, and a Merchant of Manilla went on shore, a distance fully two Miles from Harbour into the River to Landing Place. On going on Shore I offered the Boatman half [a] Sovereign, but the Spaniard objected to take it saying Dollar. My Companion said if you will come a short distance to our Establishment I can change Dollars for Gold. I thanked him and off we went the boatman bringing up the rear, and we walked fully $1\frac{1}{2}$ miles before we came to his Place of business and I requested Dollars for seven Sovereigns and [a] half. For this I received 30 Dollars and offered the boatman one Dollar which he took and departed. He hav[ing] refused half Sov^r. In a short time I left my friend the Merchant and departed to retrace my steps near the Landing Place, and took up quarters at Madam Barbaries, a very good private Hotel. On being shown into my Sitting Room the Bed room joined it the Window facing the River, but in the corner of the Bedroom there was a Large glass Case containing a representation of our Saviour as he was taken down from the Cross on Mount Calvary, hand and body nearly covered with Blood. I returned to the Ship and brought a few Parcels and my wife. I had a quantity of Luggage on board, but this I could not get till the following day, as it had to pass through the Custom House. Our Quarters was very comfortable but the Mosquitoes were abominable in hundreds every night. Although we had good bed curtains we could not keep the Mosquitoes from us.

I found out a Dollar was only reckoned Value for four Shillings. At this rate I had lost 4/- out of each Sovereign. This was terrific loss and on making inquiries I found a Sovereign was only Value 4 Dollars and each dollar Value 4/- and every Sovereign I changed I lost 4/-. On the other hand things were very cheap. As I passed my Luggage through the Customs I ascertained that a large ship was going to Sydney in 10 to 12 days, so we made ourselves at Home and enjoyed ourselves, nearly every day driving about seeing all the Lions [?] of the Place. I often went into the Country, also visited old Manilla, the Cigar Manufactory 2000 Spanish Girls working making Cigars. Every evening at Sun Set a Bell tolled and you would see all Spaniards go down on their knees, and such as myself if walking the Street stop and uncover your head. On the bell ceasing, up they would jump and in a few Minutes Dozens of Spaniards hurrying towards the Quay on the River each man carrying a Game Cock, and the next hour you would see several Cock fights and after dark the Dancing Saloons would begin and till Midnight Dancing Saloons would be crowded and hundreds of pretty Spanish Girls and Women doing the Fandango and other dances. I must say every one appeared to enjoy themselves in Manilla. If you wanted to take a Drive into the Country, you could get a carriage with Driver and Postillion, a fine turn out, for two Dollars per day. There were two Barracks full of Spanish Soldiers, their Bands playing every evening on a splendid Drive near a large Battery overlooking the Harbour, and for Miles on Sunday afternoon on this drive would be horse Soldiers posted about 200 yards apart, with drawn Swords, to keep all Vehicles to keep the left hand or near Side of the Road. No fear of a collision as all Carriages leaving the City would keep on [one] Side and all Carriages returning would keep the other Side. Youngsters running about with Cigars and a light for sale the same as at Home in England.

I made several friends while I stopped in Manilla and only for the heat and Mosquitoes I very probably would have gone into business. At this early Stage since leaving the Army I was intent to be at some thing. For the last two years I had a great wish to See the Australian Colonies, and as there was a large Ship the *Duke of Northumberland* in the Bay loaded with Sugar and Cigars for Sydney New South Wales, I took a Cabin Passage, and after staying in Manilla about twelve days, we embarked and on the 1st November 1854 set Sail. By giving the Custom House officer two Sovs. all my

Luggage was let pass without inspection. Madam Barbaries Son put me up to this dodge. During my Stay in Manilla the Governor visited the Part I was living in and it was a great Gala day. The *Duke of Northumberland* was a fine Ship. I had one of the State rooms right astern the Stern Windows with Horse hair Sofa was very Pleasant and comfortable. I occupied the Port Side and Captain Robinson the Starboard Side cabins. I had a fine Double bed and my Wardrobe 7 feet high stood up right in the Cabin. Expecting a longish Voyage, I took on board a Supply of wine, biscuits and Square Gin. We soon found out the Ship was a poor Sailor, a regular Slow Coach, but could stand a rough Sea. The other Cabin Passengers were an elderly Lady with three sons, and two men in the Steerage. Considering the Poop was 45 feet long, and only 6 Saloon Passengers we had plenty of room. The other occupants of the Saloon were the Captain [and] first and second Mates. We were a nice little Party.

In about a week we were off Singapore, in very hot weather, from that through the Straits of Borneo into the Java Sea and Straits of Sunda. Here we anchored and got a Supply of Turtles Coconuts and several Monkeys. I bought a lot of Coconuts and a fine little monkey, but a very mischievous one. One Turtle weighed nearly 4 cwt. These made very good soup. We had some very fine Pigs and Poultry. The Captain did not intend us to starve. After leaving the Straits of Sunda, we entered the Indian Ocean, and crossing this we experienced for weeks very little wind. It took us seven weeks to make Cape Lewin, the S.W. Cape of New Holland (now Australia). It was a very tedious time. The day we were off Cape Lewin we got a Gale of Wind and the Ship was short handed and one day boating ship the Captain asked me to take hold of the Steering Wheel as he required all hands at the Ropes. The Ship would not go round. I took the Wheel and as the Sails were being hauled round the Wind threw all them aback, and sent the Vessel astern nearly burying the Stern of the Ship into the Sea, and wrenched the Steering Wheel out of my hands. I tried to stop it and it caught me on my Knuckles and one Knee and sent me hopping on one leg along the Poop. In a Second the Captain and two Sailors ran to the Wheel, and after some rough knocks secured the Wheel this time with strong ropes. For myself I was a cripple for the time, and received the Consolation it was a good job it was not worse and the Captain said he had seen two men thrown over the Sides of a

Ship by the Wheel when the Sails had been suddenly filled aback and sent the Vessel astern. He never got me again to take the Wheel.

When we were crossing the Indian Ocean one fine calm day very hot, the Pigs were let run about the Deck for exercise, and the Captain had his Stern Windows up and all Saloon Doors open, and one of the Monkeys had got loose and was amusing himself aloft and as some of the Crew were amusing themselves with another Monkey, this one ran along the deck and frightened the Pigs and the next minute all the Pigs went follow my leader, straight through the Saloon, through the Captains Cabin and out of the Stern Window into the Sea. Here was a jolly mess, all our fresh Pork overboard. Boats were manned and went after them. A slight breeze had sprung up and we soon left Boats & Pigs behind. After all the bother not one Pig was saved. We waited for the boats, and the Sailors said the Sharks must have taken the Pigs. This was a serious loss. The Poultry were nearly all gone, also the biscuit was mouldy and mostly dust. By the time we made Cape Lewin, the rations in the Cabin were very bad, so much so I spoke to the Captain and complained about the poorness of the rations. One day he opened a trap in the floor of his Cabin and under the floor he had a Stock of Salmon, Sardines and various preserved Provisions, and he inspected the Stock of Biscuits and flour. He had several Casks of flour and ordered about 3 lb. loaf to be baked every afternoon. The Crew also came aft and complained about their Rations, saying the Lime juice was bad and only made out of the Medicine Chest. My Stock of Biscuits and Square Gin had run out some time since, and one day I was in the Captain's Cabin talking to him and he showing me the Chart as he often did, before he told me he had a Supply of Port & Sherry Wine on Board but if he sold any to me he was liable to be fined one hundred Pounds. He told me he could sell it at 27/- per doz. but he was afraid. On me pledging my Word not to tell anyone, but he could make me a Present of the Wine, I would make him a Present of a Parcel. However it ended that I could get and did get as much Wine as I liked after this at 27/- per doz. Being short of rations I became a good Customer for the Wine.

On Christmas Morning 1854 as the Crew had been very obliging to me on several occasions getting any Box I required out of the Ships hold, I gave them a Bottle of Wine between each two of the Crew not knowing I was doing anything wrong. The Captain also (unknown to me) gave the Crew one Bottle of Wine for each three of the Crew so between us the Crew done very well, and made several of them very talkative. During the afternoon some of the Crew came aft and demanded better rations and lime juice. [The Captain] got to hear about me giving the Crew Wine, and he called me into his Cabin, and spoke very seriously to me. If the Crew got too much Wine the matter might become serious, and cautioned me from giving the Crew any more wine, and as several of the Crew including the third mate talked insultingly to the first mate and the Captain. I did not interfere with the Crew again or give them any more Wine.

A few days after this the Captain came into my Cabin, and informed [me] he had been informed the Crew were going to mutiny and he handed me a revolver to protect myself he saying the first and second mates and himself were well armed and if the Crew did not behave themselves, there would be some shooting done. I was surprised at this, and it put me on my mettle and if it came to anything, I should do some shooting also. I had a good 5 chamber revolver and plenty of Ammunition. That afternoon I kept a strict watch on all the Crew's movements. The Women and boys knew nothing about what was going on. Two of the Crew I never did like during the Voyage. I had made free with most of the Crew but two of them I could not do so with. Myself Captain and first Mate had very little rest that night. Next day about 10 o'clock some of the Crew came aft and requested to see the Captain. I went forward and spoke to some of the Crew, in a Second I could see how things stood. About 4 of the Crew with the third mate was the Cause of the ill feeling. Several of the Crew assured me my safety and the ladies were all right, but I told them all hands in the Saloon were well armed with some new revolvers and Ammunition I had on Board taking to Australia, and it would be madness for the Crew to attempt to do anything. I also had to chat with the two Steerage Passengers, and they said they had been watching events, and blamed the third Mate and 3 of the Crew.

Things got so serious that we did not know the hour a Mutiny would take Place and several days the loaf of Bread the Steward had baked in the oven in the Galley, in Charge of the Ship's Cook, for the Saloon Passengers, had been taken out of the oven before it was properly baked. The disappearance of this loaf caused some Want in the Saloon. The Captain was very vexed about it and one day he spoke harshly to the Steward and the Cook and Steward kept such strict Watch on the oven they discovered the culprit, and he was reported to the Captain. He was one of the ringleaders of the discontents. The captain did not know what to do. Next day a Sailor upset the poor Cook near the Galley and his head came down on to a beam with such force that the poor fellow's eye was banged up and his scalp was severely cut above the right temple. This fellow was brought aft and put in Irons. The two Steerage Passengers and Captain two mates and myself with the two young boys in the cabin made a very good Show with revolvers. I could see so many armed cowed the Crew and we had Peace after. The loaf of Bread was allowed to see the Saloon table every day. During this discontentment amongst the Crew, the monkeys belonging to the first and Second Mates one Steerage Passenger and some belonging to the Crew all disappeared. My own monkey was the only one left on board. This was pure spite against the Ships officers. The last few weeks on Board had been a very anxious time.

During the heavy Gale off Cape Lewin a small Schooner was about two miles seawards of us riding the high seas like a duck. We ran down the Great Australian Bight off Port Adelaide with a strong breeze, afterwards very little wind. One day the Captain pointed out to me on the chart that if he could have sailed the Ship the way the compasses pointed the Vessel would have been 600 to 700 miles on dry land. The Ship *Duke of Northumberland* was an iron one, and affected the compasses that much. The Captain had been sailing the Ship since she was built, some years, and he was a large Owner of it.

At last we made Cape Otway the entrance to Melbourne and we were very short of rations at this time seriously so, and the Crew had been complaining (rightly so this time). We had a head Wind also dodging about Kings Island, making near the entrance to Launceston next day Melbourne side of Bass Strait. Myself and the Lady Passenger consulted together and we asked the Captain to take us into Melbourne or Launceston. He said it would cost £80 Port charges etc and we agreed to give the Captain £50 between us if he would take us into Melbourne. He answered under present circumstances he considered he would [not] be justified by doing so he would give an Answer next day. Early next morning a large Ship came in Sight coming from Melbourne bound for Callao and the first Mate took a boat's Crew and boarded it and got a good supply of fresh Provisions Tobacco etc. Another large Vessel came in sight and came within hailing distance. A strange coincidence. This Ship left England the same day as we left Manilla and being 76 days out loaded with Passengers. After we got the fresh Provisions it was no use trying to get the Captain to go into Melbourne. The Ship leaving Melbourne told the mate about the Ballarat Riots, and we thought the Goldfields were all done. We had a tedious time to Sydney.

IV

Tasmania and Victoria,
1855–63

Great Britain founded the colony of New South Wales in 1788 partly to provide a dumping ground for convicts now that the American colonies had broken away from the Empire. But there were also commercial and naval motives, notably to give Britain a southern base from which she could challenge her imperial rivals, the Dutch and French, and secure access to naval supplies such as spars and flax. The Van Diemen's Land and New Zealand settlements were off-shoots of New South Wales.

James Bodell's first home in the southern colonies was near Hobart in Van Diemen's Land, where he ran a hotel. Van Diemen's Land and New Zealand had both been discovered by Abel Tasman in 1642. Small areas of the former country were occupied by the British in 1803–4 partly, at least, to assert British claims. It became a separate colony, with a Lieutenant-Governor, in 1825. Eventually it offered a site for a very large convict establishment as well as providing land for numerous free settlers. Governor Arthur established a severe—and dreaded—prison at Port Arthur in 1830 where re-offenders and violent prisoners were kept. Altogether some 122,600 men and 24,900 women were transported to New South Wales and Van Diemen's Land.[1] Discipline was maintained principally with the lash, which was administered, as in the army and navy at the same time, with what would now be regarded as extreme cruelty.

Transportation ceased in 1853 but there were still thousands of convicts when James Bodell arrived in 1855. It is of the convicts, or ex-convicts and partially freed convicts, that he writes in his reminiscences. They were his rough customers. There was another Van Diemen's Land of which he says, and presumably knew, very little. That was the world of the Governor and his lady and the clergy and gentry which is recorded, for instance, in the letters of the Inspector of Schools,

[1] L. L. Robson, *The Convict Settlers of Australia*, Melbourne, 1965, p. 4. On Port Arthur, see W. D. Forsyth, *Governor Arthur's Convict System*, 2nd edn., Sydney, 1970.

Thomas Arnold the Younger.[2] *Van Diemen's Land was about to be renamed 'Tasmania'—which Bodell does mention—and to have its first elections, moving from being an imperial gaol to becoming a self-governing colony.*

One reason for the abolition of transportation, or, at least, an argument against it, was the discovery of gold in Victoria in 1851. To send hardened criminals to that 'auriferous region' seemed likely to reward crime. In 1856 Bodell and his wife sailed for Melbourne and he settled on the gold fields at Maryborough, about a hundred miles inland, where he ran several hotels.

The Port Phillip district (later Victoria) had originally been settled by pastoralists from Van Diemen's Land in 1834. Within a few years the whole of the Western District was occupied by sheep farmers— squatters and other pastoralists. Melbourne became a small town, but the population was not great—77,000 in 1851, in which year alluvial gold was discovered. By 1854 there were 236,000 people, and over half a million by 1861. Further gold rushes occurred throughout the 1850s, which James Bodell describes in his reminiscences.

While Bodell was in Victoria his wife Sarah disappears from his reminiscences and then, or soon after, from his life. He refers to her presence in 1859, but never again. He went to New Zealand in 1863 and remarried in 1866, describing himself as a widower.[3] *Whether he deserted her, which was common in the colonies, is unknown. Perhaps she left him—he freely confesses to excessive drinking at that time. What is known is that she did not die in the Colony of Victoria, at least in the years 1859 to 1868.*[4] *The mystery will probably remain, for if she left Victoria she could have gone anywhere, Hong Kong or England, for instance, and perhaps remarried herself or changed her name.*

The diggers were a restless mob of Europeans and Chinese. Bodell describes them rushing off to this or that new digging. Some of them sought gold in California in 1849, Victoria in the fifties and then Otago, in the South Island of New Zealand, after the 1861 discovery of gold there. That discovery attracted Julius Vogel, a future New Zealand premier, to leave Victoria. Bodell, who had lost the considerable

---

[2] J. Bertram (ed.), *Letters of Thomas Arnold the Younger 1850–1900*, Auckland, 1980.

[3] See below, p. 169.

[4] A search was made in the records of the Registrar-General of Births, Marriages and Deaths of Victoria for the years 1859–68.

wealth he was amassing, joined the militia which was being recruited to
fight the Maoris in the North Island.

―――――

We arrived in Sydney Harbour on Jan[uar]y 29th 1855 and as we were entering this fine Harbour a Sydney Brickfielder was blowing and as we went up Harbour it was suffocatingly hot and the City of Sydney appeared covered with a red glare. The heat was so excessive I turned quite faint and had to sit down. For the last six weeks I had nearly lived on Sherry Wine. We had not anchored many minutes before several Waterman's boats came along side and off I went on Shore, to get a Place to take my Wife and Luggage to. This I soon found and returned on board and fetched my Wife, and right glad I was to get on Shore again. 90 days from Manilla, a Voyage we should have done in six to seven Weeks.

Next day I had all my Luggage and the Pet Monkey removed to my Lodgings. Sydney appeared a large Place to me, but many rookeries of Buildings about the lower Part of George Street and near the several quays, lots of Shipping in the Harbour. About the third night on Shore, my Monkey got into the Passage where the Bedrooms were, and damaged a Lady's silk Dress, so much so I had to purchase another for the lady and the monkey became a very costly pet. I could not keep him out of mischief so I exchanged him for a small Terrier dog.

A few nights after this I was aroused out of sleep by some one calling to open the bedroom Window and on no account to strike a light. On awakening and jumping out of bed I could not get my eyes open and felt quite giddy. I opened the Windows and then the Door and the Landlady and house Maid were standing close at it. For mercy sake don't strike a light, your room and the house is full of Gas. I directly went to the Chandelier in my Bedroom and sure enough on putting the light out I had turned the Gas off and on again. The Screw worked too easy. All windows and Doors were kept open for about one hour then all danger was over.

One day passing along George Street who should I meet but the Gent who brought Mr Dent, Merchant of Hong Kong, Race Horses from England and who was such a Friend to me in China. I had forgotten Sydney was the Place he had left Hong Kong for with two of the Race Horses. Of course the Meeting was quite unexpected and right glad we were to meet again under such changed Circumstances, and I introduced him to my Wife, and we had a happy time of it until he left for the Country on business.

When I had been about two Weeks in Sydney, a Proclamation appeared in the Papers, by the Governor and Parliament of Tasmania (then Van Diemen's Land) offering £15,000 for a Gold Field in Tasmania. The various reports about the Ballarat riots[5] made me think the Gold Fields of Victoria were done, and as I did not care for Sydney I made up my [mind] to try Tasmania, and in a few days I took Passage in the *Emma* Brig, Captain Brown, and bid adieu to Sydney. I felt Sydney hotter than China. The day I landed three men fell dead in Sydney Streets during the hot Brickfielder I mentioned before.

During the trip to Hobart Town, one day the Wind went all round the compass in one minute. The Captain said he never before experienced such a peculiar Wind. The *Emma* was a nice smart Vessel and a nice little Cabin 7 Passengers in all. When we arrived off Cape Pillar the entrance to the Bay going down towards Hobart Town I caught 4 Sharks. This was off that dreadful Penal Station Port Arthur I heard so much about afterwards. 8 days from Sydney we arrived at Hobart Town went on Shore and secured a nice cottage as I had enough furniture to do me. Next day went down to the *Emma* to get my Luggage and the Agents would not allow me to take my Wardrobe until I paid £3. Now in Sydney I had paid for our Passage including my Luggage. The Captain argued that my Wardrobe was so large I must pay the £3 and this I had to pay. I had been paying and paying so long I began to think it was time I began to receive.

On our arrival in Hobart I did not hear so much about the expected Gold Fields as I had heard in Sydney. The rumour was that Gold had been found at a Place called Avoca the Launceston end of Tasmania so after being on Shore a few days I began to look about for business and in a few days more I had been offered various Public Houses, from 500 to 1400 Pounds for Goodwill Stock and Furniture. At last I took a fancy to one two miles from Hobart in Newtown, the Crown and Anchor. After a few Visits I concluded the Bargain, to give £575 for the Goodwill Stock and

[5] He is referring to the well-known Eureka stockade episode in late 1854 when the gold diggers rebelled against paying miners' licences. There was much Chartist and republican talk. They were put down by force.

Furniture, and had to pay the Landlord Mr John James £120 Per Year rent. I paid £300 down the balance on transfer of the Licence. I took Possession on 17th March 1855 (St Patrick's day) and as the transfer day did not take place till first Monday in May, I considered during the time I should have the Balance of the money £275 ready.[6]

The day I took Possession I began to have a little experience of the sort of People I was going to live amongst. Mr Newton the Lessee I bought from, left his Wife to stay in the House a few days, and a bonny Wife she was. She was drunk a few hours after I took Possession, and the expressions she made use of made my blood run cold. Then other Women came to drink with her, and their Conversation was abominable. At Night the bar Parlour Tap Room and Bar was a regular Pandemonium and a fair business doing. Where all the She Oak as they called it (for Beer) went to I know not but Gallons after Gallons went in to Tap Room (mostly) and Bar Parlour and Bar. The Beer certainly disappeared in a wonderful way. They certainly drank most of it, very little was carried away. That Night I sold fully one and half Hogsheads Beer retail 3 Pence Per Pint. I Paid Brewer £2.10s per Hogshead of 54 Gal. At that Price I made fully 100 per cent. Very little Spirits and Wines sold mostly Beer and Rum. For the first week I was very sorry I had come to Hobart. I had certainly got amongst about as rough a lot of Neighbours as I could have picked in all Van Diemen's Land. Twice each day gangs of Prisoners passed the House to and from work dressed in the magpie Prison dress and very often several would run in — give us Glass a Rum or Pint of Beer, put the money on counter and gulp it down, and off in a twinkling. The day after St Patrick day I found nearly all the Palings taken off my Garden fence.[7] These were taken for Shillelaghs as there was a row at the next tavern about a Mile and half further along the main Road to Launceston. The first three months I and my Wife put up with more insults from both Men and Women than I ever thought it would have been my lot to endure.

[6] On 7 May 1855 the Licensing Court approved the transfer of the 'Crown and Anchor' from James Newton to James Bodell. On 3 November 1856 the Court approved the transfer from James Bodell to Samuel Blackall. LC269/4, pp. 229, 261, Archives Office of Tasmania.

[7] The palings are shown in the drawing of the 'Crown and Anchor' in Plate 3.

One evening a big burly Stone Mason or quarry man had insulted my Wife several times, and I beckoned her to speak to me in the Parlour. I begged of her to go into her Bedroom and if there was any row not to be frightened as I would certainly try what this burly fellow was. In a few minutes I went behind the Bar and he commenced his insults and would not pay for a quart of Beer he and two others had drank. I said a few words to him and all at once he was going to smash the 'new Chum', as several called me. In a moment I was in front of the Counter and I made the Blood fly about all over the Wall into the Tap room. I had floored the burly one. Another tackled me, I had him in the Tap room, and in 10 minutes I had nearly every one willing to assist me. One rough took a few Bottles off the Shelf, and ran away with them. This I did not care about. After this if any one insulted me or my Wife I was into him in a twink and in a short time I had nearly all hands ready to do any thing for me. The two fellows that I had dressed down did not come into the House for Months after but my business improved. Coaches, Buses stopped at my door for refreshments, and I was improving the trade to the house.

I found out nearly all my Customers and Neighbours were either Passholders or Ticket of Leave.[8] One day I found it out this way. Many times I had read the Papers from Hobart Town and many Names had letters after their names which I took for a Title. This day I was reading the Papers, as usual about the Highwayman Dido and others, and scanning over the Police News, I asked a Man in the Parlour one of my Neighbours who I had got familiar with the meaning of the letters after these names, and he at once cautioned me not to ask any one else about these letters, and then after having a good laugh at my Ignorance he told me the letters of Title I referred to were to denote Pass holder for P.H. and Ticket of Leave for T.L. That some of the richest Men and Women in the District held these titles, and had to answer their names once each Month and some every three months. They certainly were letters of Title

[8] After a probationary period a convict could be granted a pass which permitted him or her to work for wages and keep part of them. The next stage towards freedom was a ticket-of-leave. This entitled a convict to work for himself and to acquire property, but subject to restrictions such as attending musters. Then came the conditional pardon and the absolute pardon. On the convict system, see W. D. Forsyth, *Governor Arthur's Convict System*, p. 4, as well as L. L. Robson's *Convict Settlers of Australia*.

such as I would not like to have attached to my Name. My companion in the Parlour also gave me lots of information about the antecedents of some of my Neighbours and the leading lights in the City of Hobart and Suburbs. Many times I have talked to *Gentlemen* who have been transported for Life 15 & 10 years very common, and I can assure the Reader and some have been real good honest English, Irish and Scottish Ladies and Gentlemen in every sense of the word, again some with all the outside appearance of Gentlemen are or were hardened Villains.

After being in business about six Months Myself and my Land-lord (John James Esqr Spirit Merchant etc Collins Street Hobart) became great friends. He had been one of the Originals. During my Visits to Hobart we often had a Glass or two together. One of his Daughters was the Wife of Alfred Nicholas also Spirit Merchant, both real Gentlemen. On one of these Visits I was taken into one of the leading Hotels and we went upstairs after my friend knocked very mysteriously at a door. We were admitted into a large room, with several Tables surrounded by dozens of young and old men. Some of them if I had met them in the Street I should have taken to be [a] Minister of the Gospel. I should say 60 to 80 men were in this Room in Groups around each Table. Each Table had upon it a Carpet or Hearth Rug, and all hands were gambling and that very extensively, three up[9] and various Games with Coin and Cards. I did not stop long, but I seen enough to tell me it was one of the Gambling Hells which infested Hobart Town in these days 1855.

Whelan the Murderer and Bush Ranger was hanged in Hobart being the last public execution. Dido caused great commotion. One day I witnessed about twenty Parties of Police three in each Gang start up the Country to capture this Dido and other Desper-adoes. At last Dido was taken, tried and only got three Years at Port Arthur.[10] I became acquainted of Mr Frost, one of the Char-tists of Frost, Williams and Jones.[11]

[9] A gambling game played with three coins, resembling 'two-up'.
[10] John Whelan, known as 'Rocky' Whelan, was a cold-blooded killer who had been tortured in the prison on Norfolk Island. 'Dido' was William Driscoll: in fact, he was sentenced to five years in prison and was later pardoned. He had previously been frequently given the lash. See L. L. Robson, p. 98 and L. Norman, *Sea Wolves and Bandits*, Hobart, 1946.
[11] Zephaniah Williams, John Frost and William Jones were leaders of the

About this time I had my Photo taken and sent to my Parents in Leicester. One day a tall young Man walked into the Bar, and on hearing him speak I could tell he came from the Central Counties in England. After a little Conversation he proved to be Jack Shipley from Oxford Street Leicester, the young Man who was rejected as a recruit when I enlisted. Some time after I left Leicester as a recruit, he enlisted into the Royal Artillery and after serving about two Years he foolishly struck an Officer, and for this offence and previous bad Conduct he was tried by Court Martial and sentenced to 10 Years transportation and at present he was a Ticket of Leave holder and was on his way to Hobart Town to have a holiday, and he had received £200 capturing some notorious Outlaw up Country. I believe somewhere near the Town of Green Ponds[12] and after taking dinner he requested me as a favour to accompany him to Hobart to select a good silver Watch and other things for him. We went to Hobart and in the Evening we went to the Theatre to hear Mr G. V. Brooke, Miss Catherine Hayes[13] and other theatrical Notables. During our Rambles about Hobart it rained and we got wet, and went to the Theatre with our wet Clothes on. When the Performance was over I could scarcely rise from the Seat my Knees were so stiff. However I managed to get to the Street and took Cab straight to my home the Crown and Anchor Newtown. On arrival I did not feel at all well and was soon in bed. Next Morning I was suffering with a bad attack of Rheumatism in both legs and back. Here was a fix, sent for a Doctor and was laid up for six weeks.

On another occasion I had to put a quarrelsome She Oak Drinker out and this brute drew his Knife and plunged it into my forearm, and ran away. I had a Policeman after him. Two days after I received a note begging all kinds of Pardons, and several of his Friends interceded for him for me not to prosecute him and the Policeman was willing not to say more about it and I also was told I

Newport uprising in 1839. They had been transported in 1840. They are described in some detail in G. Rudé, *Protest and Punishment*, Oxford, 1978.

[12] A town which was situated twenty-nine miles north of Hobart. It no longer exists.

[13] Catherine Hayes was an Irish soprano and actress who toured the USA as well as Australia. Gustavius Vaughan Brooke was an Irish Shakespearian actor who performed frequently in Australia and New Zealand. See W. J. Laurence, *The Life of Gustavius Vaughan Brooke*, Belfast, 1892.

should make more by letting him off than by prosecuting him and make far more friends if I allowed it to drop. The same man became a staunch friend afterwards.

On another occasion one of my Lady Customers, and as I considered a respectable married Woman, who had often made free and sociable with my Wife, and who had been privileged to go into my bedroom for certain Purposes on several occasions. This Night I noticed her go in and on my closing the Bar and going into my bedroom to count up the days takings I found some one had opened my Drawer and taken about six Pounds out. I immediately left the House and repaired to her Residence. On arrival there her Husband was at home and he said his Wife was not in. In a few Minutes she arrived nearly tipsy, the husband promised to see me next Morning. In the meantime I had ascertained she had been at the next Public that same Night spending freely. Next day her husband came to see me and said his Wife was insulted by me thinking for one moment she could be guilty of such Conduct. All that day the inquiries I made convinced me she was the thief. About 5 p.m. I went to her House and told her direct I had got such convincing Proof she was the Person who had taken the Money, if it was not returned to me by next Morning by 9 o'clock I should have her arrested. Just at this Moment her Husband came on the scene. He called me aside, and told me if I would go home he would see me in the course of the morning. He came and paid me the six Pounds, evidently found out his Wife was the Culprit. She never came into my house after. I found out both of them were T.Ls holding a good Position in Society. M⁰ Penny was a Master Plasterer and in a good business. I used to look on M⁰ˢ Penny as a decent Woman and M⁰ Penny as one of those honest straight forward men, and I still believe he was.

My business had improved wonderful. I was making Money. About Nov⁰ 1855 a large Building had been erected nearly opposite my house, and this Building was intended for a Public House. The Person who was having it built had a Public House in Hobart. Of course I was bound to do all I could to oppose the Licence and when the time came I did oppose Mr Trowbridge from getting a Licence, and drew up a Petition to the Licensing Bench. The first name on this Petition was His Lordship Bishop Nixon[14] and many

---

[14] Dr Francis Russel Nixon, first Bishop of Tasmania.

influential Residents about Newton and on licensing day the Licence was refused. I considered this a grand Victory. I afterwards leased these Premises and let the Corner for a General Store and the other Side of Main Entrance I let it to a Butcher. The Yard Stables, Kitchen and Servants Bedrooms I had for myself when required.

In a short time the Cordial Manufacturer who supplied me came one day and said he was going to sell out. His Wife had got into trouble again. She was a bad one and whilst she was in Gaol he was determined to sell out and clear out of the Country. He offered his business to me first, and if I would purchase he would stop two weeks [to] learn me the Business. After considering about it till next day, I agreed to purchase his Goodwill Horses Carts Stock in trade for £150. This I considered was a good Bargain for me. Here I was with another responsible business on my hand. I was determined to make Hay whilst the Sun shone and I worked very hard during the day at this business. Mr Neath introduced me to all his Customers and I initiated myself properly, as the boss of the New Town Cordial Manufactory. The Stables, Kitchen and Bedroom was just what I required. I had a large copper boiler erected in Brick with chimney. I put the Lemonade Engine in the Kitchen and my Stock of Essences and Sugar, Corks Wine Labels etc in the Bedrooms. Just the very Place I required. I erected a Shed to wash Bottles etc and commenced properly, and done a good business with the Public House on one side of the Main Road and the New Town Cordial Manufactory on the other. My two Businesses kept me going. Still, I only found it a Pleasure to attend to it. Of course this put more work on my Wife and another General Servant for the Crown & Anchor. I also engaged a Man used to working the Lemonade Engine, two boys for washing, cleaning corking and tying Bottles, and another two Men to drive the Cordial around Hobart and twice each Week to O'Brien Bridge and Bridge Water two Villages also Risdon Ferry and all roadside Publics on the road to these Places. Things went on very well for some months.

Early in 1856 I was very busy on a Saturday. I had run out of Lemonade and this necessitated to have some made on Sunday. By this time I had learnt the working of the Engine and this Sunday morning I was hard at preparing several Dozens for Monday morning, and whilst I was working a Detective caught my Wife selling a quart of Beer to a Neighbour. I was sent for and was told a

Gent had knocked at the Door and demanded admittance pulled out his watch and retired. This turned out to be a clever Detective Gordon. In a few days I received a Summons to appear at the Police Court for Sunday trading and was fined £2 and costs. The quart of Beer Cost me £4.14.6d. George Babington Brewer the eminent Barrister acted for me on this occasion.

At this time I kept my Gig and Carriage. Every Sunday I would take a Drive with some friends into the Country. When only myself and Wife the Gig would do. The Butcher who occupied Part of the front of the Building where the Cordial Manufactory was became very intimate. We used to call him Doctor as his name was Crowther after Doctor Crowther of Hobart. During the Green Pea Season, one Sunday I would find Lamb then he Green Peas and another Sunday he would find Lamb and myself Peas. During this time he made acquaintance with a young Girl about 22 Years old. Himself I should say was 54 Years and about 15 Stone in Weight. One Sunday after the two had their Dinner they went to Hobart, and when the Doctor came back alone he looked very sullen, but nothing particular only he told me on his arrival in Hobart another man was waiting for Miss ————. This seemed to trouble him. He used to sleep behind the Butcher's Shop across the Road. He left me appearing all right about 10 p.m. Next morning I was working in my Garden about 5.30 when a man came running across the Road shouting the Doctor has hung himself. I was scarcely willing to believe him, but on myself going over, sure enough there he was dead and stiff, hanging to the iron Shambles with one foot near the Butchers Block, as if he had tried to get on to the block where he had evidently toppled from. He was in his shirt and one Sock on. I directly sent a Messenger for the District Constable, and on his arrival he had the body taken down. An inquest was held, and a Verdict of Self destruction by hanging was returned. Next day none of his friends would take any Part in the Funeral, not so much Kindness shown him as to get four men to carry him from a dray they had sent into the Church Yard, so I paid four men to do this for him. The Butchers Shop was closed, and I lost a Tenant and a good Customer. My Friend Detective Gordon called on me to apologize for having me fined for Sunday trading, saying if he had known I was such a jolly good fellow, he would not have interfered with me, he being a Stranger in the Place he did not at the time know one from another. This would not take with me. I was not the

Mark for any tip. Most of these Gentry looked for it, as a Publican I was not a P.H. or T.L. and was determined not to bribe any detective. However afterwards they did not trouble me.

I received a Circular that a Meeting of all Cordial Makers was to be held in an Hotel in Hobart town, and I attended the Meeting. I mention this to relate a little incident that took Place. When the Meeting was ended refreshments was ordered. About 9 of us remained for the Supper and I suggested a few Plates of fresh Oysters, saying 9 dozen would be plenty. One tall individual remarked 9 Dozen was not enough, he could eat 18 Dozen himself. I thought he was jesting. I looked at him incredulous he saying he would bet me he could eat 18 Doz of large Oysters with Vinegar Pepper etc and if he did not he would pay for them, and if he did eat them all I was to pay. I agreed, the Oysters was ordered and counted. In about 20 minutes the whole 18 Dozen disappeared and I paid. 12 Doz more were ordered for the 8 Men who had none and this glutton assisted to eat his Share. I considered this a prodigious undertaking. The Oysters were the large flat round Variety not the small rock oyster. To do my utmost 1 doz would satisfy me, and I was the bigger man of the two. He was the long lanky Kind his tucker going through him like a crane.

During my stay in 'Van Diemen's Land' as it was called at this time 1856 I found some very good honest People. Of course I found exceptions. A large Whale was caught near the Iron Pot and exhibited alongside the Quay. He was a Monster. I had made many Acquaintances, and was welcome every where. One Evening after I had been collecting my monthly Cordial accounts I was sitting in a Parlour having a chat with the Landlord. All of a sudden a Publican from another street rushed into the Parlour picked up the fire Shovel and before I could prevent him, he struck me across the head sending the head of the Shovel across the Parlour. The blow stunned me for a second the blood pouring down my face. The assailant cleared off directly but the Landlord knew him. I was taken to a chemist and had my head dressed. I had a Scalp wound about three inches long and down to the bone. Next day I went to Hobart and found my Gentleman out, and I was going to give him in charge, but he begged so many Pardons and his friends interceded for him. All of them declared he had taken me for another man, and if I prosecuted him he would lose his T.L. and have to go to Prison. He had a Wife and Family, so I did not have him arrested. This man ever after respected me and always recognized me very courteously. Several times I could have had men and Women punished, but they never forgot a Kindness. They looked upon any one who got another punished as a deadly enemy, but forgive them instead of punishing them, they will do any good turn and highly respect you after. All of them look upon going to Prison with the greatest abhorrence.

A Mrs Ladds the Wife of a rich ex cattle Dealer and Slaughter Man frequented my Place and on these occasions she would ride up on a splendid grey Charger. When ever it was known Mrs Ladds was inside, plenty of old acquaintances would make their appearance, and Mrs Ladds always stood treat for her old friends. Some times herself would take a glass too much. At those times I should have a regular Concert. She herself was a fine looking Woman, and generally conducted herself as a Lady but an extra Glass often let the Cat out. She must have cost her Husband a deal of Money, but I heard he had plenty. It was amusing many times in the Parlour or Taproom, to see perhaps a Dozen Women, some dressed and Manners of a lady others in fair Circumstances and several in a poor Position and all these drinking together, a few Years before the lot of them in Prison together. Such is life. I made the acquaintance of Men who told me they themselves had been transported for life, others 20–14–10 years and nearly all said it was a good day for them, that a 10–14–20 Years and lifers were sure to be sent to Van Diemen's Land. A 7 years would often stop at Home.[15]

About this time it was reported that Parliament intended to have Tasmania instead of Van Diemen's Land for Name of the Island and a very good change. 17th March 1856 the first Anniversary as a Publican and the great Saint Patrick's day was held in true Irishman's style. I must say they made very little row at my Place, but at the other Publics, fighting was carried on all day and half the Night. During the Night I had a little of it. I did a roaring inside and outside trade. The Races were held at the Race Course about 1 Mile above my house. Towards evening of the second day of the races, a large Elephant that had been exhibited at the Course was

[15] Nevertheless over half the convicts had seven-year sentences and another quarter were 'lifers'. Only a small proportion had ten- to fifteen-year sentences.

on its way to Hobart and one of the drivers came inside to refresh himself and some one went outside and drove the brute in front of my Counter. He had no sooner got there than he let fall about three buckets full of manure, splashing the filthy stuff all over the front of my counter. I soon had Mr Elephant outside, and made them have it cleaned up. This day several of the Hobart Gamblers called and took Possession of my large Parlour. In a few minutes they put the Hearth Rug across one end of the long table and were doing the three up. In one hour they spent about 20/- in Drinks but did not stop above 1½ hours, and I was glad when they cleared out. They said they called to give me a turn. I always took great Care they would not get me to give them a turn. By this time I had become a good Player at Skittles, having a good alley in the Yard. I played several Matches with the crack Players on my own Ground, but they tried to get me into Town to play but no use. I was always open to play any one on my own Ground.

Several fires had taken Place in Hobart and burnt 3 Hotels down, all Gambling Places. The day I waited on my Landlord to ask him to repair several Places, and to paint the front. He consented to do it but when finished I requested him to put several lengths of Spouting up, he said if I wanted the Water I must put up the spouting at my own Cost. He was a strange old chap. I was told the following about my Landlord Mr John James. Some years before he was in poor Circumstances in Hobart, and a brother of his was in the Regiment stationed in Hobart Town. One night this Brother was on Sentry on the Treasury, and Jack James broke into and robbed the Treasury. His brother the Sentry was made a Prisoner and did not tell of his Brother or any one else, but stuck out the Treasury was not broken into during his Sentry go. However it was said the Soldier got seven Years and dismissed the Service. However I always found Jack James a very good Landlord, and a good Companion to have a Jollification with but always out of sight of the Public.

About July 1856 I purchased a grey Mare from Mrs Ladds and one morning about a month after one of my men who drove my Cordial Cart requested me to let him take the mare in the Cart. I gave Permission. About 12 o'clock, a young Girl came running to inform me my man was nearly killed at her Father's House the Harvest Home Inn about half a mile nearer Hobart than my House was. I put a horse into my Gig and off I went and about centre of a rise just past the Harvest Home I could see my Cart upset the Mare standing bleeding and on going into the Public I found my man in a fearful bad Condition. I was told Bill was returning home all right until he got about halfway down the Hill two Women in a spring Cart crossed rather close to my Mare's head and caused her to shy and ran the near Wheel of my cart on to the high Kerb and so upset the Cart thrown Bill out and jammed his body between the Wheel and the stone Kerb, the contents of the Cart many Dozens of stone and glass Bottles going on top of him. On my entering the Room where he lay he heard my Voice, in a tremulous way he called me and tried to lift his right hand. I saw in the hand the leather bag [in which] he usually carried what Cash he took during his rounds. Directly I touched the Bag he let it go. Poor fellow he was fearfully mangled, his left Arm broken his left eye out and he could not speak.

I jumped into my Gig and off to Town for a Doctor. I drove all down Elizabeth Street Liverpool Street and only found one at home in Macquarrie Street, Doctor MacNamara. I begged him to jump in and I would relate what I wanted him for on the Road. In a few minutes we were rattling along Elizabeth Street and soon arrived. On seeing Bill the Doctor ordered him to the Hospital. I galloped Home got a Stretcher and engaged four men, and had him carried to the Hospital. On arrival there on stating the Case etc I was asked if the wounded man was free or bond. I said he had only been about 12 months in the country, he having come as Steward of a Ship. They said then before they could admit him into the Hospital I should have to pay £5.5s. I was astounded at this. On my asking them if he had been a bondsman what should I have to pay they answered a Prisoner of the Crown have nothing to pay. I could scarcely believe what I heard, an old Lag to be admitted free and a Person who was free had to pay to be admitted into such a public institution as the General Hospital Hobart Town. I was half bewildered to think I was in such a Country.

On the Sunday two days after the accident I received notice that my man William Marston had died that morning and I was required at the Inquest next morning at the Union Hotel near the Hospital. I attended. Mr A. B. Jones was the Coroner, and on the Jury going into the dead house to view the body I had to step forward and identify the body as William Marston my Servant. In a Second two men standing ready turned the body on its face and a

5 Maryborough in about 1881. *The Australian Sketcher*, 22 October 1881, p. 340.

6 The house of the Maori King,
Tawhiao, Ngaruawahia, about 1864.

7 The tomb of the first Maori King,
Potatau, Ngaruawahia, about 1864.
James Bodell refers to both
buildings in his reminiscences.

8 Tauranga in 1876, showing James Bodell's shop (*top section, right*).

9 Tauranga in the 1870s,
looking towards
Monmouth Redoubt.

10 Tauranga in the
1880s, showing the
beach.

large opening about 12 inches long was in the poor fellow's back. However he lived one hour was a wonder, the ribs on one side of the spine were broken. I could have laid my forearm in the Cavity. On my turning round to go out of the dead house a large skeleton stood before me. This and the sight of the poor fellow's back made me feel very glad to get into the open Air again. After the Inquest I called at the Hospital to see about the Funeral and I was told they would bury him free but it would be in the Prison Ground amongst the dead Convicts. On stating I would not have him buried there, they answered by me paying £2.14.6d. I could have him buried in any Burial Ground in the City. I paid the money and had him taken to the Burial Ground in Elizabeth Street.

I was so disgusted with the whole affair I was determined to sell out and leave such a country. The following day I advertised both my Businesses for sale, and in a few days had many applicants for the Crown and Anchor Inn. Ultimately I sold the Public House to Mr Blackall, this Gentleman four years before had sold the same House to Mr James Newton, the Goodwill Stock and furniture for £100. I sold to him the same for £600. This is £25 more than I gave and it was considered I paid £300 too much. After selling out I had to wait two months for Transfer day, and took a private House. In the meantime I found it difficult to sell the Cordial Manufactory. This I sold partly to Doctor Crooke and a Mr Weaver a chemist of Elizabeth Street. They bought the Engine and all Bottles and Essences connected with the Lemonade and Soda water Engine. The remainder I sold partly privately and balance by Auction. Early in November 1856 the Licence Bench sat for transferring Licences etc and two days after I sailed in the *City of Hobart* for Melbourne with about twelve hundred Pounds in Gold round my waist in a leather belt made for the Purpose. The two days on board the Steamer I found the weight round my body very inconvenient and was glad when I landed.

We arrived in Melbourne on Saturday Night about 9 o'clock and I had a Card to go to 197 Collins Street East. This Place I found after a little trouble, and found it a large Mansion in the aristocratic Part of the City, the Rev Dr Lang[16] and several Members of Parliament stopping here. On Monday morning I went to the Hall

---

[16] John Dunmore Lang, Presbyterian clergyman, politician, author and republican, one of the best-known settlers in New South Wales.

of Commerce, and took two berths [to England] for myself and Wife in the Ship *Ocean Chief* at eighty Guineas each, and paid £20 deposit to secure them and note my name in Pencil on the Cabin shown on a diagram of the Ship. On my way Home, I called into an Hotel Corner of Elizabeth and Collins Street to have a glass of English ale and picked up the *Argus* Paper, and my eye at once seen a Notice of an Hotel for sale or to be let situated at Simpsons Ranges Maryborough apply to 147 Russell Street. During my short trip to and from the Hall of Commerce I was very much taken up by the busy appearance of all branches of business, and the large and costly display of Gold manufactured and in its raw State. I thought I should certainly like to be on the Gold Diggings where all this Gold came from, and on my arrival Home I showed the Paper to my Wife and as she did not care about going to England. We said very little that day about 147 Russell Street. Next morning after Breakfast, I repaired to Russell Street. On inquiring for Mr Armstrong he was not in. I called again in half an hour and found the Gentleman in the house, and on inquiries about the Hotel at Maryborough, he told me the terms, but stated as the following day was the first day of Melbourne Races, he had business there and he had great Pleasure of inviting me to accompany him and a Friend in his Carriage to the Races. I accepted the invitation, and I returned home and told my Wife the result. She appeared quite pleased to think we had a chance of getting into business on the Gold field. Next morning I had made up my mind to forfeit the Passage Money I deposited at the Hall of Commerce on Monday previous, and all my thoughts were business on the Victorian Gold Fields. I was there at the time appointed, and a very grand looking turn out we had, three of us with a Coachman and footman. As we drove through the City of Melbourne, and along the Flemington Road to the Race Course, We certainly cut a great dash. On arriving on the Course I was introduced to Hector Norman Simpson,[17] and other leading Turfites, and owners of some of the best Blood [stock] in Australia. H. N. Simpson['s] Mare Flying Doe won the Derby, and we enjoyed ourselves very well. I was determined not to be led into extravagance by my friend Armstrong. I noticed he tried me to

---

[17] A wealthy pastoralist and horsebreeder. 'Flying Doe', which won the Melbourne Derby in 1856, was sired by the most famous stallion in Victoria, 'The Premier'.

bet on several Races, but it was no use. We returned to Town about
6 p.m. and on arrival Home I retailed to my Wife my afternoon
experiences during the day. I could see I had got amongst some
apparently fast men, but I was determined not to be asleep while in
their Company.

Next day I took my Wife to the Races by Steamer up the Salt
Water river this River runs alongside of the Race Course. We
enjoyed ourselves very much. The following day I was anxious to
be off up the Country to see the Hotel, and on seeing Mr Armstrong, I told him so. He promised to start next morning. Next
morning I could not find him until after the Coach had left. I began
to fancy Armstrong did not care about going that day. He said
come out to the Race Course, and I will start after dinner. I took a
trap, and about Dinner time I told Mr Armstrong if he did not start
by 3 o'clock I would not go at all, but complete my going to
England in the Ship *Ocean Chief*. This brought him to business.
He said, why, there is no coach to be got and how can you go. I
there and then bought Horse Saddle & Bridle and off we went to
Melbourne. Armstrong went to his Residence and I went to my
Wife to tell her I was off up the Country to look at the Hotel and
about 5 p.m. off we started.

About 6.20 we arrived at the Junction Hotel corner of the
Ballarat and Castlemaine Road. Here we made up our minds to
stop and make early Start in the morning. Having seen the Horses
cared for we repaired inside. Certainly the inside of the Hotel did
not impress me with much comfort. However we got Tea and went
to bed. In the Bedroom we had one double bed and a cross legged
Stretcher. Armstrong took Possession of the double bed and I had
the Stretcher. I am sure it was not above two feet across. It was the
narrowest bed I had ever lay on. Some time during the Night I fell
out on to the floor, and on my striking a light there was Armstrong
laughing at me. I said very little but was determined not to be out
done again. I would try to be as cute as him.

I was up about 5 a.m. and went to the stable seen the Horses fed
returned had Breakfast and on mounting the Horses Armstrong in
addition to paying for our accommodation he gave the Groom 5/-. I
looked at him and I gave him 5/- also. I began to think if that was
the Custom of the Country, there were many worse billets than a
Groom at an Hotel. When we got on the road I told Armstrong I
considered it extravagance to give the Ostler 5/- each. He answered

it is the usual thing. This day was Sunday and we rode to Carlsruhe and stopped at Englishes Hotel, first class accommodation. In the Saddle early in the morning and arrived at Castlemaine before Noon. Here we were on the Goldfields in earnest, the last 15 miles we had passed several small Goldfields with Quartz Machines at work and several alluvial Diggings. We stopped at the Freemason Tavern Moystyn Street. After taking Lunch as the Horses had not finished the feed we took a stroll and over the Bank of Australia a notice was posted up that a large quantity of Nuggets from Mount Korong were on view within. We went inside and requested to have a sight of the golden Nuggets. We had to pay 1/- each for the Privilege for the good of the local Hospital. On one end of the Bank Counter a Table Cloth was spread and on our paying the Shilling each the Banker took hold of the end of the Cloth and uncovered the Gold. It was a wonderful Sight. Nuggets as large as common Bricks and others in Dozens from that size to Pigeons Eggs, covered about three feet square of the Counter, and the lot would fill a good sized Wheel barrow. It was a magnificent Sight, and no Wonder it made me more anxious to be a Resident on the Goldfields of Victoria. I have never seen such a Sight of golden Nuggets since. The Banker said to me you Sir appear to be a strong man, try if you can to lift one of the large Nuggets with one hand with a straight arm. I tried but could not. At first I thought to do it quite easy. All this wonderful lot of Gold was got in a Pocket three feet from the Surface, by two Scotsmen who had experienced very bad luck for some time previous, and this lucky find made their fortunes. I heard some time afterwards the Gold realised about £12,000.

We returned to the Hotel and mounted our Horses and proceeded on our way. At the time Castlemaine was a flourishing Mining Town the Capital of the celebrated Mount Alexander Gold Fields. During our afternoon ride we passed through several Mining Towns Muckleford, Tarrengower and other Towns, and crossed Charlotte Plains into the Village of Carisbrook. We had travelled this day from Carlsruhe about 56 miles. We stopped at Carisbrook and next morning after riding four miles we arrived at our destination. The Victoria Hotel Simpsons Ranges (now Maryborough) [had] the Police Camp only about 200 yards from the Hotel, and Chinamans Flat Diggings about one & half miles away. Here was a Population of 30,000 all canvas buildings. I considered the Hotel was doing a good Business, and about 10 Lawyers Police Inspectors & Goldfields Wardens were Boarders amongst them being Inspectors Hare & Cholmondley, Wardens Templeton, Oarm, Lawyers MacDermott, Pretty, Prendergast, Owen and others. I was anxious for business and during the Evening I concluded the Bargain with Mr Frank Armstrong, took charge of the Bar, and put Armstrong's Brother John in charge (at present a Dentist in Dunedin). Frank Armstrong treated all hands and after a Jollification we retired to Bed. Next morning I was up early, and by Mistake I opened the Door of Warden Templeton's Bedroom for F. Armstrong's. For a moment I could not take in the Sight that met my eyes, for as I opened the door of the bedroom, two naked legs projected out of the end of the stretcher, nearly to the Door. The occupant greeted me with good morning, and I apologized and retired. The occupant of the Bed was Warden Templeton (at Present Resident Magistrate for Collingwood near Melbourne). Templeton is I should say a man fully 6 feet 4 inch in his Vamps.[18] The usual stretchers in these days were about 6 feet overall, and the sleeper had got down pretty well in the bed and so his legs projected fully two foot over the end of the stretcher. The bedrooms also were not built above 8 feet to 9 feet in length and this accounted for the legs being so close to the door. I was some time before I could refrain from laughing.

However about 7 a.m. I was on my way in the Coach to Melbourne to purchase Goods etc to fetch my Wife and Servants. In these days the Coach always stopped one night in Castlemaine and the Bank had received many Visitors to inspect the Nuggets of Gold. Next day I arrived in Melbourne and on imparting the news to my Wife she appeared much pleased with what I had done, particularly so when I related the great Show of Nuggets I had seen, and all the Gold Fields I had passed through to get to Maryborough. In two days I had done my Purchases, engaged Servants and saw the departure of two large American Waggons loaded with my goods. On the 4th day after leaving Maryborough I was on the Coach again with all my worldly goods bound for Maryborough. It being Saturday one week only since I left Melbourne Race Course, and on arrival at Castlemaine we had to stop all day on Sunday. Monday morning on the road for Maryborough

---

[18] Socks.

and arrived early 5 p.m. at the Victoria Hotel. John Armstrong had done a good business during my absence. At this time the same John Armstrong was contesting an Election against D[r] Blair and Mr Aspinall the Barrister for Parliamentary honours. Armstrong & Aspinall were defeated by D[r] Blair.[19]

The Victoria Hotel at this time 1856 was considered about the best in the District. I will describe it. The Dining Room, Parlour and Bedroom were in a wooden Building about 24 feet by 34 feet something unusual on the Diggings in this District. The Bar with several Bedrooms and a bar Parlour for the Diggers. This Building was Canvas over a wooden Frame, with bark roof and Mother Earth for the floor. Behind in the Yard was a long Stable and cook house the Stable 50 feet long. On south Side of Bar was a large Building partitioned off in from about 12 feet for Mr John Armstrong to keep his Shop as a Dentist. The remainder of the Building about 20 feet by 30 was for Hay & Corn Store. As far as Buildings went I had plenty.

After my arrival I took an Inventory and about 9 p.m. I called M[r] Frank Armstrong into a bedroom M[r] MacDermott the Lawyer being there on my behalf and M[r] Owen the Lawyer acting for Armstrong. Papers all ready, I counted out of my belt 500 Sovereigns to M[r] Armstrong. This was for Stock, Furniture and Goodwill, and took the Hotel for three years at £300 Per Year rent.[20] Before I had done counting the Sovereigns MacDermott left the room saying I cannot sit there and see so much money changing

---

[19] In fact Butler Cole Aspinall and David Blair were both elected as Members of the first Legislative Assembly for Talbot. *Victoria Government Gazette*, No. 143, 7 November 1856. Blair was a journalist, not a 'Dr'. He was later elected to other seats. Aspinall was another radical, a lawyer and journalist.

[20] The names of hotel licensees were rarely published in the *Victoria Government Gazette* at that time: in any case, Bodell's name could not be found. Nor are there any Licensing Court records for the period in the Victorian Public Record Office. However, with the help of a local historian, Mr Trenear DuBourg, confirmation of some of Bodell's hotel ventures was discovered in the Maryborough Municipal Council Rate Books, held upstairs in the Maryborough Town Hall. In 1857 Bodell was the licensee of the Victoria Hotel. Its annual valuation was £250 and the assessment was £12.10.0. The owner was F. C. Armstrong. The hotel was well out of town, near the present golf course.

hands. If I had went about half a mile farther up the town I could have purchased Hotel, Land and all for £250 and at this day the Land is worth £3000, Hotel included worth £10,000, so much for being in a hurry. However I tackled to business, and for some months done very well. My bedroom being behind the Bar was in the canvas Building, and when the Wind was strong the lining of Bar and my bedroom ceiling would go up and down fully three feet and cause immense dust, and the fleas were so numerous I could not sleep. I often lit the Candle and put it on the floor alongside of the bed and on looking at my legs hundreds of fleas covered them. This I could not stand, so I determined to build a brick Building. I bargained with Mr Edwards Bricklayer of Carisbrook to erect a Building 44 by 24 feet 12 feet Walls with large Cellar, the wooden Building formed one Side so I had front Back and one Side brick Walls. In this Building I had Bar, Bedroom and Billiard Room, Cost £540. In a few months I took Possession of my new Building, and within two months after a new Rush at the Emu and Ararat took nearly all the Diggers from Chinamans flat[21] the Police Camp was removed about half a mile into centre of the Town. Here I was within six months I was left nearly all alone in my Glory.

I could see I had made a mistake, but it was no use repenting. During this time I had purchased two freehold lots of land directly opposite the Hotel and on these I erected a Slab Building 30 feet by 20 and opened a Cordial Manufactory and commenced to serve other Hotel[s] and Shanties. In a few weeks I had a fair trade. A small rush at the White Hills took Place but did not last long. A Butcher called on me one day and offered his Butchers Shop Block tools Weights and the canvas Building for a small sum. I purchased the lot and divided the front of my Cordial Manufactory about 14 feet and in front of the Building I had a butchers Shop and behind a Cordial Manufactory. Across the Road was the Victoria Hotel. I was determined not to lose ground if possible. My Groom Dick Gillman assisted me very much. I sent Dick round with the Cart for orders and delivery and I found enough Work for all hands. The Servants were reduced and I began to make ahead.

---

[21] The original 'rush' to Maryborough was in mid-1854, as was the rush to Back Creek—later Talbot. These gold rushes are described in detail in James Flett's *Maryborough Victoria. Goldfields History*, Waverley, 1975, pp. 17 ff.

As I left things not all cleared up in Tasmania, and I considered I could make some money by going there I determined to take a trip. This was before I turned Butcher and opened the Cordial Manufactory. I received news I had to start at once. It was Friday and if I did not catch the Coach at Castlemaine I should have to wait in Castlemaine on Sunday so about 3 p.m. I started in the Spring Cart with my henchman Dick to show the way and bring the Horse & trap back. Dick Gillman my Groom was a Hunchback from County of Cork Ireland and as he said had been a Jockey and Steeple Chase Rider. He certainly was a good rough Rider. One day he came to me and said if I would give him leave for the day, he would return by six o'clock with £5. I gave him leave and he according to Promise returned to time with the £5 which he insisted on my taking. He earned this money by breaking a thoroughbred Colt for two hours.

Myself and Dick started for Castlemaine in the spring Cart and arrived at Tarrengower all right. Here we stopped at Edwards Hotel to bait horse and have refreshments. About 11 p.m. we proceeded on our way. It was a beautiful moonlight Night and when as I thought we were half way to Castlemaine from Tarrengower, we proceeded down a hill at a good Pace, when Dick ran the near Wheel against a dead Tree, and in a moment the Cart was upset, going a complete over, the Horse kicking the wind with his Legs Dick underneath the Cart, and myself on my back looking at the full moon, with one Wheel across my thighs, completely pinned. It took a few moments to collect my thoughts, and then I took in the Situation at once. By great exertion I managed to lift the Wheel as to get myself clear of the Wheel. Dick he was moaning under the Cart, the Horse plunging away. I felt great Pain in both legs, but no bones broken. With some difficulty I got the Harness loose and then lifted the Cart up by the Wheel on one Side and Dick crawled out. He was all right a few Scratches and bruises. We had two Boxes in the Cart we were taking to Mr Michael Prendergast the eminent Barrister and Chairman of Castlemaine Borough Council. These Boxes bruised Dick badly. In a short time we had things all right and as I believed we were on the wrong Road and Dick was not certain, I was determined to turn back to Tarrengower. Dick begged of me not to turn back, saying he would be disgraced if I did as he could not say if we were on the right Road. I ordered the Horse on to Tarrengower. About 2 a.m. to our great surprise Mr Dick took me into what turned out to be a Digging named Nuggity Gully, about 4 Miles out of our Road to Tarrengower. Here I decided to stop till daylight, and we knocked up a Store, got some horse feed fed the Horse and took refuge alongside of the furnace of a Quartz Crushing Machine and about 8 a.m. we arrived at Tarrengower, and about 5 p.m. arrived Home. Dick was crestfallen for days after. Both my thighs were black with the Cart Wheel falling across them.

As I was determined to go over to Tasmania, I started again in about three weeks, by the Coach and arrived in Melbourne took Passage in SS *Derwent* had as companions the noted large Land owner Big Clarke[22] and his Wife. I was told this Gentleman owned fully 50 miles of Property on the Hobart and Launceston Main Road and to look at him, you would take him to be a hard up Cockatoo Farmer, with a short black Pipe, old wide awake hat, and when on shore driving a Gig you would not give £10 for. Many a time I had seen him driving in that said Gig during my Residence in Tasmania. We arrived in Hobart Town the second day after leaving Melbourne, and I remained four days in New Town [and] finished my business. Blackall who succeeded me in the Crown & Anchor Inn grumbled very much at the poor business he had done. The Building I had leased (to prevent a Licence) was now a licensed Public House or Inn. What a change in a few months. It appeared Mr Blackall could not prevent opposition the same as I had done. No wonder his business had decreased, with such a fine Building in opposition. However I bid a final goodbye to my Friends took Coach to Launceston, stopped two days here visited all Places of interest and departed for Melbourne, and in less than a fortnight's absence was at my business in Maryborough. Found business had been carried on correctly, but the Inhabitants on Chinamans flat and all round the District were leaving for fresh fields and Pastures new. Several Business People subscribed one Pound Per Week to organize Prospecting Parties between Maryborough and the Bet Bet on the Dunolly Road. Two Parties were sent out, each man to get 30/- Per Week and his rations. At this time a Rush to the Emu Diggings occurred and as I considered business was not good, on

[22] Sir William J. Clarke. 'Big Clarke' was a very wealthy landowner. On his death in 1874 he owned 5,000 acres in Tasmania, 50,000 in New Zealand and 120,000 in Victoria.

3rd June 1857 I paid these Diggings a Visit, and purchased a large canvas & wood Building cheap, and intended to open a branch of the Victoria Hotel. On the Gold Fields at this time, anyone could go into business on a Rush by paying fifty Shillings every 3 months. The Building I had purchased was the Victoria Store and by a little alteration I could have opened it as an Hotel. In the Evening I returned Home to fetch some money to complete the Purchase.

It had been a brisk business day with the Lawyers at Maryborough and during the Evening a great deal of drinking was carried on. On this day I had a treat for my Boarders at 6 p.m. Dinner in the shape of a large Loddon Cod[23] weighing 9 lb. This fish cost me 18/- or 2/- per lb., as all fresh fish did in those days. This fish Dinner was the cause of several extra Diners invited by friends. Towards Midnight it got known that the following day was my 26 Birthday and directly 12 o'clock midnight struck, I was rushed by my Boarders and friends to celebrate the event. This was done by liberal Shouts of Champagne. When my treat was finished others stood treat and this game was carried on till 3 o'clock a.m. on my Birth morning. At that hour, instead of going to bed I called an able bodied man named George King who I had engaged to take Possession of my new Purchase at the Emu Rush, and off we started.

On our way several road side Shanties were roused up and drinks obtained, but the Walk had taken much of the Drink out of me and on approaching the Diggings about 5 o'clock, the morning was very misty and I was afraid we might miss the canvas Building[s] that constitute the Main and only business Street at the Emu. I told King to go to his left front and I would proceed straight ahead, and who found the Main Street first were to cooee. We had not parted 10 minutes when I struck the Canvas and found an opening between two Buildings. I found myself in the Main Street, looking up to read some of the numerous Business Boards to ascertain which way I had to turn. I found I had to turn to the left. I had not gone many Paces, before I had a man on my back his knee in the small of my back and his arm under my chin with my head forced back and my belly forced forward, and I noticed a man with a Moustache close to my right Shoulder. In a second I could see I had been waylaid and I was properly Garrotted. The next instant I had my

[23] A very large fresh-water fish, from the Loddon River, usually called the Murray cod.

Garrotteer over my head and he lying in front of my feet, going with a heavy thud on the Ground. At the same instant I called out George as loud as I could. As luck had it he was not far away he having struck the Main Street about the same time as I did. He came running up to me, the man with the Moustache decamping, and the Garrotteer I had safely at my feet. I gave him several unmerciful Kicks and then put him on his belly and tied his hands behind his back and then made him get on to his feet. About 100 yards brought us to the Victoria Store and into this we went and I could hear some one out side, his Mate I expect. I ordered George to get the revolvers so as to be heard out side (we had no revolvers) and after questioning our Prisoner, I considered it was my Duty to give him in charge, and we marched him off to the Police Camp about half mile away on the Carisbrook Road and gave him in charge of the Serg[t] of Police, signed the charge Sheet, and returned to the Store. The noise we had made caused some Commotion and many were the inquiries made about the Affair.

My back became painful on the spot his knee had been. By this time the Champagne had evaporated and I felt fatigued and although it was breaking day I lay down on a Stretcher for two hours, as I had to be in Maryborough by 10.30 o'clock to prosecute my assailant at the Police Court. About 9 o.c. I tried to get up off the Stretcher, but if I got all Victoria to do so I could not. A Doctor was sent (always plenty [of] Doctors on Gold Fields) and after examining me he got the Stretcher lifted on one end with a man on each side of me to see if I could stand when on my feet. I could stand with less Pain than lying down and with assistance could walk. The superhuman effort I made to throw the Garrotteer over my head with his knee in the small of my back had caused me the hurt. However I did it I know not. I knew if I did not do something my Pockets would have been rifled of the contents.

My assailant was a man short stout about 12 stone, as I looked at him during the examination in the Police Court. We got a trap and arrived in Maryborough just in time for the Court. All the People in Maryborough had got the News about me being garrotted before I arrived. Both Detectives Slattery and Duffy knew the Prisoner, belonging to a rough Gang. The Prisoner was dressed in Yankee Style with a red Sash about his waist. In a short time after myself and George had given evidence, he was committed for trial at the General Sessions at Carisbrook and I sent George King back to the

Emu with Authority to arrange with the Parties I had bought the Store from, to cancel the Purchase and forfeit the Deposit. So much for the Emu Rush. As it happened I saved money by forfeiting the deposit, as the Rush to Mount Ararat took all the Diggers away in a few Weeks. The Emu Rush was a very poor one, very little Gold got. To finish with the Garrotteer, about five Weeks after the Prisoner was tried at the Carisbrook Criminal Sessions and was ably defended by the celebrated Barrister McDonough. He was sentenced to two years' imprisonment.

After this the Prospectors we had sent out struck Gold below the White Hills on the Dunolly Road and caused the large Rush known after as the Havelock Rush, and all the way for 7 miles from my Hotel to the Bet Bet Gold had been struck. I had kept two Diggers prospecting about 200 Yards from the Victoria Hotel on the old Maryborough Lead paying them 30/- each per week and found them in rations. They struck Gold averaging 4 Penny weights to the tub and directly Gold was struck at Havelock they left me for the new rush. This rush turned out very good whilst it lasted, and brought business to Maryborough. A Murder was committed on the Rush [when] a man by name Lopez killed another man. I am writing of the year 1857. About this time another rush took Place at the celebrated Mount Hope some hundreds of miles away and thousands of Diggers made for Mount Hope. This Rush it was said turned out a hoax. Some said a Storekeepers rush, it was also said the Diggers were nearly lynching a Storekeeper for causing the rush. Several men died for want of Water.

My business was going on, satisfactorily, but I was impatient of doing more. My Hotel had become only a road Side House, although in the Main Street of Maryborough that Street was fully one mile long and the business Part was half a mile from my Hotel. I still kept the butchering and Cordial business going, [but there was] the loss of bottles in the Cordial business, and bad debts as many of my Customers were Shanties on the various diggings around Maryborough. These People would be in full business today, and when you called next day, no Signs of your Customer or the Shanty. Bakers, Butchers, Brewers, Cordial Makers and everyone had to meet these losses. About Augt I found myself £1000 out of Pocket with my Victoria Hotel Spec., a fine large Hotel part Weatherboard and part Brick building. My first Landlord, Armstrong, had sold the freehold for a good round Sum. During this time a large two Storey building was being erected in centre of Main Street, and in September a Law Suit took Place over this Building which was being erected for an Hotel. This Building was the largest in the District. The owner lost the Law Suit and his opponent was to be the Tenant, but after the case would not take the Building which was not finished. Mr Tom Lawson the owner came to me repeatedly to take the House. At first I did not know what to do as I had the Victoria Hotel on my hands at £300 per annum rent. Several Friends advised me to take it, and I considered the matter over. I came to the conclusion to chance the Spec. On October 5th I paid £150 down as Part Payment of the first Year's rent which was £5 per week for 12 months with the option of keeping it for 3 years. As the House was not finished I had Carpenters put in at once to fit the Bar up and finish the Dining Room, and two Parlours. I paid Carpenters 25/- per day of 8 hours for this work and some of them made a half day overtime that is they worked 12 Hours and received 37/6 for the 12 hours. I came to the Conclusion that Carpenters and Builders was a splendid trade and picked up as much of the trade as I could for months after.

On October 10th I opened the House as the Commercial Hotel. I had to substitute Dick Gillman's name for my own as I could not use my own name as I was Licensee of the Victoria Hotel. I ran this House for 3 months without a Licence and Licence day came the Licence was only £25. The previous year the Licence was £100. Of course Magistrates knew all about me not having a Licence for the Commercial Hotel but they knew I had been taken in by Armstrong for the Victoria Hotel. On Saturday 10th October 1857[24] I opened the Commercial Hotel having engaged the Cornish Band from Chinamans flat (here I may say Chinamans flat is turning out good gold this day April 1885). That day I took between £20 and £30 and the following six Months I had cleared over a £1000, and expended lots of money in altering and improving the Building.

I had a large Room directly behind the Bar, this I furnished and altered making 3 Rooms into one, and opened the Theatre Royal, Maryborough. I did well for some months out of this Theatre. On

[24] The Rate Books show that Lawson was indeed the owner, and that Bodell was the proprietor by 1859. Gillman is not listed, but there is no reason to question Bodell's accuracy here. Presumably Gillman had ceased to hold the licence when the list of ratepayers was made. Maryborough Council Rate Books.

one occasion I had Professor Eagle the Wizard of the South and he learnt me several tricks. On one occasion I agreed to do several conjuring tricks for the Benefit of the Local Hospital, and it was announced that a local Gentleman would perform on the Stage of the Theatre Royal Commercial Hotel for the benefit of the local Hospital. I was to do the inexhaustible Bottle trick, and give 200 Drinks out of a common Porter Bottle, and 6 different drinks, also the Ladies Punch Bowl and other tricks. This brought a crowded House, and I commenced operation about 9 o'clock after the Professor had done several tricks, my man Sprightly being the principal means of the tricks being properly done. First I commenced the Bottle trick. Several days before I had been drilled by Professor Eagle. The inexhaustible Bottle is a bottle made for the Purpose in fact there is two Bottles really. You take the bottle in your right hand and there is small Valves for each finger and thumb, and by Pressing them on the Valves, you can turn the bottle upside down and nothing will come out, but directly you take your finger off the Valve the liquor you require will appear, Brandy, Rum, Gin, Whisky, Port and Sherry Wine. Gin & whisky are mixed. When you are ready Sprightly will appear with a large tray, with 2 to 3 dozen of small thick glasses, each glass looks large but they are so thick they hold very little. When you ask the Audience what you will have the Pleasure of serving them with, about a 100 drinks are asked for, and Sprightly holds the tray whilst I filled the glasses and off he goes amongst the People giving them the Drinks. Sprightly knew when the first bottle was getting empty. He came on the Stage and by his humorous talk kept the Audience's attention off me, whilst I changed the Bottle in the Slips. Directly he saw I had the Bottle I again wanted to know what drinks they wanted and so it went on the Professor having a bottle ready filled. I gave nearly 200 drinks this way.

When the bottle trick was over I commenced the Ladies Punch Bowl. This Article is a large brass Bowl with a Stand fully one foot long. As I take the bowl from the back part of the Stage which is filled up with all the Wizard's professional implements gorgeously arrayed, I approach the front of the Stage asking the Ladies whether they will take a glass of hot Punch. I get many orders and before I fill the Glasses I turn the bowl bottom up to show the Audience the bowl is empty. Although the bowl appears large it is so thick and hollow that the space inside would not hold above a quart. When you want the liquor to appear, holding the bowl with left hand and the Ladle with the right hand, you press the Thumb of the left hand on a Valve. This raises a small round Portion of the bottom of the bowl and out comes the hot Punch. Sprightly standing alongside with the Glasses and dozens of Glasses of reeking hot Punch is served out, amidst the applause of the Audience.

The third and last trick, was the Cannon Ball trick. On the rack back of the Stage [is] a Ball about the Size of a 20 lb Shot made of leather and hollow in appearance like a cannon Ball. After telling the Audience what you are going to do Sprightly rolls the Ball across the stage and you pick it up making believe it is very heavy. You ask for a Belltopper hat and fortunately there was one amongst the spectators. Doctor Laidman['s] hat I got and introduced the Cannon Ball into it and after Sprightly had amused the Spectators with some Jokes, he introduced myself and in a few minutes I had Part of the Stage covered with feather down fully 3 feet high and several suits of clothes (tiny ones) and the last Article is a tiny Pair of Ladies drawers. This caused amusement, and as you hand the hat back, just as the Gentleman is going to take it you suddenly draw it back, and you discover the Ball which you roll on the Stage and Sprightly runs away with it. I should have said the Ball is not seen by the Spectators till the last, as Sprightly gets the Ball into the Hat, unobserved by the spectators they thinking of all the stuff you take out of the empty hat. The ball has a spring and by pressing the spring it opens in two Parts and when you have emptied it you close it again then it is taken out and rolled across the Stage. 28 years since is a long time to remember. The Audience left well satisfied with the Entertainment. Next day we handed over £60 to the Hospital Committee.

Shortly after this we had a Visit from the Melbourne Cricketers, and they all stopped at the Commercial. Mr D. S. Campbell, Merchant of Melbourne bossed them. George Marshall the Grand Wicket Keeper from Nottingham was amongst them. This Gentleman I had met in Tasmania about two Years previously. At this time I was Caterer for the local Cricket Club and also one of the Players. Any Games at home I did not play as I did the catering. I had erected on the Cricket ground about 400 yards from my House a large Booth. All home matches I made lots of money. The match with the Melbourne Cricketers lasted two days. On the 3rd night a Grand Ball took place at the New Stone Hospital. I had the

Catering for this Ball and the next night Billy Barlow performed for the Benefit of the Hospital Funds. Barlow sang the Blue Tailed Fly, and other popular Songs. The friends of the Hospital increased very much with all the Benefit. All this time my business at the Commercial was going on grandly. Many days I made £50 Profit, the business took a great amount of energy. In these days I could do a fair Share of business by my own exertions and I was well supported by my Wife and good Servants.

You will inquire what about the Victoria Hotel all this time. I will finish with that unfortunate undertaking. I removed nearly all Furniture and Stock from the Victoria to the Commercial Hotel and left a man in charge. In about 3 months I found this a bad spec so I closed the House, and as the Licence was in Dick Gillman's name for the Commercial, I knew no one dare interfere. At this time I had a splendid entire House and a Dog Cart the Turnout costing about £100. I had a Friend a Lawyer's Clerk, and he volunteered his Services, to go to Melbourne to interview Mr W. M. Bell, Merchant of Melbourne, owner of Victoria Hotel and try to get out of the lease of the Victoria Hotel. We started in my Dog Cart and reached Melbourne early the following day doing 60 Miles the second day by 4 o'clock in the afternoon the last 10 miles being very heavy roads being laid with new metal. The day after our arrival we waited on Mr Bell and after a deal of talk I got the lease cancelled by paying £150. I was very pleased to get clear at that Price.

We stopped in the City three days to do some business and returned to Maryborough. An incident occurred about 26 miles from Melbourne. We were ascending a stiff Hill, and for several miles my companion sat in front and myself behind and to ease the horse I jumped off telling my mate to stop for me on top of the Hill. To my great Surprise he whipped the Horse when he got on the Level and was out of Sight before I reached the top of the Hill. I commenced to run and several men were alongside the road in several Places, hooting me as I ran and they making fun. After running fully two miles there was the Horse and trap waiting for me. It appears Mr Hall turned round to speak to me and then found I was non existent. He said he did not miss me before. However, I made up my mind if I ever stopped or walked up another Hill, I would make sure the driver should know it. In a short time we arrived at Gisborne, being late before we left Melbourne. We only made 31 miles this day. Next day we made Tarrengower and early the following day, arrived Home, highly pleased with the result of our Journey. I was free now to have the Licence transferred to myself. I had this done in a few days, my own name over the Door, and business was going on first rate. At this time I had made a good name for my business tactics, and I certainly attended to business.

About this time June 1858 I wrote a letter to my eldest Sister Elizabeth at Leicester England, to come out to Australia and I did not get any Answer for years and then I ascertained that she had sent me a letter telling me she would come. That letter never reached me.

About July 1858 I purchased a Thurston Billiard Table, done away with the Theatre as I found many of the travelling Players did not pay, so I erected and altered the Theatre into a Billiard Room also a large Dining Room as [there was a] Passage going through the Building to the Dining Room. My business became more select, and not so much bother. Many of the Play actors at this time on the Gold fields were not profitable to do business with so I was glad to do without them. I was doing the largest business in the Town. Each Evening Bankers, Lawyers, Magistrates, Merchants, after 11 o'clock took charge of my front upstairs Parlour including the Present Sir Julius Vogel, then our Editor for the local Paper the *Maryborough and Dunolly Advertiser*.[25] He was very fond of unlimited Loo.[26] These Gents would occupy the Parlour till 5 a.m. About 2 a.m. I would serve an Oyster Supper on the Side board, and let them help themselves. About 11 p.m. all Servants and Wife would go to Bed and about 5.30 a.m. I would rouse the Servants up, and if in Summer go down the Cellar. Here I had a Chinese mat and several feather Pillows, and sleep there till about noon. I often regretted having done this night work, as it led to bad habits, and made undesirable acquaintances, and gradually made me become fond of Drink. I never gambled, that was one good Point.

I had done a good business since I opened the Commercial Hotel I had purchased a New Thurston first class Billiard Table costing with all appliances & Freight £220 and paid a Billiard

---

[25] One of the most prominent of nineteenth-century New Zealand politicians and premiers. He was responsible for initiating a large borrowing programme in the 1870s to pay for roads, railways and immigration.
[26] Loo was a card game.

Marker 60/- Per Week with Board and Lodgings. I have always blamed this said Billiard Marker being the Cause of being robbed in this way. About Oct[r] 1858 a Gold Digger Rush took Place at Port Curtis,[27] and a great exodus of Diggers took Place from Maryborough and all other Towns in Victoria. During this Port Curtis Gold Fever a strange young Man respectably dressed came to see the Billiard Marker, an old acquaintance. The Billiard Marker asked me as a favour if his Friend could stop a day or two. I consented. During this day I had on several occasions been into my Bedroom for change. On one occasion I noticed this strange Gent looking very hard at me as I was leaving my Bedroom, but at the time I thought no more of it. Next day about 11 a.m. I had occasion to go there again for change, and the bedroom Window was partly opened, and on going to the usual Drawer for my Cash Box it was gone, and another small Box I used to keep my Jewellery etc in was opened and nearly all the contents gone also. I could see at a Glance I had been robbed and on proceeding down the Yard through a right of Way into a back street I picked up Part of the Cash Box. I returned and informed my Wife what had happened she having lost like myself all our Jewellery & valuable trinkets. She commenced to cry, but that was no use. I went immediately and informed the Detectives of my loss. They caused telegrams to be sent all over the Colony. I had lost £22 in money and fully £120 worth of Nuggets, gold Watches & chains, Silver & gold Rings. My Wife lost her gold Watch and chain with rings and other valuable Articles including a massive Pair of gold Earrings. I had that morning banked between £60 & £70 so my Gentleman missed some of the Booty. As it happened the actual Coin was less than it was usual to keep in the bedroom. When I missed the Billiard Marker's friend at Dinner I suspected him as the thief and on questioning the Billiard Marker, he pleaded Ignorance about his friend, but next day the mystery was cleared up as at Dinner the Billiard Marker was not to be found and I have never seen either of them since, 27 years since.

A few days after the Wife of a Digger called on me and handed me several Letters I had received from England from my Parents and Sisters. These letters were in the Box with the Nuggets and other Valuables. On asking her where she got the letters she said

---

[27] In Queensland.

about one & half miles up the Main Lead against the Stump of a Tree. I asked her to come with me and show me the Place. She consented and I had the Horse put into the trap and off we went, and sure enough, there was the Place where the Robbers had divided the spoil. An old Tom Bottle with about 2 inch of Candle in it (a Diggers lantern) and amongst the short Grass I picked up a crooked Sixpence, part of the works of a Watch a silver Chain Purse and other Articles I knew as my Property. From that day I never heard anything of my Billiard Marker.

In the Year 1858 (the year of the Great Comet) I cleared in business fully £3000. I really done a splendid Business. I was in a good business monetary Position, a good balance at my Bankers, a large Hotel well furnished and a cellar well stocked. This cellar I had dug and a large Verandah and Balcony erected. During the time the cellar was dug a good show of fine Gold was got about 5 feet from the surface. During those days it would take a good show of the precious Metal to consider it payable. As I stated before the two men I had working back of the Victoria Hotel ran away from four Penny weights to the Tub (a large fortune in these days).

February 1859 arrived and a Rush took Place to Back Creek near Amherst, and my Baker Thomas Dale Wrigley. This Wrigley Family were our particular Friends, Lancashire People. Mrs Wrigley arrived with her young Son to join her Husband who had a flourishing Bakery business. In March 1857 the Bakery (the Lancashire) was situated about halfway between the Victoria and Commercial Hotel[s]. As I said the Rush was commencing to Back Creek. Mr Wrigley as usual called in the afternoon when he had finished his delivery Rounds, and we had seven Games of Billiards. During the Evening he called again and requested me as a great favour to go with him to Back Creek as he intended to start in another line of Business, he having met with many losses in the Bakery business the last six months, the digging Population so continually shifting from Place to Place and supplying road and other Contractors, he had lost heavily.

The following morning about 2.30 a.m. I repaired to the Bakery and found Wrigley nearly ready. Whilst waiting I was going to lean against as I thought a wooden Partition. The Bread Moulders were working from a trough about five feet below the floor. I was on this Partition of only flour Bags hung up and only for being smart I certainly should have went head first amongst the dough, but I saved myself by a spring so got clear. We started and arrived at the New Rush about 5 a.m. a fine Summer's morning. I told Wrigley to proceed on his rounds and meet me when finished on a certain Place pointed out. I had not been left alone many minutes when who should emerge out of a small tent but a Carpenter that I knew. After a Conversation he told me he had two lots of Sections of Land. He showed me them, he certainly had his eye to business for the two Sections he had marked as his were at the turn of what was afterwards known as the Scandinavian Crescent Back Creek (now Talbot) the very Centre of the Crescent. I had the choice of either for a small Consideration as the Carpenter expected I was going to erect a large Hotel on the lot. About 7 a.m. my Friend Wrigley returned, and after driving Pegs well into the Ground alongside of the Survey Pegs, we took our leave and returned home.

Wrigley was well satisfied with my bargain, and he tried very hard for me to go into Partnership with him. I declined as I had plenty of business in Maryborough, but before a Month expired I considered business had [so] declined that I determined to have a Speculation at Back Creek rush, and with that determination, I waited on Mr White a Publican on Mount Greenock Creek about 2 miles from Back Creek rush, and he consented to join me, and we bought the right of a Section of Land in Oxford Street Back Creek, and erected an Hotel and called it the Exchange Hotel, opened business, and before three weeks had expired Mr White asked me to buy him out as his business had increased so much at home, the Diggers sending their wash dirt to a Creek that ran through his Property. I came to terms with him and took over the business. I may here remark this Back Creek speculation was the first Step to my ruin. If I had been satisfied with my good paying business in Maryborough, and not have been so ambitious, I should have remained at home, and not speculated, but it was ordained otherwise.

Back Creek rush was a very poor one for the Numbers that settled there. However I tried to bring business. On Easter Monday 1859 I gave £15 Prizes to have a contest in Wrestling. I had a large Ring roped off, on a spare Piece of Land behind my Stables, and erected a Bar and opened the back of the Stables for refreshments. The Wrestling came off and gave great Satisfaction, but the digging Population were so poor I did not take more money than I gave away in Prizes, during the day I had hundreds of applications for drinks of Water. In Oxford Street we considered a large Theatre it would have been an inducement to bring Custom, and I was very near coming to terms to build a Theatre with Clarence Holt, Webster and other Theatricals, but fortunately for me their demands were not satisfactory, and I would have nothing to do with them. Afterwards they negotiated with Mr Johnson of Amherst, a Publican to build a Theatre, and by Subscriptions from all business People in Oxford Street and all the money Johnson could raise. The Theatre was opened in May, cost about £2000 and in three months Mr Johnson was ruined and the Theatre shut up. All Speculations in Oxford Street turned out bad. The Town extended towards Maryborough, from the Crescent to Ballarat Street and along the old Daisy Hill Road. In July I sold the Exchange one third Cash and three Promissory Notes 6, 12 & 18 Months. The two latter P.N. I never got. I lost altogether £1000 by Back Creek, and my friend Wrigley who I bought the Land for in Scandinavian Crescent was making a fortune. His Commercial Hotel (named after mine at Maryborough) had the Police Court sitting there and all Cobb & Co. coaches stopping there, and the best Part of Back Creek.

In July I returned to Maryborough for good and about one Week after, I had business at Carisbrook and on returning home from Carisbrook I was alone in my Dog Cart, my horse shook its head so much that I got down to see if anything had got into its ear. On examination I could not find out the Cause, but as I left the horse's head to get into the trap, off he went at a Gallop and me running after. When he had gone about a three quarter of a mile it came in contact with a dead Tree lying alongside of the road, the trap was upset and the horse on his back. Close by a small diggings was there and several diggers digging and by the time I came up to the horse & trap three diggers came to my assistance and helped me right the horse & trap. I was very much blown by running so far. I gave the men 5/- to drink my health, (nothing was broken) so proceeded on my way home. I had not gone half a mile before I felt sick and commenced to vomit and by the time I arrived home I felt very unwell and felt very cold. On arrival in the Stable Yard my Groom came to meet me as usual and I threw him the reins, he remarking Master you don't look well. I went into the Parlour lay down on a Sofa and told my Wife to bring me a strong Glass of hot Brandy and Water. This I tried to drink but could not. I went to Bed and ordered several Gin bottles of hot Water to my feet. About two hours after I had a severe Pain in my right Side, and on sending for the Doctor Laidman he examined me and said that I had a slight attack of inflammation of the Liver. I got worse and he tried 2 Doz leeches. They would not take. He tried 2½ Doz more and scarred my side and all took and filled themselves. After three hot Poultices of Bran was put on the leech wound in succession. Next morning alongside of me in the bed I had a mass of congealed Blood as large as a Bullocks liver. He gave me some kind of Medicine. I went delirious for 6 days, all that time the house was shut up and all hands in the house had to wear Carpet Slippers. During my delirium I thought I was in England, America and other Places, and I thought I had brought back £2000. This I made sure I had placed in a large Camphor Wood box I brought from China. This box was in my bedroom and I could see it as I lay in bed. The worsted knobs on the bed curtains I took to be Grapes and I was told held my hands under them to catch the Juice as it dropped from them. However on the sixth day I got my reason, and to my great Surprise I was in my own Bed, and there was the Box I had placed (supposed) £2000 in and a man sitting in a chair. On my calling him by name asking him where I had been, he looked at me and gave an exclamation and disappeared for a few moments (I ascertained afterwards) to tell my Wife I had my right senses again. I asked for some bread I was so hungry. I was eating this **bread** on the Doctor coming in, the first thing he did was to send **the bread** flying out of my hand. He allowed me only dry toast & Tea, no Milk or Sugar. That morning a Boot Shop opposite and next to the Bank of Victoria took fire, belonging to Alexander & John McLandres now of McLandres Hepburn & Co. Dunedin, a narrow escape of the Bank and other Buildings.

In three weeks I could walk about but very weak. One day I went across the Street to May Garlands, Merchant and weighed myself. I only weighed 12 Stone two Pounds, having lost 2½ Stone. As I was getting strength I was attacked with a violent Cough, and the doctor sent me 8 oz. of cough mixture every morning. About the third morning of this cough Sunday, house shut except for travellers, an old Gentleman came in and heard me coughing very bad, remarked that Cough comes from a strong man I believe I could stop it for him without seeing him. He left the recipe which is as follows, 3 oz of oil of sweet Almonds 3 oz honey 3 oz treacle 7

Drams of Laudanum, ½ Pint white wine Vinegar all mixed together and simmered before the fire one hour, one tablespoon full to be taken three times a day or when the Cough is troublesome. A Chemist lived next door and on Monday morning I sent for the Medicine and only cost 4/6. That morning and every morning after I used to empty the 8 oz of Medicine I had from the Doctor out of the bottle into the Yard and used the old Gentleman's Medicine and in four days I was cured. The Doctor don't know from that day to this but his medicine cured me.

After that I recovered rapidly and got my man nurse to drive me out every afternoon in the dog Cart. About the time I was first attacked with the cough Dr Laidman took a trip to Melbourne, leaving his assistant Dr Black to look after his Patients, and about the second time I took a drive out I went towards Carisbrook and as I was driving along the Race Course about one mile from Carisbrook who should I meet but Dr Laidman bringing his new married Wife (née Miss Ford, Sister of Dr Ford of Melbourne) to her new home at Maryborough. The instant he seen me he remonstrated and ordered me back home at once. I told the man to go back, and we travelled back at a good smart Pace, getting home before the Doctor. On his arrival, he called on me, and on examining me he said I was much stronger than he expected, and allowed me out on fine days.

In a few weeks I was as I considered all right again, and the first thing I did was to listen to People to build an Hotel at McCallum Creek.[28] This I did do as I felt I should be doing a good turn to my Man [i.e. male] Nurse for looking after me so well during my Sickness. So I built an Hotel and put this Edward Carver in charge. I opened it the very day the first Champion Race was run and won by Flying Buck 1st October 1859. This proved a bad speculation. Directly Mr Carver knew the Licence was in his name, he commenced to act independent of my orders. In two months I could see I had made a Mistake with trusting Carver.

I must return to 1st January 1858. This day was a memorable day for Maryborough as the first Gathering took Place for the Highland Sports. These were held on the Cricket Ground and my wooden Booth suited fine for Refreshments. A very large Gathering took Place, a fine beautiful day, and I took in Cash £126. I was proceed-

[28] Near the present-day Craigie.

ing home about 400 yards from the Cricket Grounds about 5 p.m. to deposit about £100 that I had taken up to this time. On approaching the Commercial my next door Neighbour Mr Michael Prendergast, Barrister at Law, and considered one of the best learned in the Law in the Colony and eldest Brother to the Present Chief Judge in New Zealand (1885).[29] This Gentleman as I approached the House was on the footpath with only Trousers and Shirt on, smashing the front Windows of his house. I could see in a moment what was the Matter. He was a heavy drinker, and he was suffering from an attack of delirium tremens. I touched him sharply on the Shoulder and beckoned him to follow me. He stared at me fiercely and then quietly followed me into his house. I put him into his Bedroom and left a Man to look after him. This same Lawyer, a few Years after, was through Drink quite childish and about 1872 I heard he got lost in the Mallee Scrub near Inglewood Diggings and died a miserable Death. His Wife was about as fine a looking Woman as there was in Victoria but she had to leave him. It was a grand Sight to see Mrs Michael Prendergast in a Ball Room. I returned to the sports, and finished the day by a Supper at the Commercial. 1st January 1859 Highland Sports again, more Money taken than the previous Year. This Year after playing all the Cricket Clubs, such as Castlemaine, Dunnolly, Avoca, Bet Bet, and other Clubs we received a Challenge from Ballarat and we went and played a match there, and got beaten. Then we had a single wicket Match and we beat Ballarat Club. We stopped at the George Hotel. During our Stay the New Theatre Royal was opened by Mr Hoskins, and we were all presented with Tickets to patronise the Theatre on its opening Night. We took to play the Match two Diggers paid Players, and this trip cost us about £120. I paid for refreshments as I ordered them, others ran a bill of between 70 & 80 Pounds, and of course I had to pay my Share of this. We had a jolly time of it. We returned Home via Back Creek.

For several Years I had always given Sports on Boxing day and [in] 1859 gave them as usual. Early in the afternoon, I saw Mr Carver on the opposite Side of the Cricket Ground with a Lady on each Arm. I considered this was outrageous and I immediately sent for him. He did not come but sent word he was short of Bottle Ale & Porter. I sent it out at once and I thought he must have done a

---

[29] Sir James Prendergast, Chief Justice of New Zealand, 1875–99.

good business. Early next Morning I went out to the Hotel at McCallum Creek. Instead of being short of Ale etc he had plenty without what I had sent. I remonstrated with him and he actually ordered me off the Premises. I was taken by surprise, [although] I knew the Hotel stood on Government Land and Possession was nine Points of the Law. As the 1st Jan[uar]y 1860 was very near and I had to make ready for the usual Sports I did nothing till about 3rd Jan[uar]y 1860. On this day I went out to see if I could not arrange with Carver, but no he was in Possession and he was boss. I was determined to take strong measures and next morning I engaged a strong German to go out with me. I let him take a large dray and I rode out instructing him to leave the dray in charge of another man, and for him to approach the Hotel by the back door and in five minutes after I had been inside I instructed him directly he heard me call to come in back way. I rode up to the House shook hands with Carver and told him that I had made up my mind to let him have the House on condition he paid me for the Stock, and during Conversation I got him near the front door. In [a] favourable moment I pinned him by the Collar and swung him head over heels into the Road shut the Doors and called out for my German friend. He was inside in a minute, and up came the dray. I barricaded all Windows & doors, loaded the dray engaged others from the Crushing Machines opposite and in two hours had all Drinkables on the way to Maryborough and next day all the Furniture. This completely non-plussed Mr Carver. I did not see him again for about a Week. I was told he was out every Night with women and one of the Engineers belonging to a crushing Machine took charge of the Hotel. However it was a very bad Spec. to try to do a good turn to a man like Carver. I lost heavily.

In a few days I purchased a lot of Land near [where] the Supreme Court was to be built and near the Post office for £106 and in about two months I had my McCallum Creek Hotel removed into Maryborough and by expending about £500 making it larger I opened it as the Supreme Court Hotel, and put Mr Henry Cable as Manager.[30] This Mr Cable was a good business man and he done a good business in this Hotel. The Reason I expended so much

[30] The Supreme Court Hotel still exists. Bodell does not appear in the Rate Books as the ratepayer but, again, there is no reason to doubt his word. The records are clearly incomplete.

money on another Hotel was my Lease of the Commercial Hotel was coming to a close, and I considered the best I could do was to have an Hotel on my own Property. Mr Cable done a larger business in the Supreme Court Hotel than I was doing at the Commercial Hotel. At this time drinks had been reduced to Sixpence each instead of a Shilling. During my Tenancy of the Commercial Hotel Mr Lawson the owner had to pay Mr Henry Miller, Chairman of the Bank of Victoria £90 Per Annum interest on £600 Mortgage on the Hotel. This interest I had paid out of my rent every six Months. The first six Months of the last Year of my lease Mr Lawson came to me and said he had settled with Mr Miller for the £45 Interest and I paid him the money and also the last six Months making £90 paid Lawson. I got a Notice from Mr Miller that as he had not received any interest for twelve months he as Mortgagee would sell the Hotel and Land and gave me the first offer to purchase the Premises, but I was doing a better business at the other my own Hotel, and did not bother about the Commercial.

At this time a Volunteer Corps had been formed and I was Senior Sergeant and in May 1860 a Grand Review was held at Barkers Creek near Castlemaine and the Maryborough, Bendigo, Kyneton and Castlemaine Volunteers attended, about 500 foot and 60 Horse. This review was held in honour of Her Majesty['s] Birthday, and a glorious day it was. We chartered several Coaches to take our Company, and during the day we fired a *feu de joie*. At noon our Company of which I was the Covering Sergeant, got cheered the regular way the firing was done and during the afternoon we were on [the] Side of a large Hill, the Kyneton Cavalry charged us. I shouted out rally and square at top of my Voice, and during the rally to form the Square Captain Tucker of the Cavalry galloped up shouting Surrender. One of our Men fired a blank Cartridge straight into his face, his head went back with such force I thought he was very badly hurt. He was taken away, and one of his men got savage and tried to cut at one of our men but broke his Sword in two across the firelock, and for 10 minutes the Cavalry tried all they could to break our Square of only 22 men but could not and our enemies retired. On going down to the Booths our Captain Jack Dunne shouted a Doz of Champagne, he was so pleased. That Night we had a grand Dinner officers and non com invited and on Captain Tucker making his appearance, his face looked very bad, peppered all over with Powder and Eyes was badly blood shot in fact it would take some time for him to get his face right again. One man fired his ramrod away and another trooper received [such] a Wound in the neck that he had to seek a Doctor's advice. Next morning Papers had a glowing Account about the Review, and called the Maryborough Volunteers the Iron Square, gave us great credit for 22 men resisting 60 Cavalry. One time one tall man of ours got so warm parrying a trooper's Sword, that he rose from the resist Cavalry to follow the trooper and I had to seize his Coat tails to pull him into his Place and did it with such force that I tore one Coat lap off. After enjoying ourselves well and all of us had received Tickets for the Theatre we returned to Maryborough.

In Decr 1860 I left the Commercial expecting the incoming Proprietor to buy my Furniture. This he promised to do, but did not, but went to Melbourne and bought nearly all new furniture. He deceived me and by so doing I lost heavily as I had to remove my furniture and realise on it as best I could. My Manager Mr Cable left me on my taking Possession of the Supreme Court Hotel and got the Managing of the Golden Age Hotel. Early in 1861 the Great Rush to Otago New Zealand took Place, and thousands of Diggers and business People flocked to New Zealand. Such glowing accounts were spread about the immense quantities of Gold being found we lost a number of our best business Men. Amongst them who went to New Zealand was the present Sir Julius Vogel, then Mr Vogel our Editor of the *Maryborough and Dunolly Advertizer*, a McLandress of McLandress Hepburn & Co. Dunedin his Brother John, Mr Blackall at present an MP of New Zealand,[31] John Armstrong, D. K. Campbell, Merchant, Henry Cable and many others. All cleared out for New Zealand and business fell off in Maryborough. Mr Henry Cable passed through Auckland New Zealand on his way to England in 1880 with over £30,000 in 18 years. He accumulated this money from Gold Digging to Sheep Farming. Mr Henry Cable came to the Colonies as a commercial Traveller, in Manchester, soft goods line, went digging, from that to Hotel keeping. At this time 1861 all drinks in Hotels were reduced to Sixpence. This made a great difference in business, and

[31] This is one of Bodell's few errors, and one difficult to explain. There was no New Zealand member of either House of Parliament of that name or of any similar name.

so many leaving the Town and District made business very dull. I could see I had made another mistake by leaving the Commercial Hotel, although the Supreme Court Hotel was my own Property, and no rent to pay. So many Hotels in Maryborough, there was not business for all. Rushes to Lambing Flat and the Loughland in New South Wales had also reduced our Population.

The month of November I sustained the greatest blow I ever received by over speculating. After this event I got so disgusted with Hotel Keeping, I got reckless, and drank very hard and in a few months I closed the Hotel and sold all off, and a few months after I sold the Hotel for £400 what had cost me £1200. I had about £1300 due to me from People I had given Credit and lent Cash to. For several months I was travelling about trying to get some of this money, but I found I spent more than I received. The Person I sold the Back Creek Hotel to he cleared out to New Zealand, and left £300 due me in Promissory Notes dishonoured. And other supposed Gentlemen holding good Positions repudiated their debts or pleaded Poverty, that one day I got so disgusted, I burnt all my Books and so put an end to business in Victoria. For years I had been very obliging to many by lending money but I did not know my friends or supposed Friends, until I commenced to press for money. I will just state one debtor. I went to Avoca to see Mr Macaboy Wise, the Auctioneer and Land owner. This Gentleman I had lent Cash on several occasions, and he owed me a tidy Sum. So I went to Avoca, and called on him, making sure I should get some money. I went up to his house standing in about 300 acres about two miles from the Town of Avoca. He received me very graciously offered me a Chair etc but he pleaded Poverty, and invited me to spend a few weeks with him, at the same time letting me know he expected a large Cattle Sale at the Springs near Ballarat in a few Weeks and if he had a good Sale he would pay me part of my debt. I stopped with him for two months, and I certainly enjoyed myself very much. Fishing, Kangaroo hunting etc and often visited Avoca. At last the Cattle Sale came off. I went to the White Hart Hotel, the Springs near Lake Learmouth but this Sale was not such a Success as Mr Wise expected, and I had to take a very small Portion in comparison to what I expected. I was satisfied Mr Wise did do his best, but that was poor Satisfaction for me, so I had to leave him. During my stay with him a great demonstration took place at Avoca to celebrate the Marriage of the Prince of Wales May 1863. I believe this event took Place in England in March 1863 but was not celebrated in the Colonies till May.[32]

I proceeded on to Ballarat. Business here was very dull, and on I went to Melbourne. Several Parties here owed me money and I was also disappointed, getting very little. I was intending to go over to Tasmania as I had an interest in two cottages at New Town opposite the Public House I formerly kept. I had not been in Melbourne two days before I met a friend and as he was doing a fair business, we went a pretty fast pace for about two Weeks when large Posters were posted all about Melbourne requiring Volunteers for New Zealand. My old soldiering propensities revived, and my Friend and myself put our names down for New Zealand. I would have gone to any Part of the World to get out of Victoria. In a few days about 200 was enrolled and in a Week between 400 and 500 was mustered, and signed the declaration. I shall never forget the morning we mustered behind the Port Phillip Club Hotel Flinders Street. A few days previously Volunteers arrived from Ballarat, Geelong, Castlemaine and Sandhurst. We enrolled 420 this morning and as I had sent in my Credentials from the Army and had been Serg[t] of Volunteers I certainly expected to be Sergeant. I was about the third called in to Colonel Pitt. Directly he heard my name and as I walked into the Room he said I believe I have some Papers belonging to you. You have been a Serg[t] in the Army. I said Yes Sir, and you made me Serg[t] of the Maryborough Volunteers. M[r] Bodell what do you expect. I answered I don't know Sir. Will your old rank satisfy you. Yes Sir. The next moment he introduced me to Captain Goldsmith as his senior Serg[t] and I passed out taking my Papers. A few minutes after I could see I had made a Mistake as the next four applicants although never been any higher in Rank than Volunteer Serg[ts] came out either Lieutenants or Captains. Myself had been a Serg[t] in HM Service and a good drill, still I did not care much. That day I enrolled 75 men out of 107 for our No. 1 Company. 407 was enrolled that day and 4 companies formed. Each man gave his address and many had no Place of Residence. One man gave his Residence No. 7 Boiler Queens Wharf. At this time there was great depression in Victoria. The Municipality of Melbourne was only paying 5/- per day for Labourers.

---

[32] The Prince, later Edward VII, married on 10 March 1863.

About 1000 Volunteers left Melbourne for New Zealand in 14 days. The Conditions were we had to serve the New Zealand Gov^t three years. If required each man would be entitled to [a] 50 acre Farm and a Town lot free, and 12 months free rations after your Services were not required. Corporals 60 acres Serg^{ts} 80 acres Subalterns 200 Captains 300 Majors & Colonels 400 acres each. Pay Privates 2/6 Corporals 3/- Serg^{ts} 3/6 Subalterns 10/- Captains 15/- Field Officers Majors 20/- Colonels 25/- per day and Rations free, not bad terms. The day after our first muster, many men applied for Rations and they had no Place to sleep. Colonel Pitt gave me a quantity of Tickets. These **tickets** on presentation at the Immigrants Home on St Kilda Road, entitled the holder to three Meals and Bed. The first two days I gave these tickets away freely, but on the third morning I was called into the orderly Room, and Colonel Pitt told me that some of the tickets had been disposed of for Pints of Beer. It appeared these tickets entitled the holder to 1/- Cash or 3 Meals and bed. I immediately suggested to Colonel Pitt that all applicants for Tickets, I would parade them and march them in Rank and file to the Immigrants Home. He approved of this, and each morning I was seen marching a motley Crew across Princes Bridge. On arrival I presented tickets for one each man and each man got a 2 lb loaf and was marched to a large room. After that Publicans got no more tickets for Pints of ale.

On the 31st August 1863 at 9 a.m. we all had to muster to go to Williamstown to embark on Board the Ship *Star of India* for New Zealand. That morning myself and Mr Bailey Surveyor my Melbourne Mate, could not make up our minds to go so I tossed up a Shilling heads we go tails we stop. The Shilling came heads, and I said go we must and off we went. On approaching Spencer Street Railway Station we heard the Melbourne Volunteer Band playing. If we had been ten minutes later we would have been too late. We only had time to get a Seat in the Railway Carriage when off we went straight up to the Quay at Williamstown, and a few Paces took us alongside of the Ship. In one hour the Ship was in mid stream, so as no one could get on Shore. Here Mr Dillon Bell[33] of New Zealand gave us a Speech, and who should I see close to me but Mr Call. He was our Magistrate in Maryborough, and recently been appointed

[33] Francis Dillon Bell, a leading New Zealand politician who served as a minister in several governments, and was then the Native Minister.

to Williamstown. At present he had and has been for many years Stipendiary Magistrate for the City of Melbourne, and Inspector Hare of Maryborough is Police inspector in Melbourne. Directly I seen Mr Call I popped down below, so as he should not see me. I was ashamed to be seen with such a motley Crew.

V

New Zealand: the Waikato Campaign, 1863–65

New Zealand had been settled in the early part of the nineteenth century by sealers, whalers, runaway seamen, traders and missionaries, mostly from New South Wales. By 1840 there were about 2000 settlers. In that year the British sent out Captain Hobson to negotiate with the Maoris for the cession of their country to the Crown. The British Government acknowledged that it was the Maoris' country and that their consent to annexation was necessary. A large number of leading Maoris did sign the Treaty of Waitangi, which guaranteed them the rights of British subjects and in their landed and other possessions. In return they ceded their sovereignty to the Queen.

It was hoped that the Treaty would lay a basis for peaceful and Christian colonisation, but in fact, almost from the start, there was to be fighting near some of the settlements. The first conflicts were in the mid-eighteen forties. The next went on from 1860 to about 1872. James Bodell was a soldier during this conflict, in the Waikato area to the south of Auckland, and at Tauranga—in 'one of England's little wars', fought in many parts of the Empire in the nineteenth century—in South Africa, in Canada, in China, in Burma . . .

The Anglo-Maori war of the Sixties began in 1860 over a disputed land purchase at Waitara in Taranaki. A Maori called Teira (Taylor) offered to sell some land to the Crown. Most of the tribe, including their chief, Wiremu Kingi (William King), who were living on the land, denied that he had any right to sell, and resisted the surveyors. Fighting went on in 1860 and 1861—when a truce was made. A new Governor, Sir George Grey, investigated the purchase and concluded that it was defective. Before returning it to the Maoris, however, he sent troops to occupy some land in southern Taranaki. Some of them were ambushed and fighting broke out again.

After inflicting a defeat on the Taranaki Maoris most of the troops went to Auckland and prepared to invade the Waikato, a rich region south of Auckland. Some of the southern tribes, including Ngatimaniapoto, had helped the so-called 'rebels' in Taranaki; indeed, their chief, Rewi, had *ordered the ambush. More important, Grey was hostile towards the Maori King, and the 'Kingites' in the Waikato. Some of the main tribes had chosen their own King, Potatau, in 1858. In 1860 he had been succeeded by Tawhiao. His mere existence seemed a challenge to British sovereignty.*

It was at this stage that Francis Dillon Bell, the Minister of Native Affairs, and some officials went over to Melbourne to recruit volunteers for the Waikato Militia. It was proposed to confiscate 'rebel' land and to establish military settlements. Free land was the bait used to attract volunteers.

Bodell's unit was in the area where actions occurred in the Waikato campaign, but he missed the main battles, in some of which the British suffered severe losses. His narrative gives, however, a vivid picture of what life was like in a Victorian army. There was much drinking— Bodell was often 'locussed', that is, drunk—and he is very frank about the looting. On one occasion he actually breaks into the tomb of the first Maori King in a vain search for loot. Like many soldiers he had a considerable respect for the Maoris as fighting men.

When the Waikato campaign ended the First Waikato were transferred to Tauranga just as a new phase of the war was beginning. A new Maori religious movement, Paimarire, the 'Good and Peaceful religion', had appeared in Taranaki. Its followers, the Hauhau, believed themselves impervious to bullets. They revived the practice of cannibalism. The resistance to the British army became more savage and implacable. Some bands of Hauhau came into conflict with the militia near Tauranga.

After his three years' service had expired Bodell was discharged in 1866, but fighting continued in other parts of the North Island, so that he still had to take his turn on guard and other duties. For some years Tauranga feared Maori attacks. But in 1872 the war was over and the way was open for the progress of European settlement.

It should be added that many details in Bodell's narrative are confirmed in the army records. He volunteered on 1 September 1863 in Melbourne, giving his occupation as 'Carpenter'. On 28 September he was given a Regimental Court Martial and reduced to the rank of private. After the war an officer certified that he had been under fire and he was awarded the New Zealand War Medal.[1]

[1] References in AD76/1 and AD32/2239, files in the New Zealand National Archives, Wellington.

Next morning early we were sailing out of Port Phillip with a topsail breeze, and I had enough to do to get things in order. Each man was allowed two glasses of Rum each day and this necessitated a Companies Roll being made out, Mess Rolls also. The first few days I was kept occupied, being about the only Serg^t who understood these matters. We were very liberally provisioned, Cask of Biscuits being placed along the decks, good Butter served out in fact the rations were very good. Every day I had to drill a Squad on the Poop, so with one thing and another my time was well occupied. In fact I was glad to have plenty to occupy my time. I could scarcely realize my Position or believe I had come to be soldiering again, and as there was plenty of Grog, I often used it freely to drown dull care. I could not reconcile myself to the Position I occupied. I was almost afraid to think.

On the eleventh day from Melbourne we sighted the New Zealand Coast. This morning we had a strong Breeze, and on going on deck, every one seemed as something was the matter. The Captain of the Ship was on the fore top, two men at the Wheel and the Mate passing orders to the men at the Wheel. I looked around but could see nothing unusual on the Sea. I went below to get Breakfast. Just as I got seated in the Serg^{ts} Mess with my coffee only about four of us out of twelve Serg^{ts} and as we got seated and commenced to take our Breakfast, the Ship struck a Reef and it sent her on her beam ends. Myself and others went head first into the Scuppers, Coffee Buckets, Biscuits, Meat Butter Tables and everything broke clean away. The next moment tons of Water came down the after hatch and flooded the tween decks. In fact for a short time I thought the Ship was turning over. Myself and others were slightly hurt, and on account the Vessel was heeling over so much we could not get up. All tables all along the starboard Side was carried away and the Breakfast lost. Forward hundreds of men were huddled together. I certainly thought it was the finish of my career, but presently the good ship commenced to right herself and every timber in this Ship of 1750 Tons shivered again and righted herself. I managed to go on deck, every one I met Crew and all could not answer my inquiries. There was the Captain still on the foretop all the Crew waiting for orders, but presently the Captain came down to the deck and said all danger was over but the Ship had [had] a narrow squeak. I went forward and looked over the port Bow, and between the Bow and Midship about 10 feet of the Ship's copper covering was torn from the Ship and swinging about in the water, and out as the Ship rolled along astern I could plainly see a reef and broken Water. It appeared the Captain knew of this reef, but he was certain he could weather it, but just struck South West of it. In a short time all danger was over. That morning I shall never forget.

Towards Night we were making for Auckland and on Saturday Night 12th September 1863[2] we anchored in the beautiful Harbour of Auckland doing the trip in 12 days, a very good Passage. It generally took a Steamer 10 days from Melbourne to Auckland. The next morning being Sunday we had to pass the time as well as we could. During the afternoon we noticed a Funeral. This was Captain Swift of the 65th Reg[t][3] being buried he having died from Wounds received from the Natives fighting at the Battle of Cameron Town near Tuakau on the Waikato River. All kind of Rumours came on Board, about the New Zealand Natives killing the Soldiers, some of the 40th Reg[t] being killed and losing 40 Stand of Arms. In fact we expected to be fighting the Maoris in 24 hours. Next morning we disembarked in the Gov[t] Steamer *Sandfly* a small Steamer carrying 2 guns (small ones). Auckland appeared a poor dirty sludgy Place. We went straight up to the Barracks. Here we stopped about one hour to get refreshments at the Canteen, and we indulged rather freely, before proceeding to our first Station Otahuhu. We formed advance Guard. This I had charge of and as I was a Stranger to Otahuhu I took a man (a [Military] Pensioner) who had only been out of Auckland about six Months, to show me the way to Otahuhu Barracks. We marched on, and this old Scoundrel took me and the advance Guard straight to Rogers Criterion Hotel Otahuhu passing the turn to the Barracks about half a Mile. Directly I found I had passed the Barracks I turned my men to the right about and went into the Camp, about half an hour after the headquarters. I was told off to a hut with 20 men and a Corporal.

---

[2] The arrival of the *Star of India* was reported in the *Daily Southern Cross* on Monday, 14 September 1863, with 'James Bowdell' listed among the passengers. She brought the first detachment of 'volunteer military settlers' from Victoria, four officers and 403 men.
[3] Captain R. Swift of the 65th Regiment was killed in a small action at Camerontown on 7 September 1863.

Each of us was marched to the Canteen and received one Pint of Ale. This was my first interview with Captain Hunter our future adjutant. Next day we were served with our Regimentals and in two days from landing we were soldiering in earnest.

The third day I was drilling a squad and that night had charge of the outlying Picket. Next day at drill. In a few days I made too many Visits to the Serg^{ts} Mess, and about the sixth day we got our Pay. I went down to Otahuhu and got in Company and got locussed, managed to get to Barracks all right, and lay down on my bed and missed Staff Parade. Every night all non commissioned officers paraded at 9 o.c. Tattoo, this Parade I missed being fast asleep on my bed. Another Serg^t who I found out was afraid of me being made Colour and Pay Serg^t brought the Sergeant Major to my hut and told him I was drunk. This the Serg^t Major told me himself next day, and next morning I was brought to the Orderly Room and Major St John spoke to me very sharply, and I answered him back, saying not to speak to me like that, I did not care about the Stripes. This of course was too much for the Major and I was told off for a Garrison Court Martial, tried next day and reduced to the Rank and Pay of a Private Sentinel [soldier]. The dose I got when locussed made me very bad for about a Week. The very day I was reduced another 400 came from Melbourne and the next day we marched on to Papakura. I was very bad this day. Here the glass of Rum was served out twice each day as we were considered in the Field.

After two days Papers came into Camp reporting that Doctor Pollen,[4] a Member of the New Zealand Parliament then sitting in Auckland, in a speech, he referred to the Volunteers from Sydney and Melbourne as the scum and riff-raff of the Streets. This riled every man, and we went to Captain Goldsmith and demanded an Apology from Dr Pollen. Our Captain took the matter up rather warm and in a few days Dr Pollen sent apologies which was in the Papers, and read out in Orders. One man on Sentry threw his firelock and Bayonet away from him, in fact if Dr Pollen had not apologized a Mutiny would have taken place.

In a few days some more Volunteers landed in Auckland from Melbourne and Hobart Town and we marched on to Drury. This was a muddy Camp. About 200 of the 18th Royal Irish Reg^t were

---

[4] Daniel Pollen, a Member of the Legislative Council.

stationed [here]. One morning on turning out (it had been a wet Night) the form of my body was plainly seen in the Mud I had been lying in all night. We dug a deep trench around the tent and got more fern and made sleeping more comfortable. 20 men in a bell Tent is too many. However we had to put up with every inconvenience. I have seen men fall down with their great coats on in the Sludge and could not get up again without assistance. Drury was a muddy Place so much traffic, about 100 transport Horses and 50 carts were here to take Provisions to the Troops as General Cameron advanced.

We had not been in Drury a Week before the Maoris were reported in force at the Mauku about 10 Miles distance. About 200 were told off to go and strengthen the Mauku Volunteers as it was said the Natives had surrounded them in the small church. Our Company was told off for Martins Farm,[5] about 5 miles nearer to Queens Redoubt, General Camerons headquarters. During our Stay at Drury the 3rd Waikato Regt was formed, and our Company being 127 strong we furnished the odd 27 towards forming the 3rd Regt. I was entrusted to pick out the 27 men. One man offered £5 to let him stop but I did not take it, he had to go. Although I had been reduced still I was treated well by both officers and men. The Officer went Second in Command to the Mauku was on Picket with me the night before he went to that Station and when I seen him leave the Camp with a brace of Pistols and Tomahawk also Sword I remarked he looked as if he intended to slaughter all the Maoris. The day after Part of our Company went to Martins Farm. Here we found 50 of the 18th Regt and 50 of us making 100 in a small redoubt. This redoubt overlooked the Great South Road the Main Road to the Interior or Waikato Country where General Cameron intended and did do, take about 4000 of British troops. We arrived at Martins Farm on Octr 20th 1863 and four days after a Battle took place at the Mauku,[6] and our men were decoyed into an Ambush by the wily Enemy, and the officer I referred to being too well armed, was killed and another one and 9 Men killed. The Mauku was only about 3 Miles from Martins Farm. During the fight about 50 of us went into the Bush, intending to intercept the Natives but

[5] Waikato Maoris had ambushed a party of the 18th Irish Regiment at Martin's Farm on 17 July.

[6] The action at Mauku was on 23 October 1863.

they did not come our way, and we returned to camp with the loss of several Bayonets, being drawn out of Scabbards by the Supple Jack that grows in the New Zealand bush.

Martins Farm was about the best Station on the Great South Road. I was told off as the Engineer to the Redoubt, that is I had the charge of the Redoubt to keep in good repair, and strengthen it where required. I also made a fine bathing place for the Men a few yards outside. All the Bridges on the Great South Road were guarded every night by orders of the General. About half mile from our Redoubt was a Bridge and every night a Guard of 12 men 1 Serg^t 1 officer took charge of this Bridge. 4 Sentries were posted at each Corner, remainder remained under the Bridge, a miserable place it was running Water and Sludge under the Bridge, and every hour Artillery men galloping over the Bridge with despatches from the General, on to Drury and Auckland. As they crossed the Bridge the Sludge came down on our heads and [we were] not allowed to strike a light to have a smoke on Sentry. Each one stood still, anyone approaching did not answer the Challenge 'Who comes there' at once we had orders to fire. This lasted some months as it was reported the Natives intended destroying the Bridges to prevent the Convoy of Horses and Carts loaded with Provisions for the Troops at the front.

Every day a large Convoy went with Provisions. One day I was sent for to go and assist a Man with Dray and two Horses who was proceeding to the front with 3 large barrels of Ale in the Dray. About half mile from our redoubt the heat of the Sun burst one of the Ale Barrels, and the Horses took fright and ran the dray into a ditch. I had to return to the redoubt to get some men to assist, but I knew the best Preventative to prevent the other Barrels from bursting was to draw a Bucket of Beer from each Barrel so I got the Men to take 2 Buckets and large Gimlet, being the Engineer I had plenty of Carpenter's tools and off we went. I persuaded the Carter to have a bucket of Ale taken from each Cask, and on filling the Buckets one was drunk and by a little dodging I drew the third Bucket full and then we got the Cart on the Road and the Barrels in, and sent the drayman on his way. We returned to the redoubt intending to fill some bottles with part of the Beer, but the troops seen us approaching with two Buckets and they concluded what we had in them, and rushed us. The Ale was soon all disposed of without bottling it.

One morning myself and 11 others came off Bridge Guard and as usual we got our 12 o'clock Grog early in the morning, about 6 o.c. a.m. Being under the Bridge all night each Guard coming off had Permission to have their midday Grog on coming off Guard. This morning we noticed a peculiar leathery taste and weak about our tot of Grog. I went to the officer and on inspection it turned out the Batman to the acting Serg^t Major was a Shoe Maker and the Guards' Grog was left in charge of the Serg^t Major and the night before his Batman or Servant got at the Grog and drank some of it and replaced it by water he had been soaking his leather in and so spoilt the Rum. For this offence which was proved against him he was tried by Court Martial and got 50 Lashes and two months imprisonment.

On Christmas Eve 1863 we went into the Bush and got a quantity of evergreens and decorated the Redoubt for Christmas day. The Redoubt looked splendid as the New Zealand Bush has splendid evergreens for such Purposes. That afternoon I made a large Plum Pudding. I got the flour Raisins Suet etc from Mrs Martin (the Farm House formed one side of the Redoubt). I was a favourite with M^r & Mrs Martin. We had received no Pay since September and all of us were short of Cash. Our Captain had our Pay at Drury and I wrote a letter to the *Daily Southern Cross* Auckland Paper complaining about the way we were left without Pay etc Signed my name Biddle.[7] On Christmas eve I had the large Pudding boiling in

---

[7] His letter was published on 30 December 1863:

WAIKATO VOLUNTEERS' PAY.

To the Editor of the *Daily Southern Cross*.

Sir, – Considerable discontent has been caused throughout the 1st Waikato Regiment in consequence of the irregular payment of the men. Mr Dillon Bell apprised us before sailing from Melbourne that we should receive our pay in such a manner as would give general satisfaction – either daily or weekly. Many of us are in duty bound to send from time to time, remittances to our friends or otherwise. Now, sir, we are very anxious to know where the fault lies. At present there is six weeks and four days pay due to us.

ONE OF THE 1st WAIKATO REGT.

Camp, Martyn's Farm, December 24.

The reference to 'remittances' possibly suggests that Bodell's first wife was still alive.

a Copper Boiler lent by Mrs Martin, and some of us considered a few head of Poultry would be very good for our Christmas dinner. We made a small party of four, and left the boiling Pudding in charge of others. After making it all right with the Sentry about 10 p.m. we four slipped out of the Redoubt for the Purpose of visiting two Farm Houses about two miles away being between us and the Mauku. These Houses we had seen during the scouring expedition we made on the 24th Octr (the day of the Battle at the Mauku). Being dark we made very poor Progress through the high Fern and Scrub, besides we lost our right track. About Midnight we came in sight of one Farm house. For the two Miles we must have travelled six. On approaching the house dogs commenced to bark and lights flitting about, so we had to withdraw and make for another house. We approached near to one about one o'clock a.m. These People were on the alert also. Here we did not know what to do. We had to retire into the Scrub, and not one of the Party knew of any other house, and after travelling till approaching daylight through a rough Country, we came in sight of the Redoubt at Williamsons Clearing occupied by 100 troops. This Redoubt was about two miles nearer Drury than our Redoubt at Martins Farm. Here was a pretty go, if the Sentry had seen us we certainly would have been made Prisoners and a nice plight we were in. The Sole of one of my Boots had parted Company with the upper [and] my feet very sore, all our clothes torn more or less. When daylight had fairly come, we cut a sorry Plight. When we got well clear of the Redoubt we examined each other and we came to the conclusion we had been fools, and got into our Redoubt as quickly as possible. This we did and was laughed at for our Pains. When we considered over our expedition we agreed by a little forethought that all houses in the district was guarded every night to prevent being surprised by the Natives. This Christmas day turned out glorious, the large Plum Pudding was done to a turn having been kept boiling all Night, and we passed a merry Christmas.

I must return back for a few Weeks. About the last week in November I had been on Pass to Headquarters at Drury to try to get a Pass to Auckland. I done it in this Way. I wrote a letter as if I had received it from a Brother just arrived in Auckland and I showed the letter to our Colonel and adjutant, and from them to the Garrison Adjutant. It passed Muster with all and I got the Pass for three days. This was on a Saturday. That day on my way to

Auckland I had to pass several redoubts. About 10 miles on my way I met a man I knew in Maryborough Victoria. Some years previous this man was delivering to me several Barrels of English Ale, Bass's. About the third Barrel being put down my Cellar this Barrel would not aright itself on its end. This man put his feet on the end of the Barrel to put it upright, he being half down the Cellar with his feet on the Barrel and when I put force [on his shoulders] the head of the Barrel gave way and the Man went into the Barrel of English Ale Value about £14 (54 Gal) and of course the ale had to go back to the Merchant. On meeting this man on my way to Auckland he was very much surprised to see me in Militia dress knowing me two years previously as a Man in a good business and in good Circumstances. We had a Jollification all night. Next morning we arrived at Otahuhu 9 Miles from Auckland and about 9 o'clock this Sunday morning after getting several Drinks we were in a merry mood and who should pass us on horse back but Major St John (our Major). He knew me and in half an hour I was taken into Barracks.

Next morning I was given in Charge of a Sergeant of the 2nd Waikato Militia to be taken back to Drury. This Sergeant called at every public house on the Road and drank at my expense. We had emerged from the Papakura Hotel about 3 Miles from Drury, he appeared to be getting tipsy. We passed a redoubt about half mile from the Hotel. All of a sudden he seized my firelock and marched me a Prisoner into the Redoubt. The officer could see the state of the Serg^t and would not keep me a Prisoner but retained my Firelock. So we proceeded on our way minus my firelock. I considered this very bad Conduct on the Part of the Serg^t after drinking at my expense to put me in Chokey to save himself. I was determined to have revenge if possible. We had to pass two Hotels as we entered the straggling Town of Drury, and we called into each of these and when we arrived in Camp my beautiful Serg^t was as tight as possible and your humble Servant sober. As we approached our Orderly Room the Adjutant met us. He asked me where my firelock was. I referred him to the Serg^t. He was so unsteady the Adjutant in an instant called the Serg^t Major to take the Serg^t to his Tent a Prisoner. He was marched there and when I explained matters to the Adjutant, he said you must get your firelock. I told him if he would let me go for it I would be back in 3 hours with my firelock. He laughed, as much as to say I do not think so. In a Second he said do you promise to be back in 3 hours with your firelock. I say I do Sir. Off you go and fetch it. I did and was back in 2½ hours with my Arms.

Next day Bailey my Melbourne Mate who I got made Corporal in Otahuhu had been Pay Serg^t of our Company, but had misbehaved himself and the day I reached Drury got reduced to the Rank of Private. This morning he came to me and showed me a large Roll of bank notes, saying are you game for a trip for Auckland. I consented at once and off we went. We got into an Hotel about two miles on our way. We had stopped here fully one hour, Bailey had gone into the Yard I was in the Bar talking to the Landlord when who should come in but 4 men and a Corporal. I was taken Prisoner and on they inquiring for Bailey, I told them he had gone on to Auckland. They took me back to Camp, and Bailey got to Auckland.

I did not see him again for 11 months when I met him on the Waikato River, Engineer for the erection of a large Bridge and receiving 22/6 per day Pay. After his Spree in Auckland he being a Surveyor and Engineer, he got put on the Staff, and got his present Position. This time we had another spree.

During my stay in Drury I put my name down as a Volunteer to take provision boats up the Waikato River to follow General Cameron, and all the troops at the front. I was anxious to see the Country and more active Service. Still I was very comfortable at Martin Farm Redoubt but the Sameness Week after week, inactivity did not suit me. I regretted this Step afterwards. For my trip with Bailey I got 10 days Grog stopped, and joined my detachment at Martins Farm. The letter I [was] supposed to have received from my Brother he [having] just arrived in Auckland caused many a laugh afterwards.

Three days after Christmas after we all gave a days Pay to erect a Monument over the men killed at the Mauku an officer and one man came into the Redoubt to take me with about 50 men from Drury to the Mangatawhiri Creek that was the headquarters for the Boats plying up the Waikato River. Commodore Wiseman and 100 Sailors belonging to Men of War Vessels on New Zealand Station were stationed here and we had come to relieve them. I forgot to mention the 25 Octr 1863 the day after the fight at the Mauku, an expedition went out to bring in the men killed the day before and on arriving at the Place, where the fighting had been, all the killed 9

Men and 2 Officers, Lieut[s] Percival and Norman.[8] The dead bodies had been placed in a row and an officer at each end, the dead officer on the right had his right arm erected in upright Position and the one on the left his left Arm, and all of them had their throats cut open and their tongues pulled through on their breasts, and so left by the Maoris. Their bodies were buried at Drury and a Monument erected over them each man paying a days Pay all officers also. This same Monument can be seen to this day.

The following morning after our arrival at Mangatawhiri Creek the Sailors left and our laborious duties commenced in earnest. Up at 5 o'clock load boats then have Breakfast. On Board by 6.30 and off to Meremere. Here a great fight took place a few weeks before. We did this trip twice each day. Going to Meremere was very hard Work having to pull against the Waikato River running against us at the rate of 4 Miles per hour. 8 Boats loaded for each trip on Convoy, the Creek was always very muddy and the Ground knee deep in Mud. We did this for about two months. During the last week in Jan[uar]y 1864 our boats Crew was sent to Waikato Heads near the open Sea to fetch a large Boat [of] 16 Oars. Many of these were built afterwards. The one we went for was the first built. From the Manga Creek to Waikato head is about 25 miles [and] with the Stream going with us we did not require much pulling and beautiful Scenery to be seen. About 2 miles below Tuakau, a Redoubt of 100 men, is Cameron Town the Place a great fight [took place] in Aug[t] 1863. Captain Swift that was buried in Auckland on the Sunday 13 September that we seen from the Ship *Star of India* was killed at Cameron Town (named after General Cameron).

This morning as we were passing under the waving branches of the drooping trees on the Banks of the River, I noticed a man's Body on opposite Side of the River to Cameron Town, alongside of an old small Canoe, and as we approached the Body we disturbed the Water. The Body bobbed up and down and [I] could see the red stripe in the Soldier's Trousers. We got alongside, the hair was off the Crown of the head the part out of the Water. We tied the Body to our Bow rope on Painter. Myself and Jack Appleton done this.

---

[8] He gets their names right. According to the official report six men were killed and one dangerously wounded, as well as the officers. Lt. Colonel D. A. Cameron to Sir George Grey, 28 Oct. 1863, *Appendices to the Journals of the House of Representatives*, 1863, E-5A.

This body was decomposed and gave a frightful Stench. Our officer [was] noted by the name of Bully Fraser, he was only 'Ensign'. He got on the Seat of the boat and commenced to shout Come on you B------ Maoris we fight you—you murdering D----- S----- his Language was frightful. One fine looking fellow Dick Williams fainted with fright. In a town he was all boast like our officer. If the Maoris had come and fired into us I expect Bully Fraser would have soon taken Shelter ashore. We had the body secure and proceeded on our Journey. A few miles further we came opposite Kohanga Mission Station of the Rev Maunsell.[9] This Station is about 8 miles from Waikato Heads our destination, and from this to the heads is a Succession of mud flats. None of us knew the Channel and we frequently got stuck. The River ran towards the Heads and every time we got stuck the Body came alongside smelling very bad. After several hours, we got to our destination and the *Eclipse* Man of War was inside the Heads. We called alongside and informed them of the dead body. The Captain sent a boats Crew on Shore with us. On landing the body I was examining the Socks expecting to find a Regimental number or some mark to denote what Regiment the body belonged to. As I was doing this one foot came off from the ankle. In the trousers Pocket was a Purse containing £5.2.9d. This the Captain of HM Ship *Eclipse* took he being the senior officer at the Waikato Head. Here was stationed 150 of the Second Waikato Militia. While this was going on the Sailors dug a hole and we put Branches of trees into it and lowered the body in a few more branches and then the body was covered over with the Earth, and so the body of (as was ascertained afterwards) Corporal Ryan of the 65th Regt [was buried]. The poor fellow lost his life by trying to save the Life of a drowning Sergt of the same Regt, both were drowned the Sergt body being found a few days after. Poor Ryans body had been in the water between 3 & 4 Weeks. A few months after the Victoria Cross arrived from England for Ryan and Lieut Talbot of the 65th for Gallantry at the fight of Cameron Town for rescuing the wounded body of Captain Swift of the 65th Regt.

On going to quarters provided for us we noticed a Maori Pah a few yards distant with a Notice No Europeans Allowed Inside. The Barge we came for had not arrived but was expected next morning so we made ourselves comfortable and passed the Night very well.

[9] The Anglican missionary, Robert Maunsell.

Next morning after breakfast we seen a Steamer coming seaward making for the Heads. As she came nearer we could see the Barge in tow. The Entrance was very rough and on the Steamer crossing the Bar or entrance the rope that held the Barge broke and the Barge went adrift was washed ashore and got broken up. All we got was two thwarts Mast & Sail, anchor & chain.

That morning I felt very anxious to have an inspection of the Maori Pah, and I made the acquaintance of a Pakeha Maori (that is a white man living amongst the natives). He told me how to get into the Pah and I did so. I had been in about half an hour when who should come towards me but our officer Ensign or Bully Fraser. He was half drunk and he had no more business in the Pah than myself, and if he had told me to clear out in a just and proper manner I should have done so, but instead of that he got hold of me and was going to strike me. I cautioned him not to do it again [and] when he was going to strike me again, I parried his blow and struck him. He ran away. In a few minutes he appeared with a Corporal and four men of the Second Waikato Militia and I was made a Prisoner for striking my superior officer. I certainly gave them some trouble before they got me to the Guard Tent. Bully Fraser gave me such a Character that I was chained with my hands handcuffed behind my back to a strong Stake drove well into the Ground and left there all day in a January Sun which nearly made my face as black as a Native's. At Night I was taken from the Stake and put into a bell tent by myself with my hands in front of me with the manacles on.

For the information of the reader I will describe this Bully Fraser. By some fluke Colonel Pitt when recruiting in Sydney for men for New Zealand [heard] Fraser had been in the Army and Colonel Pitt made him Ensign. He had the appearance of a fighting man or a dog fancier[10] a brutish countenance and he had often been on the Wallaby (or tramp) about the various Gold Fields and Squatters Stations. On joining the boating Corps on the Waikato he took a fancy for the boat I was in as we were all old Australians and officer & men when on the River always fraternized together. He particularly boasted about his abilities, and when he took freely of Grog he let us know that and boasted six Months before he was

[10] A 'dog fancier' was a receiver of stolen dogs who would return them to their owners for a fee.

Coal heaving in Sydney but now he was Captain of the Waikato. On one occasion we were going with Provisions to Rangiriri a travelling Jeweller (a Jew) took a Passage in our boat. About half way to Rangiriri after Bully Fraser had got several Glasses of Grog in him he commenced at this Jew. You B----- Jew you crucified Jesus Christ and by G-- I'll crucify you if you don't hand me some of that Jewellery. He kept at this poor fellow for two hours and then he got a valuable Meerschaum Pipe from him. Of course we would not let Fraser hurt the Man. This was very near getting him into trouble. On another occasion we that is a convoy of 7 boats Crews were returning from Rangiriri empty boats and stopped at an old Maori Village to loot anything we could get, and get some fine Peaches. Our boat was some distance from the others and we were amongst the Native huts. All at once a Native Woman appeared. I could just see her head above a bush and for a moment could not tell if it was a man or Woman, but directly I drew Fraser['s] eye to the object, he let a Yell out of him and ran as hard as he could towards the boat. Myself and another stood laughing at him. The Woman only had one eye. Poor thing she would not leave the Village on account of some of her children being buried there. A few weeks after her and another Native Woman we found in another Village. We subscribed a few Shillings and bought enough cotton Print to make each one a Skirt with Needles, Thread etc. Shortly after this we persuaded them to come with us to a Native Settlement near Rangiriri.

To return to Waikato heads, the day following my adventure with bully Fraser, as the boat or Barge was smashed up, Captain Parnell of the Steamer *Lady Barclay* intended going up the Waikato with the Steamer a small one of about 30 Tons and we was to return to Mangatawhiri Creek our headquarters. There were also as Passengers the Rev Maunsell and his large Family returning to the Mission Station as the War had removed 70 Miles from Kohanga Mission Station. During the afternoon I was marched a Prisoner on board had a bayonet Sentry over me, and off we went with our boat in tow. We got stuck in the mud many times and when I could see help was required to give a hand to push the Steamer off the Mud Bank I always assisted. At last we landed Rev Maunsell and Family at the Station, 4 fine buxom Girls and one Son. We got no further that night. The Pakeha Maori I referred to before came on Board as interpreter to a Maori Chief as Pilot.

During the second day since we left Waikato Heads as we lay

stuck in the mud opposite Tuakau Redoubt the Pakeha Maori Jack Duncan by Name came to me and said he was surprised to hear I was a Prisoner and he considered Bully Fraser should be the Prisoner not me. He said he had seen the whole affair between me & Fraser in the Pah and had seen Ensign Fraser strike me first. This was good news for me because the Crime I was charged with by the officer who I had struck if I could not prove my Innocence would be a General Court Martial and perhaps 10 years Penal Servitude and a flogging besides. Myself and Jack Duncan talked matters over and he said I will see Captain Parnell and see what we can do for you. That Evening was a fine Moonlight, and I had noticed Ensign Fraser looking half Tipsy by 7 p.m. He had two of the Crew one playing a Concertina and the other playing a Banjo and Mr Fraser on aft of Vessel in his Shirt and Trousers only in a State of intoxication and dancing Nigger breakdowns, bare Head & bare feet. During this time plenty of Grog was handed round and I had received my several refreshers. About 8 p.m. Captain Parnell and Duncan came to me, and after a little talk about how I was made a Prisoner, Capt Parnell told me he had got the Steward of the Steamer to draft a Petition to Capt Fraser signed by Captain Parnell and all the Crew. Shortly after I was called to go down [to] the little Cabin. On my descending there was Bully Fraser quite drunk. Captain Parnell introduced the matter and after explaining a few words to Fraser Captain desired the Ship's Steward to read the Petition. On finishing it a Silence occurred for a few Seconds, and Bully Fraser turned to me and said—You D----- B----- you know I don't want to hurt you, you are released, and go on deck and enjoy yourself. So I was got out of this Scrape by two Strangers and I was very glad to have such Friends. Afterward I could not make any Freedom with Ensign Fraser. I considered he had took a mean advantage of his Commission. That night and next day on our way Home in our own boat we all got gloriously drunk, how we got Home to Mangatawhiri Creek I know not officers & men alike.

After this we commenced duty to take Provisions to Meremere. This Place was the Scene of a Fight with the Natives on first of November 1863. On this occasion as the Steamer *Pioneer*[11] was

[11] There is a drawing of this river gunboat, and a chapter on the Waikato River fleet in James Cowan, *The New Zealand Wars*, Vol. 1, Wellington, 1922 or 1955 editions.

passing with General Cameron and a Load of Troops the Natives had a small Cannon and in the absence of proper Shot loaded the Gun with a Steelyard Weight about 4 lbs and fired it at the Steamer and it passed through the Bulwarks and lodged in a Cask of Salt Meat, hurting no one. The Maoris were soon drove out of Mere-mere (pronounced Merry Merry). On the 20th of the same month the great Battle of Rangiriri was fought. At this fight which lasted two days and nights the Natives gave the British Soldiers enough to do. General Cameron had about 1200 Troops and two Gun boats, and on the second day the Troops & Sailors charged the Maori Position three times and were compelled to retire after severe loss each time.[12] On the afternoon of the second day, an assaulting Party got under the earth Walls of the Maori defences, and during the Night were making Preparations to blow it up. The Maoris being surrounded by the British Troops and Sailors and ascer-tained they were hemmed in. At day light they hoisted a flag of truce, and the whole lot was taken Prisoners, about 183. Several hundreds must have got away by the Lake close to the left front of their Position. These Prisoners were all marched off to Auckland and put on board a Hulk in the Harbour. Myself formed one of the Escort on their way to Auckland. A few weeks after I was in the small Maori raupo Church, and it was perforated in many Places by the 12 lb Shots from the Gun boats on the river, and Blood was plentiful about the altar. People may say what they like about the New Zealanders (Maoris), if they are properly handled they make as good a Soldier as any in the world. If they had the same appliances as the British they would have made it very warm to the troops under General Cameron. As far as my memory serves me the 40th 57th 70th Regts besides Sailors from HM Ships *Curacao, Miran-da* & *Eclipse*[13] were represented at the Battle of Rangiriri and many of these sailors officers afterwards lost their life at the Great Gate Pah fight near Tauranga in April 1864. This Place is about three miles from where I am writing this Narrative.

To return to Bully Fraser at the Water Transport Corps, about a

---

[12] The British lost three officers and thirty-five men and took 183 pris-oners.

[13] The British forces were as follows: Royal Navy, Royal Artillery, Royal Engineers, troops in the 12th, 14th, 40th and 65th regiments. HMS *Curacao* and the *Pioneer* and the *Avon*.

Week after our return, a large Supply of Ration Rum came by drays from Auckland to be taken up to the various redoubts along the Waikato River. On this night a Guard of the 18th Royal Irish as usual arrived from the Queen Redoubt about one and half miles away relieving the old Guard of the 43rd Regt. A Bridge that spanned the Creek contained about 26 Hogsheads of this fine Jamaica Rum and as usual a Sentry was posted to take Charge. Next morning about 5 o'clock we commenced to load our various Boats. This task we had to do every morning at 5 a.m. At six Breakfast at 6.30 man boats two trips each day to Meremere and back, very hard work and this hard work we volunteered to do. When we did so we all understood that it was to sail boats not to pull. After a few days at the pulling Boats our arms ached a Pain from your back right through to your chest. Lumps came on the muscles of your arms, in fact we became Slaves. When at Martins Farm Redoubt I was a Gentleman compared to what I was in the water transport Corps. Still the life was exciting and that suited me, as when left alone I would get thinking about the Position I held in Victoria only 18 months before and gave me much anguish of Mind. This morning on loading the boats with the Rum several Barrels appeared light or partly empty but one Cask we could not remove and no Wonder. Some one had got under the Bridge and with a inch auger bored through the Planks of the Bridge into the Rum Cask and either carried away or spilled about 25 Gallons. A report was made but no one knew anything about it. This could not have been done without one if not all of the three Sentries knowing who did it but we found out afterwards it was a frequent occurrence. I have seen all the Guard officer & men drunk Prisoners included. I knew for a fact, and did participate in it myself. Every evening a new Guard arrived from the Queens Redoubt and during the night if any Rum Casks were waiting to go up the River that night the Guard (always after midnight after Guard had been visited by the Visiting Rounds from Queens Redoubt) would let one man take all the canteen[s] and empty bottles and with the assistance of the Sentry fill the lot, draw off as much as a 3 Gallon Camp Kettle for present use and the Canteens and Bottles would be taken about half a mile up the Road towards Queens Redoubt and planted amongst the Scrub of a small bush close to the Road and after the men dismounted Guard would return from Queen Redoubt and spring the plant at the Queen Redoubt. If you did not care about drinking it you could sell it at 10/- Per Bottle and after reducing the Strength very much one quart would make two good Bottles of Rum, each canteen held three Pints.

I now return to Bully Fraser. About three Weeks after he had released me, one morning in February it being very hot Weather and all of us were as black as the Maoris working in the hot Sun Mr Fraser sent for me. I could not understand this as he had since we returned from the Waikato Heads took his trips in another boat. Mr Fraser's duty was to go with each Convoy of boats as officer in Charge. He had made another boat his quarters. I suppose being frightened of me for the shabby affair at the Waikato Heads. However this morning I goes to him. The Officers occupied a small redoubt formerly Commodore Wisemans quarters. I made my appearance before Mr Fraser. He received me very civilly and pointed to a Bottle of Rum for me to help myself. This I refused to do, telling him in a respectful way I did not care for it just then. Then he said I have sent for you to shave me, my face is so tender my Servant is afraid to do it. I looked at him and he showed me the shaving apparatus. I noticed one of his Cheeks was more Sun burnt than the other. I would not use his Razors as I suppose they wanted sharpening so I returned for my own and I commenced operations. The good Cheek I finished very well and Part of the Chin. He wore his Moustache. On my operating on the other Chin, the Razor being a sharp one took hair and Skin the Skin being badly Sun burnt the blobs of Skin came off before I was aware of it. In a few seconds one side of his face was streaming with blood and I could not stop it. In a short time the Blood commenced to drop on his Shirt. He roared out what the Devil are you doing by heavens you have taken half my Cheek away. He jumped up and commenced to abuse me swearing I had done it on Purpose for the Waikato Head affair. I quietened him and at length he asked me again to have a drink. I took one and left him [in] a fine fright with a Patch of hair on the lower part of one Cheek and part of his Chin. He always believed I did it on purpose. To finish with him, in the following August we all joined Headquarters in Tauranga, his Wife with two small children had arrived from Sydney and were waiting for him at Tauranga and by his cruelty and unsoldierly Conduct Colonel Harrington got him cashiered. What became of him I don't know, perhaps Coal heaving again in Sydney.

The Provisions arrived at Mangatawhiri Creek so fast, at one time fully 100 Tons were heaped up under Tarpaulins that many tons rotted. About middle of March we were relieved by another company and we went to Meremere. Now our Work was to go to Rangiriri each day 20 miles and back, the Peach in abundance along the Waikato River particularly so near deserted Native Settlements or Villages, and all splendidly ripe. I sent several Casks to my mates I left behind at Martin Farm. Our Work at Meremere was even harder. Each man was allowed one and half full fresh Rations by General orders (the men of the Water transport Corps). We also had received very large boats of 18 Oars the same kind we went to Waikato Heads for, carrying about 20 Tons each Boat. We had three of these boats and several smaller ones. At this time I rather liked the Work only for many of the men were great Blackguards their Language and thieving Propensities were almost unendurable. Myself and four others kept to ourselves and had a tent of our own, so we were rather comfortable and well respected by many of our superiors in Rank. I could do a Jollification but not amongst many we had to call mates, in fact us few could always command respect from the biggest of the Rowdies.

The 68 Reg^t two companies were stationed at Meremere. On our arrival the Triangles were often in use flogging their men. A few Weeks after the 18th Reg^t replaced the 68th. After being at the Work from Meremere to Rangiriri a few weeks we had been working on Sundays also. At last 26 of us would not work on Sundays. Captain Breaton wanted us to go up the River on Sunday again and we went to our Captain and told him we must have one day in each Week to do our mending and washing. Captain Hill said quite right my men and who wants you to work tomorrow. We told him and he said I don't see any occasion for it and the least Captain Breaton could do was to acquaint me about it. Men I hope you won't be made more slavey by Captain Breaton. This was enough and to work on Sunday we did not go. During the afternoon Captain Breaton comes and has us all put into the Guard Tent as Prisoners for mutiny. In about two hours Major Turner orders us to parade in front of the Guard Tent and on getting into line read us a Lesson on Mutiny in the Field before the Enemy etc and advised us to go to work. We told him we had been worked like Slaves and we must have a half day on Saturday to do our washing and mending, that Provisions were plentiful at the front. That as long as there was any fear of the Troops getting short of Rations at the front with General

Cameron we had worked like horses. He then asked all who would go to work to take two Paces to the front. Not one man did so and we were marched back to the Guard Tent as Prisoners. We sent for our Captain Hill and told him he would be doing us a great Service if he would report the State of Affairs to General Callaway at the Queen Redoubt. He said my men I have done so already and I intend to have your Work made more easy. Next day an Order came from General Callaway for us to be released and to have half Saturday and all Sunday to ourselves, when our Services were not specially required for Urgent Service and Captain Breaton who had been Acting Commodore over all boats was removed so we done a good thing for ourselves backed up by our Captain.

We often seen Soldiers receive a flogging from the Cat o Nine tails. The Volunteer Militia used to boast that being Volunteers they could not flog them but several afterwards were flogged. A case of theft always received a flogging. One Militia man for striking a Corporal got 50 lashes. At the time we were at Meremere loaded drays commenced to go over land to Rangiriri and in March our Company were shifted to be stationed at Rangiriri the scene of the great Fight. Here also were stationed Detachments of the 70th and 18th Regiments. Our duty was to take loaded boats up to opposite the Coal Mines at Taupiri and then to discharge our Cargoes into the fine Steamer *Pioneer* who took the Cargo to Ngaruawahia (name[d] afterwards Newcastle). This Place was before the War the Residence of the Maori King, King Potatau. The present King's Father was buried here a small wooden Building was erected over his Grave. On one occasion three boats Crews took three portable Engines up the Waipa River to Te Rore to saw Timber for the Purpose of building a Barracks for the Troops. On my first Visit to Ngaruawahia (Newcastle) I had heard so much about Green Stones and other precious relics of the Natives being buried with the late Maori King,[14] I was determined to try to get some of these relics so I gave my Mates the Slip and made for the King's Tomb. I had some difficulty to find an opening. At last I discovered a small door and after using some force I slid the small door back. It left a hole about 18 inch square and into this hole I went. As I got partly through the Grave was not about two feet from the Entrance so I put my hands on each Side of the wood

---

[14] The tomb of Potatau (Te Wherowhero).

framed Grave and when I was through I only had to draw my feet up and into the Grave I dropped. About 18 inch of fine Sand was in the Grave and I commenced to grope into this, scraping away all over till the Perspiration ran off me and after working at this for some time I did not find anything and left it in disgust. On reaching the boats I found I had lost my Sheath Knife. I was very much disappointed.

At this time the Kings Palace stood near the River with a large flag staff in front. This Palace, as it was called, the late Residence of the Maori King, was nothing more than a large Raupo Whare or hut with several carved wooden figures, very ugly. At this Visit no Soldiers were stationed here but shortly after it became Headquarters of the Field Force and then you dare not go within 50 yards of the King's Grave and when I called here a few Weeks after the King's Palace was made the depository of all the Wheelbarrows Shovels Picks etc belonging to the Pioneers of the troops, and a Sentry on the Maori King's Grave. On removing the flag staff a large Green Stone was found at the butt.

In April 1864 a Township was surveyed here and sold. Some quarter acre lots realised £325. This day June 1885 these lots are not worth half the money in fact the land about Ngaruawahia is inferior, nearly all Pumice Stone. About 10 years since the Railway was made from Auckland to this Place. The Township stands at the Junction of two Rivers, the Waikato and Waipa, and I certainly expected it would have been a large Township before this, but this Place has not gone ahead, like Townships 20 to 30 miles farther into the interior.

At last we started with our Engines up the Waipa River and after two days hard pulling we arrived at our destination Te Rore. One of the Engines we left at a Station half-way between Ngaruawahia and Te Rore, Whatawhata. We put the Engines ashore and walked to the Camp. The 12th Regiment was stationed here and two Sets of triangles were erected for a Punishment Parade, some poor devil to get the Cat. The quarter Master of the 12th Regt refused to issue to us the usual Ration and half for each man. We were nearly rebelling. We got it after this trip with the Engines took us about 12 days and all that time we often got wild Pigs and vegetable Marrows and other Vegetables from deserted Maori Villages, and out of a Crew of 16 13 of us had a severe attack of Diarrhoea. Some of us were very bad.

The day after arrival at Te Rore the great fight of Orakau where the Chief Rewi[15] and about 300 Natives stood the attack of about 2000 Troops for 10 days and five days without Water. The Troops had to sap the Hill the Maori Pah was on. Here the Natives stood the attack of this superior force with the usual Rifles, big Guns Mortars and hand Grenades and after six days fighting the Maoris were asked to surrender and they shouted out Ake, Ake, Ake, 'Never Never Never.' At last the Sap got so close to the Pah hand Grenades were thrown over the Parapet, making it [so] warm for the Natives that they got out down a steep cliff and broke through the lines of the 40th Regt but many of them lost their lives by the Cavalry cutting them down. Old Rewi the Chief got clear. I met him in Tauranga some years after, he was then suffering from asthma and looked a small puny man to have been such a great Warrior. This same Chief Rewi at present has as much Power over the Natives as the so called Maori King.

This fight at Orakau was the last of the Maori War of 1863 & 4[16] and about one month after we were not required on the River to carry provisions to the troops. Roads had been made and small steamers built and the boat Corps were not required. On our return to Whatawhata Colonel Wyat of the 65th Regt was suffering from Gout and he was on his way to Auckland and on leaving Whata-whata he was put on board our boat. He lay at my feet as I was the Stroke Oar. On arrival at Ngaruawahia myself and another man went on Shore to have a look at the Township allotments of Land which had been recently surveyed for Sale. We were told 30 minutes to stop. After seeing the lots on our return the boat had left. Here was a fix. If my mate had consented as I proposed for us to go over the Ranges to the Town of Raglan on the West Coast, but it was not to be and we travelled 15 Miles to Ruapekapeka Redoubt at the Taupiri Coal Mines. Here I went straight to the Bakehouse and got a loaf of Bread and bought Sardines and had Dinner.

Fortunately a Canoe was going down the River to a native Village

[15] Rewi Maniapoto.
[16] It was the end of the Waikato war, but General Cameron now led an expedition to Tauranga, where there were two big battles at Gate Pa, 29 April 1864 and Te Ranga, 21 June 1864. In the former action, a third of the British force were casualties: ten officers and twenty-one other ranks were killed. At Te Ranga about 120 Maoris died – a bad defeat.

3 miles from Rangiriri, here some hundreds of British troops were stationed. When the Canoe got to the native Settlement we went on Shore, and I had the Pleasure of again seeing Princess Sofia,[17] a Daughter of the late Maori King and Sister to the Present King. Her knee was all but well since I had seen her at Rev Barton Station up the Waipa River. After a short Stay we proceeded on to Rangiriri, this is the Place where the Natives repulsed the British Troops three times when trying an assault on their stronghold. Here were stationed several Companies of the 70th & 18th Regts besides a company of transport Corps (Colonials) and a company of the Royal Artillery. Here again we wanted some tea and I went straight to the Baker, but got disappointed as there were no Bread on hand. I applied to Captain Trench of the 70th Regt the senior officer for a ration order on the Commissariat Stores. After telling him how we got left behind at Ngaruawahia he answered the sooner we made tracks for our headquarters 4 miles farther on at Meremere the better it would be for us. However for all that we got Plenty to eat and returned to Meremere with a Convoy of returned empty Provision Drays. I met this same Captain Trench at Tauranga the following year and I reminded him of his treatment to me at Rangiriri. Many of these British officers holding a little Power with the Rank of Lieut or Captain were ten times worse to deal with than a General or a Commodore or Admiral.

On arriving at Meremere we reported ourselves to Captain Hill and got well laughed at for being left behind and had such a long trip for our negligence. Next day I missed the iron Plough (new) I had looted also the boat Anchor. Some one had considered they had more right to them than I had, worth about £15 was gone. No use grumbling over such small things. A few days after I was off again up the Waikato River and Waipa river to Whatawhata. On arrival one of our men were a Prisoner for striking a Corporal. Next day he was tried by a garrison Court Martial and sentenced to 50 lashes with the Cat and one month's imprisonment. A detachment of the 18th Regt were stationed here and their Drummer was the flagellator. We all paraded to see the Punishment inflicted. The man was ordered to strip, the triangles were ready close by and the Culprit was in a short time pinioned to them. He was a fine robust

[17] The Maori King was Tawhiao and his sister (or perhaps cousin) was Te Paea.

well made man and we considered him one of our best men, by name Barnett. We all considered the sentence too severe. As the Corporal being related to the Captain commanding our Company we also considered that the British officers should not sit on trial of Militia men. This Corporal we knew very often had been very insulting to some of the men. In a few minutes the flogging commenced. I certainly expected to see some Blood fly about to see the attitude of the flagellator and the way he handled the Cat. On the word one down went the Cat on his fine broad back, not a quiver. Two, and so on to the end and not the sign of a drop of Blood. About the 30th stroke the Commanding officer called out Drummer do your duty, but the Drummer took no notice but went on just the same. When all was over the man's back was very little marked considering he had received 50 lashes, and all expressed their satisfaction at so light a Punishment as it was considered a trivial Crime. I was told Barnett only pushed the Corporal. When a man is flogged two Drummers are generally told off and each administers 25 lashes each. After the Punishment the two Drummers were made lions of by Militia men. The Corporal got his deserts after and he had to be transferred to another Company.

Shortly after this I went on a Pig hunting expedition and only got a few young ones. During this summer of 1864 we certainly had some very hard work. At the same time we had some very pleasant times. Now and again on a foraging expedition we ran some risks as when ransacking a native Village. Often we came across men and Women who could have popped us off. One day a Lieut Mitchell was shot dead when passing up the river. On one occasion several of us had left the Boats and gone about two miles inland and was ransacking a native Village when the Alarm was given and some Natives were in front and showed fight, but on us showing a bold front they ran away and we returned to the boats. This was the Place where the Militia Settlement of Haripepe near Alexander on the Waipa River is at present.

My Boots had cried enough and parted company with one foot and at Whatawhata not a Pair to be got. I could not knock about bare footed and I persuaded a Maori to sell me his boots for 5/-. These would only last about a Week. By that time I might be able to get a Pair of military boots or what was called Ammunition Boots about the best Boots for travelling. Through eating Wild Pork, Vegetable Marrows and other food, several of us was attacked again with Dysentery but by this time I had got some of the Native recipes for various Complaints and by taking a concoction of Koromiko this shrub grows plentifully all over this Part of New Zealand and is a sure cure for dysentery. The roots of the supple Jack, a cane like wiry stick that is very common in the Bush is capital for regulating the system and blood cleanser.

On one occasion I had a smart Engagement with the Maoris, about 50 of us were sent to reconnoitre a Native Strong hold, about $2\frac{1}{2}$ miles from the River. We approached the Pah and the Natives let fly several shots. We had to cross a Ravine and scale a steep bank. When near the top of the bank an awkward German or Dane was near me. I had just loaded my Gun again when by some means the awkward fellow handled his firelock that it struck me with considerable force on my forehead. However he did it I know not. For a few seconds I was stunned and then I found the Blood running down my face in streams, being very warm with running the blood was hot and ran the more freely. My mates thought I had been shot and came to my assistance. The Dane swore it was not him. I believe it was not purposely but accidentally. However I had a wound 3 in[ches] long on my forehead. If it was a shot as I was facing the enemy I should have thought it would have gone through my head. However in a few minutes with my handkerchief tied round my head I was onwards again and then we ascertained the Enemy had flown and we retired to our Boats after looting several articles. One man got a set of Draft Harness and another Plough Harness. I had enough to carry my head all right. This wound troubled me for week[s] after and a large Scar was left to disfigure my frontispiece. Shortly after this we got orders to return to the lower Waikato as our Services were not longer required. The War was virtually over. The Natives were satisfied for a time. At any time it never took us above one hour to ship all our wordly goods from a Station and the following day we had bid the upper Waikato goodbye for good and our Company stopped at Wangamarino about half way between Mangatawhiri Creek and Meremere on the lower Waikato River. Wangamarino Redoubt stands on an eminence about 300 feet above the Waikato and Wangamarino Rivers, a fine commanding Position. Here was erected the Battery for the 40 Pounder Guns that came from Sydney for the Purpose of firing [on] the Native Stronghold of Meremere and these Guns took a prominent Part in dislodging the Natives from Meremere on the 1st November 1863—20 days before the great Battle of Rangiriri.

On our arrival at Wangamarino we found N° 3 or Captain Stacks Company of the 1st Waikato Regiment, Colour Sergt Jackson acting Sergt Major. In a few days I was all at Home. I was exempt from all ordinary Drill Parades as it was considered I knew enough Drill and several other little indulgences. All our rations came by the Waikato River and a nice little Job it was to get the horse feed and our own Rations up the Cliff. Twice each week rations arrived and fatigue Parties told off to carry these Rations up the Hill. These Parties each second man carried an empty sack, so as to divide the sack flour or sack of Oats. The only occasion I was on this fatigue duty I scouted the idea of dividing a 200 lb sack of flour and shouldered it myself to take it up about 100 steep steps up the Cliff and some of these steps were farther apart than others which made it more difficult to ascend with a heavy weight on one['s] back. However I undertook the task and about the Centre of these steps two was I found farther apart than wanted and caused great exertions on my Part to ascend. I managed to carry my sack of flour up to the Top and down I went Sack and all as I had not strength enough left or I was afraid to jerk it off my back. I considered this was the easiest way to get quit of my burden. When I got up about 20 men were there belonging to the Contractor building a Bridge across the Wangamarino River and they hurrahed and clapped their hands at what they considered my wonderful achievement. A Gentleman came up to me and said you are a wonderful strong man but advised me never to try the like again as I might hurt my back. I told him I thanked him for his advice and if I had known the steps were so irregular and wide apart I should not have attempted to do it.

That day I found my old Melbourne friend Bailey that joined the Militia with me he being a Surveyor for the last 7 months he had been at his Profession at 22/6 per day. This is the man that was reduced from Pay Sergt at Drury in Decr 1863 who started to Auckland with me. I had not seen him since 9 months ago. Here he was Clerk of Works for the Government over the erection of the Bridge. He had a Tent to himself and we passed several jolly hours in it talking over our adventures since last December. He had plenty of fine pale Brandy and we considerably reduced the Stock before we parted. The following day a Hogd of Rum had to be got up the Cliff and I stood watching the men get this up the Cliff. Plenty of ropes and men and Rum was soon on top. To get to the Redoubt we had to go round a small Gulley. The Road was on the edge of this Gulley and when the Hog^d of Rum was going along this road a quarter of the men could get it along. By some means or carelessness the Cask took a wrong turn and down the Gulley it went dragging the ropes out of the men's hands and on reaching the bottom it busted into nearly separate staves and all the Rum in a few seconds running like a small Rivulet. Before it actually got to the bottom several men were running helter skelter down the Gulley some distance below the Barrel and on to their bellies and meeting the Rum with their mouths. Others saw what these men intended and down goes a lot more men on the same errand and there they lay as thick as herrings in a barrel sucking the rum into their mouths. Some got more than they could conveniently carry. How they got up I don't know as I left.

Shortly after this word came that several fat Bullocks were up the River behind Meremere and any Bullock so seen straying about was considered good loot for the troops and 5 of us went up the River in an old Canoe with firelocks and Ammunition. In a short time we brought one of the huge animals down the first shot. 3 men jumped out and soon had his hide off and with the entrails buried in the River after cutting it into quarters we shipped it and took it down about half mile from the Redoubt, took it on Shore and planted it in a small Plantation until night and so as to let the meat set, it would be better for carrying. That night 4 men took the Canoe and brought down the Beef. Myself and others were waiting in readiness to carry it up to the Redoubt this time a different way, very few steps but a steep round about road. Just under the big Gun Battery I took an hind quarter and before I got to the Redoubt I had a very hard tussle. When I appeared at the entrance to the Hut I could not get in. In a few seconds plenty of hands took it from me and right glad I was to get shut of my burden. Amongst us we had Butchers Bakers Builders Publicans Tailors Shoemakers Confectioners and all known trades Baronets Sons, Lawyers, Parsons from all quarters of the Colonies. The Beef was soon cut up and hung up in Joints. Early next morning we sent a nice Plate of Steaks into the officers Hut, no questions asked.

That day the route came for us to prepare to go to headquarters at Tauranga, we must do something with the Beef. I should say the

Beast was fully 1000 lbs dressed, so after having a talk over matters
we concluded to send me to sell Part of the Beef to yon Bridge
Contractor and I went there and another man went to some men
making a Road about 1½ miles [away]. By this and giving some
away and cooking some for the Road we got shut of the lot and laid
in a good stock of Rations Tobacco etc for the Road. Next morning
we bid farewell to Wangamarino and Mr Bailey and got to Queen
Redoubt that night, a beautiful night but very frosty, 26 Augt 1864
two days after in Auckland. The last day my boots blistered my
feet. On the Road I was in the Advanced Guard with the Acting
Serg^t Major Jackson. Every few miles he would call the Baggage
Cart. This Cart carried a small Keg of Rum and every few miles he
gave us a refresher. Several years after this same Jackson became a
storekeeper and made a fortune and lost it again by Quartz Reefing.
At present Octr 1885 he is storekeeping again and buys largely in
Gum and is doing very well.

On reaching Auckland we had a day to ourselves and on the 31st
Augt 1864 we arrived in the fine Harbour of Tauranga, about 3
miles from Mount Maunganui the entrance on right hand on west
Side is the Town of Tauranga. Here Vessels drawing 14 feet can lay
alongside of the two Wharves, about 2 chains from Shore. The first
object of interest is the old Cemetery, here lies some hundreds of
[remains] formerly belong[ing] to Native[s] & Europeans. On the
north west is the last resting Place of those poor fellows who lost
their lives fighting for their Queen and Country at the Battles of
Gate Pah and Te Ranga 1864. A little further south is the Landing
Places. At the time I first landed the only Building[s] of Note were
the College and on either end a Gabled Residence of Church of
England Missionaries. The College was turned into an Hospital
and the Residences were occupied by Colonel Green of the 68 Reg^t
and Colonel Harrington of the first Waikato Reg^t. Adjacent to the
Hospital were several large Indian Tents occupied by wounded
Natives and British Soldiers and Sailors the result of the two recent
Engagements. On north end of Township near and opposite the
entrance was the Residence of Archdeacon Alfred Nisbet Brown.
This Gentleman had been a Resident in Tauranga for 30 years
previous to the War of 1863. There is no denying the fact these
missionaries had suffered great hardships in the early days of their
Labours in New Zealand. Arch. Brown had a fine Residence and a
splendid orchard. At this time I estimate the Strength of all Troops

in Tauranga at 2000. A few storekeepers done a roaring trade making their fortunes fast. Detachments of 100 men each were stationed at Judea, across an inlet of the Harbour on west Side of Town, the Gate Pah, 100 Men 50 Soldiers 50 Militia 3 Miles out on Main Road named after General Cameron, at Maketu, 20 miles South East 200 men, 100 Soldiers 100 Militia. My first impression of Tauranga was far superior of the Waikato Country and I remarked 5 acres of Land in Tauranga before 50 acres in Waikato.

Next day after the Bustle of landing and settling in our new quarters I applied to quarter Master Tunks for my Box I left in his charge in Otahuhu Septr 1863. We were directed to a large heap with Tarpaulin as cover. About 20 men were anxious to get their Boxes and after a long search not one of us got our Boxes. The answer we got was those are the only Boxes we have. My Box contained some valuable documents clothing Boots etc but I did not get them nor never shall. This was a great disappointment to me.

A regular mixture of Troops, Royal Artillery, Sappers & Miners Commissariat Corps, British Soldiers and Militia, 3 canteens, in Camp. Here we met our new Colonel who had been appointed in place of Colonel George Dean Pitt. Colonel Harrington looked every inch a Soldier and a fine Drill, and the first few months Drill twice each day was the order and to see some of the officers at Battalion was something to look at considering they had been in the field for 12 months. Some of them did not know right flank from left and could not do their facings. The Colonel had the Patience of Job. In a few months he had them fairly drilled. I must say the 1st Waikatos were a fine body of men. Our right hand man was 6 feet 6 inch and the whole front Rank averaged 5 feet 10 inch.

In October Horse Racing were got up. This brought the Military to the front, money appeared no object with some of the officers. The Races were held about 1½ miles out of camp half way to Gate Pah, and gave us a grand holiday and the Races were a grand Success, the splendid Band of the 68th Light Infantry playing nearly all afternoon. Several officer Jockeys got a Tumble in the hurdle races. At this time Tauranga was a good business place. For myself I could have got a man in my place for £5 but I never thought of this. If I had done this and went into business I could have done well. I was a maker of all kinds of Cordials and could brew good ale. These goods came from Auckland and sold at 150 per cent above cost. It became known amongst the officers that I was a rough Carpenter and in September 1864 an officer came to me and asked me if I could make a Clothes Press. I said I could if I had the tools. He said he could get Tools and I went to work. In 3 days I had the Job finished and then had another to make for Mrs Major St John. One Job after another kept me going and I was doing well, erecting wooden Buildings, making rough Furniture. I was making 4 to 5 Pounds per week besides my Pay. I worked very hard. In Novr I built for myself a small House of Wood and Sod Chimney the first house in Camp. I recollect the Colonel, Quarter Master & his Sergt coming to look at my House and the Colonel remarked he must have an Orderly Room like it. About middle of Novr I had a contract to cut out a frame of a Building 25 × 15 feet to go to Maketu. I finished this in one and quarter days with a Labourer to assist. I received £2.10s. [and] out of this I paid my man 15/- leaving me 35/- for a day and quarter's work. In a few days a Pass was put into my hand signed by the Colonel to go to Maketu to build this frame I cut out. Mr Foley got this Pass, unbeknown to myself, and he would have me to erect the Building.

I expected and wanted to go to Auckland having money [and I] wanted to see a little of the great City. I was disappointed and went to Maketu. I took Passage in the Schooner *Herd* and arrived at Maketu next day. I found the Place under Martial Law, everything military 200 Troops in Colville Redoubt. Myself and Mate had use of a native Whare or native house. The Chief placed cups saucers knives forks Plates etc at our Service and for 5 weeks we had a loose leg from military restraint. We only visited the Redoubt when we wanted Rations. By Decr 21 my contract was finished and I returned to Tauranga on foot. On my arrival I found one of the Militia had took possession of my House. This I objected to and made him clear out. Next day I set to Work and brewed 15 Gallons of Ale for Christmas & New Year. Having half a Barrel and 2 Buckets and a fire Place in my Residence I could do many things that could not be done in a tent. I bought Malt at 16/- Bushel hops 4/- lb Sugar 8 Pence lb and in a few days on Boxing Day 1864 I had about 14 Gallons of the best ale in Camp which did not require a very good article to be best in Camp as at this time no draft ale to be got. It soon became known I had the ale and I bottled some and sold it at 1/6 Per Bottle and by New Year's day 1865 I was sold out. It got abroad about me using Malt and for months I made hop beer using Bran & Maize instead of Malt and made a good wholesome beer. In a few days I had plenty of Work and done very well.

I often visited the Scene of the great fight of Gate Pah and 3 miles further Te Ranga, the 140 odd Natives killed here were buried in the Rifle Pits they had made to fight the British Troops. The Trenches crossed the only road from Gulley to Gulley about 80 yards and on the level ground east Side of Road the dead Bodies were buried and you could in 1864 smell the Stench half a mile away and till today March 1886 the spot is noted by the fern growing higher on the line of the trenches than any other Place.

On April 1st 1865 [there was] a rumour in Camp that the Natives were assembling in numbers and intending having another fight at Te Ranga. 150 of the 68 Regt 150 of 1st Waikato Regt with two 12 pound field Pieces paraded. Myself was right hand man of the Militia with Captain Stack on my flank and as we marched along we were in great Spirits. When we came near Te Ranga two mounted men went ahead to reconnoitre and returned stating no natives to be seen but many had been there and evidently got cowed and retired. We piled Arms and rested for some time, and about 3 p.m. we march[ed] back halting at Gate Pah for Refreshments. The day was unusually hot and dusty and we appeared like so many Sweeps, the dust being dark and perspiring freely we certainly looked a Picture. However we were disappointed at not having a brush. I never was anxious to fight in the field, but when you commence then all else out of mind. I was glad when [we] arrived in Camp. We did nothing only being tired.

On the 7th April 1865, the detachment stationed at Gate Pah were changed and my Company was the one told off to relieve that Post and we were stationed here. I did not like this as I was doing very well at my trade as a Carpenter and had an unfinished Contract on hand. However the Colonel kindly allowed me the Privilege of going to Te Papa name of Town of Tauranga each day and return at Night until my Contract was finished, about 3 Weeks. This Contract was building a Store on the beach road Tauranga now called the Strand, and I had to purchase horse Saddle and Bridle. I lived outside the Pah and built a small house for myself and took in as mate the mounted orderly who was stationed here to take and bring dispatches to and from head quarters. We drew our rations together and lived very comfortable.

I made some bricks for the fire Place and sun dried them which answered very well. About 6 months before I shifted to Gate Pah a Victorian mate of mine got Permission to make Bricks about one mile from Gate Pah and he had a kiln of Bricks burning when the Natives were becoming dangerous and when the Bricks were about half burnt Colonel Green of the 68 Reg^t ordered all hands into the Redoubt and the Kiln of Bricks was left to spoil. Captain Tunks our Quarter Master paid this man 20/- per 1000 for the bricks he finding all firewood, a very good thing for Ned Lea and his mates. However the first and only Kiln was left and spoilt. Some of the bricks turned out fairly good. We required some bricks for to line the fire Place in the Serg^t Mess and Serg^t Burns a big strong Irishman was continually boasting about his strength and I challenged him, we to take a Wheelbarrow to this brick yard and load it with as many as we could and we would take turn about to wheel them to camp, a very rough hilly road. To get these bricks we had to carry them up a hill [and] load the barrow. We put 72 Bricks on and off we started and it was a tremendous load. We had accomplished about two thirds of the distance when Mr Burns had enough and I had to wheel them to camp. It is a light Brick that don't weigh 5½ lbs so you may calculate the load we had. This Ned Lea the Brickmaker was my mate shortly after and a canteen was outside of the Pah and Mr Lea was engaged by the Canteen Manager to attend to the Beer Counter. The Canteen was opened one hour before Breakfast & Dinner and 6 to 8.30 p.m. One night I went in for a Pint of Ale, cost 6 Pence I put down one shilling and Mr Ned Lea gave me the ale and 2/6. After the Canteen was shut I told him what he had done and he answered and very good Change too. I did not approve of such swindling and never did so again.

During May I was pig hunting and came across 110 lb Shell unexploded half buried in a Swamp about half mile from the Pah on south Side. The Battery where these Shells were fired from were about 1000 yards north of the Pah, it being a Concussion Shell falling on soft mud did not explode. Here was a chance to get a Stock of Powder for pig hunting and I pulled off coat and hat, went into the Swamp and after a lot of trouble I extracted the Shell and got it on dry Land. The next thing was to get it to camp. To do this I had a steep hill to get up and a Shell 110 lb. If I should let it slip from me as I tried to put it on my shoulder, it may explode and blow me piecemeal into Kingdom Come. I looked at the Gentleman, rolled him over several times and at last I said if he does slip I

11 The Mayor of Tauranga, 1888–89.

12 'Bradgate Villa', Tauranga, James Bodell's house.

13 James Bodell and his family at Bradgate Park, 1883.

14 James Bodell, his mother and sisters during his 1890 visit to England.

(17)

gave me of one sold out & one tenth of their
value, and by the end of the Second week I had
nothing left saleable but my Bible and Prayer Book
The big Grenidier, several times expressed himself
he would buy them, but I did not wish to part with
them, however the Pangs of hunger and the want of tobacco
carried the day and the Grenidier got my Bible and
Prayer Book, for a very small Sum I believe one
shilling or four Pence, during the third week I began
to get better, and could stand a little on my eighth forth
and on the 22nd day I pleaded so hard to the Doctor
he let me out but for the first few days I had to attend
the Hospital each morning at 9.30. oclock, and out
I went and very glad I was, before I crossed the large

15 Detail from a typical manuscript page of the reminiscences.

try and let him fall on the flat end. These shells are about 8 inch in diameter and 24 inch long and a pretty good lift to shoulder one. So there was a possibility of letting it slip. However the thought of such a trophy was too much for me and I put on my coat and after a tussle I had him on my shoulders. I found it a hard task to get up the hill, the roundness of the shell made it more difficult. When on the road I was all right and soon had his Shellship in Camp. For a while I was advised to bury it. One of the Royal Artillery came forward with a wrench and took the Cap or nut out and then the shell was harmless. I found the Powder nearly as hard as wood and difficult to get out. I got 2 to 3 lb of Powder out and then buried the Shell near the ditch of the Pah.

I was a particular friend with the Royal Artillery and they asked me into their hut and as several of us were enjoying ourselves with refreshments the Bombardier Scotch Jock put the nut from the Shell into the fire. We did not notice this being done and as we sat talking all of a sudden this nut exploded with a loud report sent all the fire out of the fire Place, smothered us all in Ashes hot & cold, and caused a Panic in Camp. It sounded to me like a large Piece of ordnance going off. No one was hurt and when it became known what caused the explosion a general Laugh took place and Bombardier Scotch Jock acknowledged he was the Culprit who had caused the explosion.

Some months after when I was up the Waikato the second time an old friend of mine named Harry Mathews found one of these shells unexploded and on that occasion he used a Hammer and Screw driver to knock the nut out, he having the shell between his legs and this monster of destruction exploded and blew poor Mathews into bits tearing the upper Part of his body from the knees upwards into fragments. He was one of the Melbourne Volunteers. The following year some Volunteer Artillery came from the Thames to do duty here. They got hold of one of these shells and not understanding them commence[d] to hammer them, exploded and killed the man. On another occasion a Settler near headquarters got one of these shells and had as he thought took all the Powder out, he having the shell in a Wheel barrow and he put a fire stick into the shell and ran away. He did not get far before the Shell exploded sent the barrow into small Pieces and the man did not stop for half a mile. The explosion was so loud that the Buglers in headquarters and detachment at Judea sounded the Alarm, and all troops under Arms. This man was not connected with the troops but was Manager for Mr Samuel Clark's Mission Farm and supplied fresh milk in Camp at one shilling per quart.

I passed away the time very well at the Gate Pah. Several times I made about 20 Gallons of Ale and gave my friends a small spree. The Natives were not allowed near the Pah but when they brought anything for sale would be allowed to come to a small hillock about quarter of a mile from the Pah and wait there until some of us would go to them to barter. They had Potatoes, Sweet Potatoes principally, some times fish. On the 18 July 1865 word came to the Pah that 300 Rank & file were ordered to the Waikato and our company was amongst them. Preparations made for a move and 8 a.m. we paraded and marched into Tauranga the Headquarters. We had made ourselves very comfortable at Gate Pah and I did not care for leaving.

One little incident I must relate. During the month of June 1865 the first European child was born and today March 1886 he is a fine young man out of his apprenticeship as a Painter and doing well. The other incident was many sheep was grazing within half a mile of the Pah belonging to the Gov^t Meat Contractor and I came to the conclusion that the contractor could well afford to lose one so I got a Mate and off we started, having a couple of good Knives and made for the Sheep. We selected several to separate from the Mob and one in particular to a race by himself and me after him. We were going at a fast Pace and I had hold of the wool on his rump and being in a thick Scrub I did not notice the direction we were taking. All at once down we went together rolling down a steep declivity and only for a bush we should have rolled into a deep river. I stuck to the bush and after great exertions I got on to the level land. What became of the sheep I know not but I seen my mate fast hold of another and assisted to kill & dress it. When dressed and the Skin and offal buried I took a good look at the Carcase and I upbraided my mate for not selecting a better one. The one we killed would not weight much above 40 lbs. However we cut it up and put the Carcase into a sack bag and off we went homewards. We had to cross a Swamp then the main Road into another swamp and along this swamp till opposite the camp. Here we planted our Mutton till dusk and then took it to our Hut and gave our friends the Royal Artillery and others a Joint each. Next day Mutton was plentiful in camp.

On July 19th 1865 300 of us embarked on Board the SS *Egmont*, several hogsheads of Ale was put on board also and these were presents from the Canteens for the troops on their Passage to Auckland. When at Sea these Barrels we opened and the Liquor was quite thick. The Head of each Cask was taken out and the Beer ladled out. To get a drink you had to strain the Beer through your teeth. Next day arrived in Auckland. Here we stopped till next day and then on to Otahuhu. We stopped here 4 days and the day we arrived at Otahuhu I tramped back to Auckland determined to have a couple of days in Auckland. Next day I suppose 150 men out of the 300 were in Auckland. On the 3rd day I with many others returned to Otahuhu and a good Job we did it was in Garrison orders any man absent that day after 3 p.m. was to be put into the Guard Room. Many of us were on Parade at 3 o'clock and so escaped Punishment.

Next day off to Mercer on the Waikato. Here were two Steamers waiting for us and it was very dark as we embarked. One poor fellow not seeing the Gangway of the Steamer walked straight into the River with all his accoutrements and 60 Rounds of Ball Cartridge. Much Rain had fallen and swollen the River which was running fully 5 miles per hour. I was near to the man as he went over but I never heard him cry out and he was drowned. About a week after his body was found some 7 miles farther down the River. The Arrangements were very bad for a dark night, it was a miracle more was not drowned. My experience has been look after yourself first and others after but many men at times act like small children being so very careless.

We had two miserable days trip up the Waikato River the steamers made such slow Progress. We arrived at Hamilton after dark, late at night remained on Board all night. Our company was to have remained here but as our Captain remained behind (courting I believe) he being the Senior Captain was commander but another Captain having Command he ordered us to go on to Cambridge and his Company stopped at Hamilton. We knew this was wrong as the Post near Cambridge 4 miles away on top of the Mount Maungatautari Southern end [was] the worst station in the whole of the Waikato called the Crows Nest. On arrival at Cambridge we complained to our Lieut and he telegraphed to our Captain at Auckland and we waited his return, when we returned to Hamilton and the other company went to the Crows Nest. We found Hamilton a fine station, good barrack accommodation much better than the Crows nest. Here we remained for 14 months. I was carpentering, making ginger beer for the Hotels and as usual making money and spending it as fast. The reason we came to the Waikato was to relieve the 2nd 3rd & 4th Waikato Regiments from military duty so as they could go on their Farms. Many of them did not like this as they would sooner be on Pay. For myself I would have given £20 to remain at Tauranga. However we passed our time away very pleasantly. During our stay here many single Women from Lancashire arrived in Auckland and married dozens of Militia men particularly the 4th Regt at Hamilton. Each morning as we went for the Rations you would meet Dozens of these Women.[18] I was sent down to Ngaruawahia to repair the general hospital and waited about 7 days when word came not to repair it, and I had to return.

In September 1866 we got orders to return to Tauranga and arrived there 14th October and found the 12th Regt. The 68th had returned to Auckland and left for England the War being over. On my going to my House that I had built I found it occupied but soon had possession also the Hut I built at Gate Pah had been sold and removed. A few days after returning the Natives were inclined to be troublesome about 12 miles away. An expedition was sent out and returned reporting no Natives to be seen.

At this time my three years was expired and I went to the orderly Room to claim my discharge, and the Colonel at first refused, but I stuck to him, and at last he told me to give my Arms and accoutrements in and bring a ticket. I had done so. In one hour I had my ticket and in another ten minutes I had my Discharge and I was again a Civilian. A fortnight after the Natives again mustered in force and for the next six months another little War was carried on and several Engagements took place within 14 miles of Tauranga.[19] In about a month we had 800 men composed of the 12 Regt Militia

---

[18] These women undoubtedly came to New Zealand under a scheme organized by Maria Rye to relieve unemployment and social distress in Lancashire during the cotton famine during the 1860s.

[19] The 1st Waikato Regiment took part in this campaign against parties of Piri-Rakau and Ngaiterangi, many of them *Hauhau*. See J. Cowan, *The New Zealand Wars*, II, Wellington, 1922, Chapter XVI. Bodell wrote a separate and repetitive account of his first years in Tauranga which has

and native allies, the tribe known as the 'Arawas' professed to be Queen Natives, and fight for her Majesty. On several occasions sharp engagements took place and several militia men were killed. All native Villages that we came across were burnt and their Crops destroyed. The Natives never made a Stand but took to the Bush and we never seen above 20 at a time. Every European in the District was compelled to take Arms and all men under 40 years of age went to the front. The 3rd class Militia men married over 40 years protected the Town. At this time I was 36 although I did not belong to the force, still I had to carry Arms and do duty. All Europeans had to do military duty. One Native Settlement we looted a fine lot of Poultry and the best Potatoes I had seen in New Zealand. We destroyed several Villages, could not tell how many of the Enemy we killed, they being in detached Parties, being in dense Bush. Their Presence were made known by the Ping of their

been deleted from the end of his manuscript. However, his second account of this final action in Tauranga deserves to be quoted:

'The Natives commenced hostilities again every morning all hands under Arms. Sentries posted all round the Town, detachments at Gate Pah, Judea and at Maketu. We had to put women and children in the Monmouth Redoubt. A building about 60 feet long was partitioned off, the Guardroom in the end and women and children occupied the remainder. In 1867 about 500 Troops went on an expedition to all the native Settlements and burnt all Crops, Poultry and all Buildings in each settlement. Hundreds of tons of splendid Potatoes Cattle and horses were all destroyed and in retaliation the Natives shot down several Militia and Soldiers. The miserablest night I ever passed was on one of these expeditions. It was a wet windy Night and I was with others in an old Whare or house and the Wind came through it like a sieve. I was glad when morning came. It is all nonsense to send soldiers on these expeditions because a body of men cannot keep together. I knew from my Waikato experience the best way was for 3 or 4 good men to keep together on these occasions and then take care of yourselves. One poor fellow was shot close alongside the eye and nose. The bullet only left a small mark about the size of a Threepenny bit. The man felt no pain he was dead instantly. Another was shot just as he was looking over a dead log in the centre of the forehead. Another was shot in the breast, and many wounded. Officers could do very little in commanding. They soon lose their men. In 1867 just after this expedition all the British

Bullets and a loud report. One of our men were killed who had volunteered, a Storekeeper, he left a Wife and 6 children. I was told by a Native Chief some years after the enemy did not muster above 50 to 60 and they harassed fully 800 men for months. About July 1867 this little war ended and Peace reigned supreme.

I should have mentioned about Jan[uar]y 1867 the Native allies became aware that a European named Peter Grant was living with the Rebels, with a young Chieftainess and was the Father of one child. The Commander gave orders to the Native allies to take this man Prisoner and after a few weeks he was taken and brought into Tauranga a Prisoner. This man Peter Grant came from Melbourne with myself and belonged to the same company, and on the occasion of 300 of us leaving Tauranga in July 1865 for the Waikato as already related, he belonged to the Company that went to the Crows Nest Redoubt on the south end of the Mount Maungatautari. Here the Captain in command and some of the non commissioned officers made it rather warm for Peter and he ran away into native territory. At this time the Maoris were very proud to have a European in their Tribe, and Peter became a great favourite amongst them and took the Chief's Daughter to Wife, and as related was taken Prisoner. I went to see him in Prison and he told me all about his desertion, the tyranny of his superiors and his life since then. That same body is an able bodied man now living in the country of Tauranga. Peter was tried by a General Court Martial and received 50 lashes with the Cat, and two months imprisonment. At present March 1886 he is a boniface of an Hotel in Tauranga but still inclined to be unsettled. The Maori Wife still hangs about Tauranga although Peter has been married to a European Woman for 17 years and has 6 of a Family.

Soldiers left New Zealand, and the Settlers were left to take care of themselves. At the time I thought this was very foolish for the Government to do but I ascertained the British Troops were very costly. Then the Men of War used to come into the harbour. These cowed the Natives.'

VI

A Tauranga Settler,
1866–83

Tauranga was the merest outline of a settlement when James Bodell first went there in 1864. There were a few mission buildings and houses, a blockhouse, a landing place and, no doubt, plenty of tents. The missionaries had been there since 1835. One missionary, A. N. Brown, actually served there for over fifty years, starting in 1838.

Tauranga had a distinct character because it was a military settlement. The army had invaded Tauranga in 1864 because some of the local tribes had been assisting the Maori Kingites in the Waikato. Moreover Maoris from further south were moving to the Waikato front through Tauranga. After the two battles at Gate Pa and Te Ranga, the government confiscated about 214,000 acres of Maori land. Much of this was eventually returned to the Maoris, but some 50,000 was retained by the government. These confiscations were later held to be wrongful and a dispute goes on to the present day over the payment of proper compensation.

The government also purchased from the local Maoris—at a very low price—huge areas for settlement. The confiscated land and the purchased land was partly subdivided to give land to the militia. A private was to receive fifty acres of farm land and a quarter-acre town section. Higher ranks received bigger areas. Once the soldiers were discharged they also received free rations for a year.

As a military settlement Tauranga was a failure. Soldiers did not easily turn into farmers. Maori hostility, and a complete lack of roads, made access to the farms difficult or impossible. Most of them sold their land if they could and left. Only a few hundred acres round the settlement was actually occupied. Bodell eventually sold his fifty acres, but he stayed on in Tauranga, earning a living in a variety of ways, revealing that adaptability, enterprise and toughness which made him an excellent settler. First of all—as he relates—he went gold prospecting. He became an auctioneer. As he wrote in a letter to his sister in 1873,[1] '. . . anybody would think I ought to make money I am Auc-

---

[1] 14 March 1873, in the possession of Mr Andrew Newton.

tioneer & commission agent. I serve Hotels with Gingerbeer I am Peirmaster [Piermaster] and now Photographer and have a [grocer's] shop besides.' He had become a professional photographer, taking pictures of local settlers and Maoris. He was also a brewer and barber.

Bodell was willing to turn his hand to anything which might prove profitable. The occupations listed by no means exhausted his activities. He was also a land agent and insurance agent. In the 1880s he was to move into even more ambitious enterprises. It was characteristic of settlers that they had to become jacks-of-all-trades. There was little division of labour. In their consecutive census returns the settlers frequently altered their description of their occupations. It was particularly common for hotel keepers and storekeepers to have a wide range of occupations. Bodell did not, at first, make much money. For some years there was little business to be had in the new township.

In Tauranga Bodell, who turned thirty-five in 1866, at last settled down with his new wife, Jane, and her four children, and he altered his ways very much. He joined the Good Temperance Lodge and became a teetotaller, that is, he abstained from alcohol. In 1882 he built a 'temperance' hotel, one which did not sell alcohol. He wrote to his sister Annie, 'in the Colonies any man never does any good that drinks to excess. I have experienced it. I had a fortune several times only for that Hotel keeping. I am different now. I am comfortabiler now than I was when I had all the money when in Australia. . .'[2] Even more of a change than sobriety was that he became a regular church-goer and eventually churchwarden, at Trinity Church.[3] Respectability had descended upon a fairly vigorous sinner. When he travelled abroad later in his life he stayed, where possible, at temperance hotels. Certainly he might reasonably have thought that he had had his share of alcohol.

He now began to take an active interest in public affairs, which may seem a surprising development, for he scarcely mentions politics in his memoirs, but it is understandable as another outlet for his restless energy. In 1881 he was a candidate for election to the Tauranga County Council, but was defeated. The farmers did not support him, but he had more success in the town, and in the same year he was elected to the Town Board.[4] The Board had severe financial difficulties and some of the citizens wanted to form a borough because a Borough Council had

[2] James Bodell to Annie, 2 January 1862.
[3] James Bodell to Annie, 26 September 1871.
[4] *Bay of Plenty Times*, 26 September 1892.

the power to raise loans. At a stormy meeting, Bodell successfully moved that the town should be formed into a municipality. In 1882 the government approved of the Board's application. Bodell was now elected to the Borough Council.[5] By this time he had become a moderately wealthy man. In 1883, after an absence of thirty-five years, he set off on a trip to England.

After Peace was settled I considered it was time I looked about for a business and as I got a lot of land on the main road from Tauranga to the country I built a House of 5 Rooms and intended to commence business in a small way at first by selling refreshments, being a Cordial Maker and a good deal of traffic passing my door I considered I might do some business. I had not finished my Residence many weeks before I could see I had made a mistake and to do Business I must be in the commercial Part of the Town near the shipping. I began to look about me for a good business site. This were all taken up but I induced one man to divide his lot with me he retaining the corner and I took the other Part for 7 years lease. In a week I had a Building 10 × 14 feet for a shop only and commenced business my Wife[6] taking charge and I rented a workshop close by. For the next 12 months we walked night and morning from the House to the Shop 1 mile each way. When I commenced this undertaking I was short of cash having spent all to erect my dwelling house. However by Perseverance I found in a few months [I] was making headway.

In September 1868 rumours of Gold in the Katikati ranges were circulated about 30 miles away when I joined two others and off we

---

[5] W. H. Gifford and H. B. Williams, *A Centennial History of Tauranga*, Tauranga, 1940, pp. 343–4; Evelyn Stokes, *A History of Tauranga County*, Palmerston North, 1980, pp. 194–6.

[6] Bodell had married a widow, Jane Munro, in Hamilton on 19 January 1866. It is not known what happened to his first wife, but in his marriage entry Bodell is described as a widower.

Mrs Munro had four children, James, Jane, Duncan and Peter. Only two of these, Peter and Jane, are mentioned in Bodell's will. James was alive in 1889 and was reported speaking at a political meeting. In the wedding entry Bodell is listed as a carpenter and Jane Munro as a 'tracer'. Perhaps she traced patterns for embroidery.

went to prospect for Gold.[7] The Thames Gold field had commenced in July 1867 and being only about 80 miles away 50 north of Katikati ranges, and a continuation of the same range it was considered Katikati was a good Place to prospect for Gold and elderly Natives stated they had seen Gold half the Size of their thumb. A Pakeha Maori (a European living with Maori Woman) declared to me it was correct, and it was agreed that 6 of us should meet at 3 o'clock a.m. next morning at the Tauranga Hotel and proceed in a boat to Katikati a Part of the Range where a Chief had seen Gold. This little Party was organized very quietly so as not to make a large rush until we were sure that good payable Gold was there. Every business man in Town sent their Contributions. A Publican sent Brandy, Baker Bread a Grocer Groceries & so on. Myself I remained in the Hotel Parlour so as to have all ready by 3 a.m. About 4 next morning off we went to make our fortunes.

About 5 miles on our way we had to call at a native Village to get the Chief and another Native to guide us to the Eldorado. The Pakeha Maori also came with us and during our stay at this Village he had made himself a jolly good fellow by giving several Natives Grog. The Contents of 2 Bottles soon disappeared and we expected to be absent several days so I remonstrated and took the Provision under my charge. By 11 a.m. we arrived within 3 miles of the Golden Ranges being a good landing Place belonging to our Chief and a Camp of Potatoes. Here we stopped and had Dinner. As we were preparing to go on a boat came in sight loaded with Tauranga People and then another boat load arrived. Such exaggerations about the large quantity of Gold to be got sent half the Population of Tauranga half mad hence the other two boat loads, they chaffing us about giving them the slip etc.

Now we mustered 19 strong and we took it in good Part and off we went a few miles up a narrow stream and about 5 p.m. we could get no farther with the boats. We put all gear ashore erected Tents and remained for the night. We had to clear fern away 10 feet high to pitch our tents. During the evening we sampled a Bottle of 3 Star

---

[7] Traces of gold were found near Katikati and in the Kaimai range, near Tauranga, in 1867–8. Later gold was mined at Katikati. There were very large gold fields a few miles north of Tauranga, at Waihi and Thames. See Evelyn Stokes, *A History of Tauranga County*, Palmerston North, 1980, pp. 275–81.

P.B. and next morning after a early Breakfast we started to prospect the Ranges near us the Place as the native said Gold was to be got as big as your Thumb. In about 1½ miles we came to a Junction of the Stoney River and we distributed into various small Parties going in various directions with the understanding all to meet at night at the camp. One hour satisfied me no Gold had never been got here. After labouring about for several Hours and not any indications of the Colour only land slips of Iron Sand and Red Clay in Places. These land slips appeared like an old Gold Digging where heavy rains had carried the clay down the Creek. At night we all met at Camp and all told the same tale, no Gold to be got.

Being so many of us and the other two Boats brought no extra Provisions our Supplies were getting short. Next morning we went back up the River to a Place called Bowen Town with a few Settlers, and after breakfast I suggested that 3 or 4 men should volunteer to remain and proceed to the ranges, about half the distance from Tauranga than the Place where we had prospected the day before. This was agreed to and myself and two others consented to remain, the others to return to Tauranga. By mid day all had left us except the 2 Natives and during the afternoon we agreed to visit a native Settlement about 10 miles nearer Tauranga than Bowen Town and interview the Chief and get his Permission to prospect partly in native Territory. The Chief Te Moananui[8] gave his consent at once and offered to send one of his Sons with us as a guide. After chaffing our two Natives about lumps of Gold as big as their thumb that we expected to get on our first inspection they departed for Home and the three of us with our young Chief started next day, the boat having arrived from Tauranga with Provisions and a Pakeha Maori came with it by name Fairfax Johnson to be our interpreter.

During the afternoon we started across the Harbour and tramped about 4 miles to the Ranges. Here we found good looking quartz in plenty. We made a Miamia[9] (a small house) composed of sticks tied together and the leaves of the Nikau Tree. The leaves of this tree are from 12 to 22 feet long and if properly put together will

[8] Moananui was a chief of the Ngaiterangi tribe.
[9] An Australian aboriginal word for a shelter, corrupted in modern New Zealand English to *mai-mai* (pronounced my-my), a duck-shooter's hiding place.

keep rain out, and [we had] mangemange[10] for a bed with a good fire opposite the door. We made ourselves very comfortable, soon had the billy boiling and took our Supper. During the night it rained, put our fire out which had set fire to the roots of the trees and by morning disappeared into a hole caused by the roots being burnt.

Next day we commenced our work in earnest and came across several good looking quartz Leaders. In a few days we shifted quarters higher up the Creek and built a good Miamia and remained about two weeks. We got some fair quartz showing very small specks of Gold, and as our Provisions were getting short we returned to the boat and Tauranga. Next day after getting Provisions we started again but this time to another Place nearer Tauranga. Our Resident Magistrate sent for me and told me he had some years since seen Gold brought in by Natives from Kaimai not above 20 miles by land from Tauranga but we had to go by boat to give several native Villages the slip as our R.M. said the Natives would not let anyone go if they knew it so we sent to a Frenchman['s] Place (having a half caste family by a native Woman) and he consented to let two of his sons accompany us as Guide[s] and interpreters. At 12 o'clock midnight off we started, one half-caste taking a pack horse by land to meet us on the Te Puna River about 5 miles away. About 1 a.m. we met at Place agreed upon. By doing this we had passed the native settlements. Just as we had the pack horse loaded he commenced to kick and plunge and in a second I could see the Pannikins billies, a[nd] small rations Box flying in the Air and one man got kicked in the knee. We knew of a small empty House a Settler had built about 1½ miles away and to this we carried our swags Provisions etc. We broke the door open made a fire and made ourselves comfortable. The half-caste took the horse back and the man with the Kick returned Home. Before dinner another horse arrived and we loaded it and started again. We travelled about 5 miles and got into the bush, pitched our tent and remained all night. The Guide took the Horse home and we agreed to go so far through the bush and remain till he came. We left the Tent with Provisions in the Box to fall back upon if we ran short of rations. We travelled to spot agreed upon and remained there for the night.

By 9 a.m. next morning our Guide arrived telling us Mr Butts's

---

[10] The *nikau* palm has leaves up to three metres long. *Mangemange* is a springy shrub.

knee was very bad. After he took some breakfast we all started along as rough a road as any one could get along with a 60 lb swag on his back, down ravines very deep and up sides of Gullies that only for the roots of Trees we could not have got along. By these we pulled ourselves along and to our surprise horse dung was seen in several Places. However any horse could get along such a Place was a mystery. By midday we came on to about two acres of a fern spur overlooking the upper Thames delta and the Waikato country. One of the best Views conceivable was obtained from this Spur 1800 feet above the upper Thames River which lay at our feet like a huge snake. I became familiar with the Country at once. In front nearly at our feet but 8 miles away at Matamata Firths Station [was] the Residence and Burial Place of the Great Thompson the Maori King Maker.[11] On our left front Mount Maungatautari, to the right of that Mount Pirongia near Alexandra[12] and to our right front was the Trig Station over the Waipa River at Ngaruawahia and on right again Mount Taupiri [and] the Waikato Coal mines and on our extreme right was the Piako river and Mount Te Aroha and on our extreme left as far as the eye could reach the Great Patatere Plains, a most magnificent View.

Here we met some Natives 1 Man 1 Woman 1 boy with 5 horses bound from Maungaturoto (Cambridge Waikato) to Tauranga. Within 500 yards on our right was the grand Water Falls called Wairere. After resting a short time our Native friends departed towards Tauranga and we commenced the descent. Many Places you had to go ahead the Path being about four feet below the ordinary surface of the Ground through the action of Rain Water and traffic, and was very steep, only for gripping the bank as we descended we must have gone by the run. The heavy swag on your back felt very troublesome and assisted to propel you forward. I was glad when we reached the bottom. Here we lit a fire and had our dinner. Alongside of us was the Waihou or Thames River and the Water from the Wairere Falls came tumbling along amongst large boulders. Whilst the Billy was boiling myself and Burrows

[11] J. C. Firth was a wealthy businessman and landowner, and a friend of Wiremu Tamehana (Tarapipipi), a very remarkable man, who was called the 'Maori King maker'. He took a leading part in securing the acceptance of Potatau as the first Maori King.
[12] Now Pirongia.

(Captain now) went to see the Water Falls and we had a magnificent View of them. A large Sheet of water 30 feet wide and several feet deep fell perpendicular for about 400 feet and then a Succession of rapids to the Waihou River. What with the grand View from the fern Spur and these falls I was well repaid for the hard toil of getting here. All through the bush we never seen any indications of quartz or Gold.

After dinner we proceeded toward Mount Te Aroha, 'Mountain of Love' of the Natives. For years Gold was seen in this locality. At present 1886 it is the centre of a large Gold field. We started to go and inspect Kaimai south of Wairere falls but as we seen no indications on our road through the bush near that Place we concluded it was not a likely Country so made north to Te Aroha. That night we encamped about 6 miles from Wairere in a gorge and for the first time our half caste friends made us a comfortable Mai Mai made of a few Sticks and plenty of raw flax. We gathered the material and they done the covering and we made a large fire near the opening and became very snug. During the early morning it began to rain and as we was in a gorge the water began to run close to us and we had to make an early start to more high land. We found some quartz and as we proceeded it rained hard and we pushed ahead to get shelter for the night. This day we met two native Women carrying a few Potatoes in Kits. These Potatoes had commenced to grow having been left in the Ground since previous season. The Natives about here, the once powerful Thompson King Maker's Tribe, the 'Ngatihauas' were very short of food. The poor women had scarce sufficient clothing on to cover their nakedness. Both them and ourselves were completely wet through. We talked to them a few minutes, gave them a little Tobacco and biscuits and proceeded on our way.

We went through numerous swamps, the Land at base of the Ranges lay low and became half swamps for miles. About 3.30 p.m. we seen a native on horse back and he waved Blanket or Shawl as we supposed indicating to proceed towards him. As we advanced he galloped ahead. At last we lost sight of him. At this time our half caste guides and interpreter appeared to be much frightened and wanted to hide in a flax swamp but I insisted going ahead and get[ting] some Place of shelter. At last we came to a small clearing about five acres the Maize just coming out of the Ground and at the farther end I noticed two partly built huts. Into the best of these I went and off with my swag as wet all over as if I had just taken a header in a river. The natives had certainly been here the last few hours as the remains of a fire were burning. I soon made this larger and my mates Burrows & Morrison soon followed suit and our half caste friends after a little delay did likewise and when we got fairly comfortable the billy on the fire one native talking a little English made his appearance [and] shook hands all round. In a few minutes 4 or 5 more came and then more including a big burly chief. This fellow would not come under shelter but sat out in the rain. By this time the Billy boiled and in a few minutes the Natives used the lot besides taking our rations. This was too much and I told our guide to get more water and boil the Kettle again letting the Natives know we were hungry having had nothing to eat since early morning. During the boiling of the second billy I took my coat off so as to dry my shirt about my waist. To do this I turned my back towards the fire and in a short time I noticed by the noise they were making I became aware I was the object of their special notice and asking our interpreter what they were talking about he told me the Natives were saying what a fine 'copper Maori' I would make, that is what a fine roasted Pakeha (or White Man) I would make for them to feed upon. On this announcement they all including my mates guide and interpreter (very consoling for me) burst into a loud Laugh.

We were told that the Chief intended to send us down the Waikato River to Auckland as Prisoners as we had no business in their territory looking for Gold. This was true. A short time previously the Superintendent of the Province had published Gazette Notices forbidding Europeans prospecting on native Territory and the Natives knew this. At this time these Natives belonged to one of the most influential and powerful Tribe in New Zealand the Ngatihaua. On opening our Swag to get some more Tea & Sugar Biscuits etc to have the second billy of tea the Chief noticed two new Tomahawks and asked for one. Our interpreter told me this and I said give him one Yes so as he don't take us Prisoners. On getting this Tomahawk he came into the Shed and had a Pannikin of tea. In a few minutes I began talking to him and got the interpreter to assist but I found the Chief Riki one of the fighting native Generals under Thompson at the great Fight at Rangiriri Waikato 20th Nov[r] 1863. We got into a brisk conversation about Rangiriri he putting out his naked foot showing he had two toes shot off at the Battle and the attitudes he put himself into during the fight and how he shot 4 English officers. A Native telling of his Valour gets very excited and Riki became very much so, the Natives paying great attention to what he said. In the long run we became great friends and we invited Riki to pay Tauranga a Visit and we would welcome him. After all this talk night was close upon us and nearly all our Provisions were consumed. Through talking so much with Riki I was not aware the Natives had been taking too free a liberty with our rations. I told him this and he promised us a Supply of Kumaras or Sweet Potatoes. At last they told us if we promised to leave at daylight next morning and go over the Ranges they would let us go. We promised and the Natives departed, one returning with a small Kit about 10 lb of Kumaras and this with a little wet Biscuits Sugar tea and Bacon fat all mixed together was all the rations we had. We were very glad when the Natives left.

We consulted what step to take next. It was agreed to take to the Ranges at daylight next morning and get to the east Side of the Ranges. Our rations all gone and two days travel from home and about equal distance from the Tent with the rations we left behind. We turned into our Blankets and at daylight we started across the ranges, raining heavily all night and all this day. After two hours toil we came across the Creek the Natives said gold had been got some years before. We certainly found good looking Quartz and a small speck of Gold. (The last five years Gold has been found here and a small Town formed called Wairongomai of about 1000 Population principally Diggers [with] good payable gold.) We had great difficulty to light a fire [as it was] raining hard. At last we managed to get a hot pannikin each of what I called Boilly Soup a Mixture of Tea Sugar Biscuit and Pork fat, anything better than hunger. After this we started and the next 6 hours we toiled about those Hills to no Purpose. About 3 p.m. we came in full View of the Place we left in early morning, we had been travelling around these Hills raining all the time. The Bush Lawyer or Supple Jack was very thick amongst the trees [and] the trees also were covered in their lower branches with bunches of Moss. This collected Water and we were all so wet the same as if we had been ducked in a river. As we toiled up the Hills the Supple Jack would catch your swag and pull you back. I lost one side of my coat and part of my cap. At 3 p.m. on coming near the spot we left in the morning I [was] very much vexed as my mates would not go by the Compass I carried. I begged of them to let us be guided by the Compass one hour. They consented. In less than an hour we found a little creek running east. This we followed and in one hour it got much larger and wider. We recognised it as the Creek we had prospected before and built two Miamias or huts. Water on account of the heavy rains was rushing down and in Places we were up to our Middles. On we went and at last we came to the Water fall. About 10 p.m. we came to our hut [and] a large tree close to we had fell[ed] on our previous Visit came in handy. We soon had a large fire. The rain had ceased the last two hours. We all stripped naked put stakes and rails around the three sides of fire [and] put our clothes to dry. We must have cut a figure all naked [and] nothing to eat. [We each] got a wet Blanket and lay down, soon asleep. Next morning our clothes [were] nearly dry. I started to find a Nikau Tree. The top Pith about 30 inch long is like eating a cabbage. I found one of these trees and got the Pith and put a remnant of our Grease Mixture and boiled it all together and had each a Pannikin of this and started homewards. We had 30 miles across Country to get to the Frenchman Farm. About mid day we had to swim a river. We managed this way. We sent one of the half Castes across the river with a long flax rope and then sent our largest tin dish across and so back and forwards. When all things were across we swam across also. I managed to throw my boots across but Mr Burrows was trying also when his finger caught in the boot and sent it down the river and sank in 9 feet of Water. The guide dived and recovered it and we started again. After this the tide being low and we had several Rivers to cross we took [to] the Beach for it and at 12 o'clock Midnight we arrived at our head quarters very tired. A strange coincidence the Ration Boat had been stuck all day on a Sand Bank and only arrived with Provisions about one hour before us. We had a good Supper and turned in. Next morning we were very tired and stiff. We concluded to leave the tent where we had left it for the Present. The Natives would not believe us that we had been to the Wairere Falls and Ohineroa. When they became convinced they want[ed] Utu or Money for us going there and even followed us into Tauranga thinking they would frighten us into giving them something. We were not to be done like that.

The quartz we brought in was analysed and a few specks of Gold found. I came to the conclusion it would take £5 to get one ounce of

Gold worth £3.10s. To satisfy myself [I decided] to give a certain Place a two Weeks' trial. 4 of us started out again and after two weeks came to the conclusion it required more capital than we had to prospect the Ranges properly. I had destroyed nearly all the clothing I had and I must try business again. Several Parties have prospected same locality on various occasions since and found indications of Gold but not in paying quantities. So now I turn[ed] my attention to business which at this time was very slack in Tauranga.

The day after my return to my great surprise I was warned for a month's Militia duty. I thought I was done with soldiering but as the authorities had let me alone so long I could not complain to do a months duty at 4/- per day and I had to tackle to. Every night a Chain of Sentries were posted all round the Town. The north end of the Town of Tauranga ended in a fork or spit of land the waters of the Harbour washing it on three sides. Across the western Estuary was only about 100 yards and this Point was considered a very dangerous Point for the ingress of rebel Natives as it was a main thoroughfare to many native Settlements. Inland of this Point three Sentries were posted one to guard the eastern side of the spit and that side of the Harbour, one at centre of spit, this being about 400 yards wide and one Sentry at the western or Judea Estuary side and these 3 Sentries could on emergency communicate with each other. On the eastern side of the base of this spit was the Cemetery the last resting Place of all those killed at the fights of Gate Pah, Te Ranga and other Engagements and the dead of the civil Portion of the community. This Cemetery was on a hill about 100 feet above the waters of the Harbour and from the north east Corner you had a full command of the western Ford before mentioned and all round the Spit. This last spot was my Post every night during the month for 3 hours. One night I was left on Sentry from 8 p.m. till 3 next morning. One morning about 2 o'clock an unusual noise was heard about the narrowest Part of the western Crossing Place. It sounded like several hundreds of Rebels moving about the Sand. I communicated with next Sentry N° 2 and he also with No° 3. It being a cloudy morning we could not see above 100 yards and this Crossing was 500 yards north west from my Post. My elevated Position gave me a good View far better than my Comrades. We were in great suspense for some time then I heard a horse snorting and swimming across. Presently I heard another and several more, heard them quite distinctly get out of the water, and shake themselves. I listened very attentively to see if I could hear anything like men walking about but could not. Presently the Horses commenced to feed on a little rough herbage. I goes to the next Sentry and we went towards where the horses were and when we got within 150 yards we lay down and listened and were satisfied that all this alarm was nothing more than several Horses belonging to Natives swimming the ford for a good feed. One night alarm was given when all Women and Children was roused out of Bed and run for the Redoubt and remained all night. At this time the Natives were in thousands all round us. I should say there were 6 then to 1 now.

My month expired without any particular incident except a little bother about a pet Pig of mine. I had a very small pet Pig. One day it came home with a fresh made Brand on its hind quarter and I recognized the Brand as being the initials of a man who was suspected of branding several Cattle belonging to another settler. I goes to this man and in his workshop I seen the iron brand corresponding with the Brand on my pet Pig. I accused him of branding my Pig. He denied it. As I had to go on duty I could not stop to say more to him. Then on going home [later] to dinner my Wife told me Harley had been and abused her and said if I did not let the Pig go he would have me put in Gaol. This was too much so I went and laid an information against him and had him arrested for branding my Pig and claiming it as his Property. For his bounce he got 6 Weeks in Gaol. I did not Value the animal at 5/- but the abuse to my Wife and threatening me I could not stand. This same man was tried for branding several Cattle not belonging to him and during the next year he was tried at Supreme Court Auckland for selling Ball Cartridges and caps to the Natives and got 8 years in Gaol.

A few months after this I paid the Penalty of prospecting for Gold. Through being so much wet I took the Rheumatic fever and was nearly going off this mortal coil. I lay delirious for several Weeks, our only Doctor could not relieve me and during my illness he left the District and there I lay for 17 Weeks before I got off my bed and then I used Holloways Pills freely and got several Pots of Jamaica Sarsaparilla Paste and dissolved it with hot water. When [it was] cold [I] added a small Portion of Iodide of Potassium. A strong constitution and plenty of this Medicine pulled me through. I was badly in need of some funds so I sold my 4 roomed House and land with 50 acres of a country Farm for £52, £18 down, balance within 3 months. I done this lying on my bed. To make matters worse my four children took the Whooping Cough. I had never seen this cough before and I thought it was a most extraordinary sickness. I was certain some of them would choke. The eldest Jim suffered most, Peter the youngest stood it like a Briton. In a few weeks they got over it and the first thing I did when able to walk I went and bought a Piece of building Land close to my shop and this proved a good speculation. This was purchased from the Proceeds of the Sale of my Residence and 50 acres.

At last after 6 months idleness through Sickness I commenced business. I undertook the duties of Town Barber, Undertaker and Builder, Cordial and Ginger beer Hop beer & Cider Maker. With my several businesses I did well. My Wife took charge of the shop and in 12 months I enlarged my Premises. The next 12 months I built a 6 roomed House for myself on the lot of land I had bought. The next year I turned Photographer having bought from a Photographer all his appliances and he agreed to stop with me 14 days to learn me the Photo Art. I built a Studio and succeeded very well. Had several engagements to photo dead Maori Chiefs and Natives in groups. These Jobs always paid me well. The following year I bought the lease of the whole of the Land my shop stood on and erected a large Store. The Studio I shifted to the line of Streets next to my new Store and made additions to the Studio as to make it a shop 30 feet × 18. This I let for 20/- per week and sold my photo apparatus and gave my attention to merchandise. In another year I have five shops built in my corner lot of Land besides my own large store. These shops brought me in a weekly rent of 60/- each week. Two years after I purchased 5 Lots of Land about 300 yards away with a House of 6 Rooms in a good Position for £600. In fact from 1870 to 1878 I invested in various Properties and I became worth fully £4000 and through Perseverance and attending to business the next five years I increased my Possessions to fully £6000 and in June 1883 I took a trip to old England after an absence of 35 years and 9 months. I visited my Parents and five Sisters in Leicester, 3 of my Sisters being born during my absence, all my Sisters being married with Families and found all in very comfortable Circumstances. In 1847 when I left Leicester I was a young man 9½ stone and return[ed] 18 stone weight. I weighed myself in October fair during my Visit to Leicester and I turned the Scale at 18 stone 8 lbs. I enjoyed myself very much during my Visit and returned to New Zealand by the Orient SS *Liguria*. Left Plymouth on 21 Octr 1883 arrived in Melbourne 29 Novr and via Sydney to New Zealand arrived in Auckland 13 Decr 1883.

VII

My Trip from New Zealand via America to England and Return Trip: June—December 1883

Although it seems unlikely that Bodell kept a diary during his soldiering and publican days, the following account of his return trip to England does seem to be based on, or a revision of, a diary. A lengthy and rather tedious account of a train journey across the USA has been omitted.

On Wednesday 13th June 1883 I left Tauranga Bay of Plenty in SS *Glenelg* and after a rough Passage arrived in Auckland next morning at 7 a.m. I remained in Auckland until Tuesday 19 June. I took a Saloon ticket and as I preferred a Cabin on Spar or upper deck I had to Pay £72 to be landed at either London or Liverpool. Having choice of several first class Steam Ship lines running from New York to England a Passenger taking a Saloon Ticket in Auckland at £66 and a Cabin below deck to accommodate four berths you have no Choice of Ship from New York but have to go to London on Vessel belonging to a certain line. At the time of taking my ticket in Auckland a profusion of Pamphlets and book are given you and advertising Sheets with various routes through America telling you the best Hotels to stop at in San Francisco and other Places on line of railway from Frisco to New York and very good Plans of line of Railway through America. If you intend stopping in any Place in America en route as I did on arrival at San Francisco you have to apply to the office of the P.R.M.Co and on producing your ticket that you received in Auckland, they will ask you what Places on line of Route you intend to stop at and you get Coupons accordingly. For instance I received one Coupon or ticket from San Francisco to Ogden as I intended to stop at Salt Lake City and have an interview with the Mormons; another Ticket from Ogden to

Chicago and another ticket from Chicago to Niagara Falls and another to New York and another from New York to England. These are together about 18 inches long.

On Tuesday June 19th 1883 I embarked on board the Pacific Royal Mail Steam Ship the *City of Sydney*, Captain Dearborn, and about 2.30 we dropped down towards the North Head. A Saloon Passenger was very near losing his trip. We had not left Auckland Wharf half [a] Mile before our attention was drawn towards a Waterman's Boat the occupants shouting and cooeeing and a passing ferry Steamer directed our Skipper's attention and he kindly eased Steam and picked the Passenger up and off we went full Steam ahead. In a short time we were clear of Auckland's beautiful Harbour and approached the Tiritiri Light House and by dusk we made the Little Barrier Island.

By this time I began to notice my fellow Passengers. I was very fortunate to have a three berth Cabin all to myself. This I found very pleasant when we came to the tropics. It was situated next to main entrance from deck to Saloon with large window opening on Passage between Bulwarks and Staterooms. My fellow Passengers were a mixed lot, several from Melbourne, Geelong, Ballarat, Sandhurst in Victoria and others from Sydney Queensland and various Parts of New Zealand, Mr Simonsen the Celebrated Violinist and his Daughter a capital Vocalist. On the morning of the 20th we were out of sight of Land with a fresh breeze blowing dead ahead. Still the good Ship made her 12 Knots per hour. At dinner this day a young 'Masher' from Sandhurst ordered a Bottle of Whisky and he nearly finished it during dinner. I considered this was doing very well he not being above 22 years old. Before night dinner, Whisky and other edibles went to feed the fishes. This young gent lived at a fast rate and was fond of gambling cards taking various bets up and as he told me his Father at Sandhurst kept a Toy shop I thought there must be great profits in selling toys to carry on at the rate he was going. I found gambling was carried on rather extensively during the afternoon and Evening. We had also in the saloon Mr Albert Fisher and his Wife on board. Mr Fisher is brother to Mrs Morrison of Ohinemutu. They appeared to take matters very easily and [be] enjoying the trip very well.

When Thursday appeared I was told we should have two Thursdays on account of Variation of time. Saturday 23 June wind still ahead but going along about 12 Knots. The Social Hall on the *City of Sydney* is a large one being on the upper or hurricane deck. The Passengers patronized it very freely. In fact I considered it the best room in the Ship. It could accommodate 100 comfortable. The upholstering was very good and a good Piano occupied the forepart. In this room many comfortable hours were passed. There was a good library on board for the use of Passengers and the Ship was a good sea boat. I consider the *City of Sydney* is one of the best Vessels I have travelled in and I consider I should be a fair Judge having travelled much during my 36 years absence from England.

On Sunday 24 June the Wind moderated. At 11 o'clock Divine Service was held in the Social Hall the Doctor of Ship officiated [and] made a very good Minister and the singing had a very good Leader, Miss Simonsen. The Doctor of the Ship was a fine good old soul a Yankee. On Monday June 25th a Concert in the Evening in the Social Hall. This was well attended and the Singing was very good. Old Simonsen played on the Violin. He is about the best Performer on that instrument I have heard. The Mail agent sang very well the 'Death of Nelson'. On Wednesday 27th crossed the line. During the Evening the Crew went through the performance of Neptune coming on board. Several Saloon Passengers were put through the Ordeal. My Sandhurst Friend of whisky notoriety he was taken forward and was in the act of being shaved when he bought himself off by paying for sundry bottles of Grog. Some of them had a rough time of it. Any Passenger the Crew was told had not crossed the line before was seized and taken forward and if he did not pay he was put through the shaving operation. About 6 of the Crew was got up very well for the occasion. Old Neptune had a beard down to his Knees made of unravelled rope with his Crown on and carried his trident. His assistant was got up very well. The barber carried as a Razor a Piece of hoop iron about two feet long and the latherer had a large tar brush, and the lather was a Mixture of Soap, tar and rank fat, not very nice to have a mouthful of. The Victim was brought before a large tub and if you did not buy off a question was asked you and when you opened your mouth to answer, the brush covered with the Mixture was shoved into your Mouth and the more you resisted the worse you got. My Sandhurst friend got one mouthful before he cried enough and compromised.

The weather was wonderful cool. As far as the heat went you would not believe we were in the Tropics. Captain Dearborn said he never experienced such cool weather before crossing the line.

Friday 29th June, [we] have run 2803 miles since leaving Auckland. Passed Navigator's Island, a large Island about 8 miles on Port Side, weather still fine and expect to reach Honolulu on Monday morning. Sunday July 1 Divine Service in Social Hall the Doctor of Ship officiating, good attendance, the service very enjoyable. We had about 60 Saloon Passengers on board. At one o'clock morning Monday 2nd July arrived outside reef at Honolulu. Fired Gun for Pilot and the next hour fired several Guns. The Pilot did not answer until 3 a.m. when we steamed slowly ahead and at 4 o.c. was alongside the Wharf. At 6 o'clock I went on Shore and took a Stroll around the City of Honolulu. I happened to walk towards the Chinese Part of the Town. The appearance of the City from the Quay is not very great, but the Part I accidentally walked into was a dirty filthy Part [with] poor Buildings and at this time I was surprised that the City of Honolulu was as it appeared a dirty Town. This was altered after Breakfast. I returned on Board about 7.30 and having informed several questioners about my rambles I was told by going towards the Grand Hotel and the King's & Queen's Palaces I should have a more favourable opinion. About 10 o.c. three of us made a Party and took a Carriage and drove for 2 Hours about the City and Suburbs and certainly when you get clear of the Business Part of the City and [in the] direct opposite direction than I took before breakfast, the appearance of the Town is very good. The town is well laid out wide straight Street[s] and some grand Buildings. The Hotel is a very good Building, I believe the only one in Honolulu worthy of the name [with] a beautiful circular drive in front. Breadfruit, bananas, and other tropical trees in Profusion. We visited the King's Palace and the Queen's Palace (each have their Palace) and the King's Monument, and all the principal Buildings including the Gaol. All Residences are surrounded by two to four acres of Land with plenty of ornamental trees, Shrubs, and various fruit Trees. On our return to the business Part of the City we called at a Tobacconist and on buying a fig of Tobacco I handed him a Sovereign and he offered Mexican Money in change. Now a Mexican Dollar is only worth 4/- and four Dollars for a Sov. would not do . . .

Honolulu is the first Place from the Australian Colonies where American Money predominates, and I got a little puzzled with the 5 cent and 10 cent Pieces. We shipped about 80 Passengers and about 800 Tons of Sugar, Rice and Bananas. On account of the increase of Passengers the Purser said he would have to give me a Companion in my Cabin and a young Gentleman from Sydney volunteered to take a berth in my Cabin, and gave his up to three Passengers from Honolulu. I was very glad of this arrangement, in Place of having a Stranger. About 2 o'clock p.m. the King's Band came on to the Quay and discoursed some excellent music. I believe this is done by the King's orders when the Australian and Frisco Boats call here. At 2.30 we let go the lines and got clear of the Quay. About 8 young men followed us in the water shouting out to send money and any small silver Coin thrown into the water they would dive and bring it up and wait for more. These natives are very expert in the Water, any one throwing a Sixpence or Shilling into the water 40 feet deep these Youngsters would have it very quick put it into their mouth and ready for another dive. On leaving the Wharf the Band Played 'God Save the Queen' and 'Yankee Doodle'.

The American Man of War *Essex* was lying at Honolulu. We had not left the Quay far before we were hailed by a boat from the American Man of War and on coming alongside they had a Prisoner for us. This man by name Kerr had been taken in Chile near Callaō for embezzling a Bank at Chicago of 150,000 Dollars from his employers. Detective Julian had him in charge. The Prisoner appeared to be very down cast. Detective Julian of the American detective force appears to be a very smart officer although under the medium height in fact rather small in Stature. He gets 10,000 Dollars for the Capture. He related the capture to me which I will tell farther on. By 5 o.c. p.m. we were on the way for San Francisco. About 6 p.m. passed a large Island. We have on board from Honolulu the Celebrated Macabe, the comic actor and delineator also Professor Humberger and Lady.

July 4th the Glorious Fourth as the Yankees say. The Weather is grand and every appearance of it keeping so, scarcely a ripple on the Water. All day things appeared very quiet for the great Yankee day. During the afternoon I noticed several old Yankees visiting the Bar rather often. At Dinner 6 p.m. the glorious fourth began in earnest. One tall old Gentleman, a Sugar Planter from Honolulu, every day since he came on board he was occupied reading half reclining in a easy chair with gloves on. On arrival of the third Course he began with a Doz of Champagne sundry Bottles of Whisky Soda Water and Claret and he invited any Britisher to join him in drinking the prosperity to Yankees and America with the dessert. Many friends assembled round the old Gentleman and were drinking his health and all Yankees and the American Nation in particular. About 9 p.m. I visited the Saloon and there was the old Gentleman gloriously drunk and many others in the same state. The old Chap was bragging he could drink them all under the Table and I seen him myself empty the contents of one Bottle of Champagne into a large Jug and added Whisky, Claret, and Soda water and took a hearty draught of the Mixture. I did not see any more of the old Chap till after Breakfast next morning and there he was in his old Chair reading with his gloves on as usual and appeared if he had not taken a Drop the Night before. As he recognized anyone of the previous Night's debauch he merely nodded his head and let them pass.

July 6th the weather still fine, Vessel averaging 12 Knots. Gambling had increased on board the last [few days] and several Parties were constantly at cards in the smoking room. Lately my young Sandhurst friend was very often in close Confab with the Purser, and on several occasions he seemed to be as if something was greatly the matter and his extravagance at Table had modified to a small Bottle of Beer for dinner. Being often in Conversation with him one day I asked him if anything was wrong as he looked so very excited. O, D----- it I have been a loser at Cards was the Answer and I found out his being in company with the Purser was to get the purser to advance him some Money on a Bank draft payable in San Francisco. He succeeded in getting the money and before we arrived at Frisco he was hard up again and a good thing for him to be hard up.

July 7th a Grand Concert in Social Hall commenced at 8 p.m. The Hall was crowded and it was a great treat. Mr Simonsen manipulated that Violin in a way that he almost made it speak. Professor and Madam Humberger played at the Piano in turns and singing with Miss Simonsen was really grand. The Mail Agent and a Mr Rothchild sang very well. The Inimitable Macabe caused much Laughter. This Gentleman is a host in himself in a concert. Professor & Madam Humberger played some high class Music and at 10.30 p.m. the National Anthem brought a very enjoyable Evening to a close. Often I have paid 5/- for a Ticket and would [not] have such a good Performance as we had on board of the good ship *City of Sydney*.

July 7th several Passengers still keep the glorious fourth up. For the last week a auction Sale were held every day about 11 o'clock. Directly after Breakfast two gents would go round amongst the Passengers and solicit your name and one dollar to go into a Calcutta Sweep as they called it. About 11 o.c. the Auctioneer would commence to sell the Tickets. These tickets would be numbered say from 250 to 400 [and] the Vessel's run the last 24 hours would be between the above numbers. Someone not interested in the Stakes generally a young Girl would draw tickets and the Auctioneer would state the owner of Ticket and Number on it. If it happened to be say near 320 the Ticket will sell for a good Sum. This day 8 July the money paid in and realised by Auction was valued at £60 and a Gent from Geelong was the Winner and took his friends down to the Saloon and shouted 1 doz Champagne and then others shouted this and the remnants of the glorious 4th kept things very lively.

July 8th this night another Entertainment in Social Hall. Professor Humberger and Lady & Mr Rothchild were the principal Performers, all Sacred Music being Sunday Evening. In the Morning Divine Service in Social Hall as usual. Not a Sail seen since leaving Honolulu. I noticed an American Naval officer on board a Lieut. from the Man of War *Essex*. The Prisoner Kerr has conducted himself very well passing his time reading smoking and walking about the Poop. Detective and myself have become pretty good friends and we often have a chat together. At noon today we have 375 Miles to Frisco.

Monday July 9th weather still fine. 2 p.m. Land ahead. Passed Seal Rocks about 30 Miles from Frisco. As we approached the Golden Gate or entrance [to] the Harbour of San Francisco, the Sea Birds are very numerous. One kind with red beak skims along the water appears [as] if not able to fly. As you near the Harbour I consider it a grand Sight. On your left large lofty Hills some covered with Trees. On your right a hill rises from the sea and you can perceive tracks over it and as you enter the Harbour the Pilot Station on left and a battery on your right and the Shipping at anchor appears. Barracks on your right and a train running along. About 5 p.m. we come to anchor in the Stream, tide being out, not enough water to let the *City of Sydney* alongside the Quay. The Whistle was sounded for the Doctor and after waiting some time he came on board. Taking a View about the Harbour there appeared to be plenty of Shipping and the various Steamers appeared to be very busy. One large Steamer I noticed always crowded steers across the Harbour. About 6.30 a small Steamer came alongside and any Saloon Passengers who liked could go ashore.

A number of us went ashore and took tram for the Hotel. The Grand Hotel appeared to be large. This is the largest Building I had seen seven Storeys high and I should say 300 feet square. Some of us proceeded to Russ House Hotel and found the accommodation very good. After depositing our nicknacks we brought with us we took a Stroll round the City of San Francisco and called in at the Grand Hotel. The entrance to the Grand Hall is very nice, here a Band was playing and the Vestibule was crowded. I met several Passengers and they said their Bedrooms were up 3 or 4 storeys high above this entrance Hall. The Balconies are in front of the dormitories, very nice no doubt but I like to be in a Building where if there is a fire or any accident I like to be where I can clear out without much trouble. At 8.30 the Band cleared out and nearly all the Crowd there did not appear to be stopping at the largest Hotel in the World. I believe I was told it cost about $150,000 but the numerous business Places on the ground floor not interfering with the Hotel should bring enough rent to pay half the interest on the Capital expended. I was told it did not pay as a speculation.

After visiting several Places of interest we returned to our Hotel and there I found Detective Julian and during conversation he told me incidents relating to the capture of the Prisoner Kerr. It appeared this man Kerr was the Confidential Head Clerk in a Bank at Chicago, and had held that Position for some years. About last February he suddenly levanted from his office and on examining his Books this deficiency of 150,000 Dollars was found out. In April the Inspector of the detectives was sent for and the Case placed in Julian's hands and as he said the Prisoner had nearly two months start. However he commenced operations and after travelling about some weeks he heard of a man answering to the description of Kerr going south and off he went in that direction and come to the conclusion that he had made for Chile or Callaō. He traced him to Chile and went to an Hotel where he expected to find his man. Here he came to a Person answering to Kerr's description but much altered in appearances. He concluded to stop at the Hotel and in a few days he got acquainted with Kerr and during another few days he became rather intimate with Kerr and at this stage

Detective Julian took a Fever and was laid up several days. On getting round again he became more intimate with Kerr and during Conversation he led Kerr [to] believe he was anxious to get away as he had done something that he was afraid he would get taken. After this Kerr related the Cause of his being where he was. As Julian said even before this he was pretty well sure he had his man but they being out of American Jurisdiction he must entice him into American locality . . . and here was the American Man of War *Essex*. To endeavour to get Kerr on board was Julian's wish. In a few days Kerr had put such faith in Julian that he accompanied him on board just to pass an hour away. However when Julian got his Man fairly on board he revealed himself and made Kerr his Prisoner. Kerr nearly fainted and could not eat anything for days. In fact Julian had to get the ship's doctor to him. In about a week they sailed to other Places and called at Honolulu to intercept the Australian and New Zealand Mail Steamer going to San Francisco and that is how we met him at Honolulu. After this I met Julian aboard the *Alaska* bound for Paris via Liverpool on another expedition.

On Tuesday morning July 10th Mr McKay the courteous agent for several railway lines to New York and other centres of Population waited on us at our hotel and offered his services in any matter required such as changing Sovereigns into dollars and giving instruction about the various railway routes and the best Places to stop at etc. and how to get your ticket changed for the several coupons or tickets required. In fact I should recommend anyone travelling through America to put himself in Mr McKay's hands. He does all this in the interest of the various Companies he represents. During the day we got our tickets changed and Mr McKay gave me a note to a money changer. Here I got 4 Dollars 85 cents in 20 or 10 Dollar Gold Pieces for each Sovereign, 5 cents more than 20 shillings for each Sovereign. Several had arranged to get a Detective to show us around the Chinese part of San Francisco. So we agreed to meet at 8 p.m. at McKay's office. During the day I went on Board the *City of Sydney* to get my traps. On going into my State Room I missed a carved Maori walking stick and I hunted high and low enquired of Bedroom Steward a Chinese, the Head Steward, the Purser and Captain but all no use the stick had gone since I was there the night before and I never seen it since. So Mr Bedroom Steward lost his fee for I believe he took it. My Cabin mate's boxes and clothes were all there. He came on board for them before I left.

I also visited the celebrated Garden in Frisco (Woodward I think). The City appeared to be a good business Place, all branches of business appeared brisk and money plentiful. At 8 p.m. as arranged 17 of us mustered with a Detective to show us round. This 17 of us was too many so on coming across another Detective 9 went with him and we commenced our rounds. Some of the sights were very good but some of them was very bad. We visited the opium dens. [In] the Joss House the Chinese Women appeared to be very numerous. Several Places would make you feel sick. The Detective appeared to have a kind of open Sesame for all and every one welcomed him and those that were with him. Several Merchants' Stores were very anxious to sell fancy goods from China and I suppose 50 Dollars were spent during the evening. About 11 p.m. I got tired and as they did not appear to be inclined to go home I called a council and totted up the expenses, including 10 Dollars for the detective. It came to something about 2½ dollars each. One Place we went into down a stair into a large room [with] a Stage erected in one end [and] I should say 200 as queer a company as any one would wish to see. Men and Women of all nations drinking swearing decoying and the Performance was even worse. At last I said to the Detective I am off Home and so was he. He said quite enough for one night and in half an hour I was between the Sheets in Russ House Hotel ready to start next afternoon for Salt Lake City.

During the day I [had] noticed my Sandhurst friend and the Purser dodging about, I believe to get the draft cashed. This they accomplished and during a few minutes Conversation with the Sandhurstite it appears he was a heavy loser on board, and he was getting short of cash and serve him right. He told me he had been brought up and educated to be one of the Medical Profession and that he had [so] sickened the old man by his extravagance and bad company that his Father had given him a little cash and arranged with an Uncle a medical man in Omaha, America to take him and see what he could do with him. I am afraid the Uncle would have [a] hard nut to crack.

Wednesday 11th July at Breakfast Mr McKay waited on us to ascertain what he could do for us and how we had enjoyed our Rambles of the previous night. Some of our experiences were related which made McKay enjoy a hearty laugh. On making it known I was off by the 3.30 train only one man consented to start the others wanted to stop in Frisco another day or two. So after taking the tram cars to various Parts of the City until dinner time and a Gent who was going on board the *City of Sydney* volunteers to find my carved stick if possible and as he did not intend to leave till Friday and as I intended to stop two days at the City of the Mormons he said he would overtake me there or at Ogden and if successful he would bring the Stick. After Dinner me and my companion made a start towards the booking office. My companion was a Sheep Farmer from Hawkes Bay and bound for Yorkshire. At 3.30 we embarked on one of those large steamers to cross the Bay of San Francisco. This Ferry steamer was very large. However we were soon on the train and bound for Sacramento. Before leaving the Railway office in Frisco we had to pay 6 Dollars for two nights Sleeping Car accommodation.

Arrived here [i.e. Sacramento] about 5.30 p.m. Here you can have tea 1 Dollar, stopping 20 minutes and then off again commencing to cross the Sierra Nevada Mountains. During early morning went round Cape Horne, 12,000 feet above sea level. This Place caused great trouble and expense as it is a cliff 2000 feet perpendicular and the workmen had to be swung on Stages hanging in Chains to excavate the rock. Several times two Engines were made fast to help the train, some of the Gradients being very steep. The train stops three times each day for refreshments Breakfast Dinner and Tea. Truly the Americans are a wonderful People. It was a great undertaking this Railway across the American Continent. By Evening 12 July we had crossed the Sierra Nevadas. The Sights are wonderful. At 9 a.m. July 13 arrived at Ogden. We could see the Great Salt Lake 20 Miles before we reached Ogden. Got my Traps together and drove to a large Hotel. Ogden is not a large Town, some very good Buildings. About 11 o.c. started for the City of the Mormons, by rail 28 miles. Stopped at Walkers Hotel in Main Street. After dinner visited the Great Tabernacle and the Temple. The last Building I was told by our Conductor has been 25 years building. It has massive Walls and not half finished. I should think it will take another 25 years before it is ready to be opened. The Tabernacle is a wonderful Building egg-shaped and has Seat Room for 12,000 and Conductor said can accommodate 14,000 People. At one end a large Organ built, in front I should say there is Seats for the Choir, room for 300 Performers. The Conductor requested me to go to the far end of the Gallery and he would drop a small Pin into his hat (hard felt) and on his doing so I could hear the sound of the Pin falling into the hat quite distinct, and he again whispered very low to me and although I was 150 feet from him I could hear him easily. There is some plan about this Building that assist[s] the Sound. I should think the Choir would make too much noise.

After leaving the Tabernacle we inspected everything about the Mormon Church and other Buildings. Not far away from the Tabernacle there is a large Yard, Building on two Sides and several Barn like Buildings on opposite end and another Building near the Centre of Yard, this latter Building standing in front of us on our entrance into the yard a load of green feed on a cart going in and a jolly looking individual opening the gates. We went up to this Person and in a few minutes we were in conversation which continued for the next two hours. He became very communicative. He told us the Mormon Form of Worship was taken from the Bible and he said the load of green Grass you have seen delivered is part Payment due for *Tithes* from the Farmer who sent it. He said all Mormons have to pay 10 per cent of their earnings, a Farmer 10 per cent on his Produce a business man the same on his Profits and in this way the Mormons get the Capital to pay for the various Elders, Bishops and other Ministers connected with the Mormon Church. I asked him if all the Residents in Salt Lake City were Mormons. He said no. Fully half of them are Gentiles and don't belong to the Mormon Church, and I said I did not know before that anyone besides Mormons would be allowed to reside in the City. Many of them did belong to the Mormons but had left as their Profits had been so great that they would not pay the 10 Per Cent and so left the Church. Still he said all are welcome to reside in Utah Valley. He asked me where we were stopping. I told him Walkers Hotel. Ah he said he was a Mormon but left on account of the *Tithes*.

When I asked him how any man could manage so many Wives he said easily enough. He said I have two and have been a Mormon 30 years and am 63 years old. Still I am thinking of taking a third Wife. I remarked I considered him too old, not a bit of it said the old chap it would be more of a Variety and would make things livelier at home. Why said he some of our Friends have 4 & 6 and look at our President (Taylor) he has 20 wives. Look over there said the old chap holding out his arm you see that Building with 10 Windows upstairs, them are 10 of the 20 Wives' Bedrooms and on other side of House there are 10 other Bedrooms but I remarked it could not be expected that one man could keep these 20 Women under subjection and keep peace at home. He said if a man has 10 wives and he takes another and any one of the 10 are dissatisfied the one dissatisfied can retire and become a Pensioner. Those wives who are satisfied know it is no use grumbling afterwards. Still sometimes there is bickerings at Home.

He said do you know you Gentiles practise grievous Sin in what way you take unto yourself one wife. You lay with her, she proves to be in the Family way and still you lay and have connection with her and by this you are disobeying God's Laws. Read your Bible and I can prove it. All we Mormons do and practise in our Law is taken from the Bible. All you Gentiles sow your Seed on unfruitful Places, having to do with a woman when she is bearing a child is against the Laws of God. We Mormons never lie with a Woman after she is proved to be in child she is left alone for 18 months. The woman is not touched for 9 months after the child is born so as the Mother can give all her strength to her offspring. I certainly was non plussed here and there were some truth in his remarks.

It was a most interesting two hours conversation and I may say instructive also. I certainly felt inclined to become a Mormon and told him so. He said we require subjects to the Mormon Church [since] the American Government have been interfering with us and the more Votes we have to return Members to Congress the more Power the Mormons will become. I asked him how strong were the Mormons in Numbers. I forgot his answer but he said we have 21 Districts in a country about 120 miles by 60—and we don't care much about the American Government. At last we bid the old [man] goodbye, and he was very slow at parting and invited us to see him again on the Morrow. This old Gentleman was from Scotland, I. McMurray by name and he sold all Produce that was received as *Tithes*.

The Valley of Utah where Salt Lake City is situated, and a fine Valley it is, the only drawback is all cultivation is by Irrigation as only 3 months in the Year there is any rain. You can see furrows made in all cultivation for the Water to run down, the Valley runs North and South. On the West is the Great Salt Lake and on the East is a range of Mountains and the Water Supply comes from these mountains. Fruit and Vegetables appears to be very plentiful and grows well. I seen many orchards in full bearing and all trees appeared well laden. I believe it is very cold in winter. Ice is plentiful during Summer taken from a fresh Water lake in Winter and preserved in Summer. The City of the Mormons is well laid out fine long broad streets at right angles and some good Buildings appear in several Streets around the Suburbs. The Houses of the well to do Mormons appear situated in fine ornamental Grounds. You can tell a Mormon's house at once by its peculiar Build and many Windows, and generally two to four females occupying the front Part of the house. It being about 5 o'clock in the afternoon I suppose it being a nice fine afternoon, brought the ladies out, some were watering the various flowers and Shrubs by a Water Pipe fixed in the Garden, water being laid on all over the City and good clear water it is. Fruit Shops were well stocked and cheap. In the Evening we took a walk round the City and several times we met gangs of 6 to 8 young Women. I was told they were Mormon lasses. The city by night looked very nice all shops and Lamps being well lit up. I met several Mormons from Leicestershire, Nottingham-shire Derbyshire and other Parts of England.

Saturday 14th July a train arrived this morning from Colorado 1100 miles [away] with about 75 Men and Women belonging to the Press on a Visit to Salt Lake City and to bathe in the great Lake. I was fortunate in making the acquaintance of some of them, and I ascertained they had engaged a special train to take them to the bathing Place on the Lake, 25 miles distant. This was the very thing I wanted and on waiting on the Boss of the Party at once he consented to let us go and a very jolly time we had. We started about 10.30 a.m. and by 11.15 we were at the Place. As you alight from the train direct in front is a partly open Building a refresh-ment Stall. On Counter at one end here you apply for a bathing dress and pay ¼ Dollar. Off you go down a planked roadway [which] takes you on to a Jetty built over the Water. On each Side were small wooden Cribs as dressing Rooms. You take Possession of one of these, and you find two towels 2 Buckets of fresh water Glass and Comb, Key in door. Here you divest yourself of your clothes and rig yourself out in the bathing dress. In a few minutes I could hear them jumping into the water and on me trying my bathing dress on I found it too small. It was the largest to be got in the Establishment. By great effort I managed to button it in front and off I scampered along the long Verandah and I had not gone many yards before the Dress in front gave way and below in the water were Dozens of Ladies and Gentlemen bathing. Nothing for it but go ahead and down the steps head first into the water about 4 feet deep. Bang I went to the bottom and I had a great struggle to get perpendicular. I could not understand it. My Position was anything but pleasant. After a great struggle I got upright and after seeing others in the same Predicament I found it was the water being so much pregnated with Salt it was impossible to sink. It made your eyes smart as much as eye wash does and the taste was as bad as Epsom Salts. We all knocked about for some time. When many had left the water I did not know how to manage my dress being in such an open State. At last my friend the Boss came along towards the steps with two ladies. I beckoned to him and he came over and on my explaining the state of my bathing dress, he said off you go up steps and if any one looks it is not your fault and up I went and as fast as possible got into my dressing room and right glad I was. After using the two buckets of fresh water I dressed and got out on to a floating Hotel at the end of the Pier watching others bathing.

About 3 o.c. a fine dinner was ready for all hands and after these refreshments was finished some went boating and others adjourned to a room and a short enjoyable Concert for about one hour was indulged in—some of the Ladies sang very well, one Lady taking the Piano. A game was got up amongst them a Kind of hide & seek. In a few minutes a young lady found the button that was being looked for on a young gent and [as] if prepared for the occasion she drew forth a needle and thread and sewed the button on the young man's coat amidst great Laughter. I understood this was the finishing of the game and it was supposed these two were to be engaged to be married.

About 5 o.c. we all assembled at the Station and the train was ready for the return Journey and by a little after six we were all in Salt Lake City again. After passing one of the most enjoyable days I ever had not forgetting the bathing dress episode the Boss invited us to pass the Evening with them. This we could not do as we intended returning to Ogden by the 8 p.m. train so as to start on our Journey in the morning by the 9.30 train. On leaving San Francisco we did not know that a train went from Ogden to Salt Lake City and continued on to Denver. If so we could have booked for Salt Lake City instead of Ogden and saved about two Pounds. This line had been only opened since May about 2 months since called the Rio Grande trunk line.

At last we left our bathing Friends and they were a jolly lot. Cleared out of the City of the Mormons and returned to Ogden. Here Chinamen were the washer women, and very well they get up linen. Sunday morning 15th July all aboard the train another Six Dollars for sleeping car to Denver. . .[1]

Tuesday, July 24th. Today I embarked on board the Queen Liner *Alaska*, the largest Ship I had seen being 5500 Tons, much larger than the *Great Britain*. About 9 o.c. got clear of the Dock at a very slow cautious manner. When out in mid stream we went ahead. It was a pretty sight to pass along such large extensive rows of various Shipping and fine Buildings in the distance. I believe we had fully 800 Passengers on board, a large number in the Steerage and intermediate. I was told a large number of the Steerage Passengers were returning to Ireland and have been helped to do so by the American Government. Amongst the Saloon Passengers was the celebrated Mrs Langtry 'the Jersey Lily'.[2] We had not proceeded far before I had the opportunity of having a good look at the celebrated pretty Woman. I certainly say she is a good fine Specimen of a Woman but have seen Prettier. She had a good figure and the many opportunities I had of seeing this beauty the next six days, I certainly say she is something above the average of pretty females but there is many in the Australian Colonies, New Zealand and Tasmania I have seen prettier and better figure. I consider the nose spoils the face. Each day both morning and during the afternoon she would promenade the deck always in Company with a Gent, very often the Purser of the Ship a jolly short stout man. She appeared to be fond of men's company. A little woman was her lady companion. This Person wore specs.

The first 30 miles from New York a Steam Yacht kept us Company with a Gentleman on board named Gilbard I believe. This Gent I heard was the owner of the Yacht and had been following Mrs Langtry about America. Several times this Yacht

[1] Several pages describing his train journey across the USA to New York have been deleted here.
[2] The famous actress and beauty, formerly mistress of Edward VII.

would come very near to the *Alaska* give a jolly cheer and hold up bottles of champagne and Mrs Langtry would wave her handkerchief but otherwise she took very little notice, and appeared pleased when the Yacht dropped astern. The first two or three days any time Mrs Langtry promenaded the deck scores of steerage and intermediate Passengers would come amidships and stand and look at Mrs Langtry. This occurred so often that the Captain ordered Ropes to be put across the deck to keep the Passengers away.

We were ploughing along at the rate of 17 Knots per hour. I believe the *Alaska* has up to the Present performed the quickest Passage on record between New York and Liverpool or Queenstown, in six days and 16 hours 20 minutes, and if we continue at the rate we are going we shall not be far behind that time. I understand Mrs Langtry cleared £25,000 by her American trip and advanced on mortgaged Property [£]16,000 in New York City. She intends returning to America in October next with a fresh company. She expects her Father & Mother to meet her at Liverpool. She is [in] no way stuck up like some beauties I have seen but talks freely with Saloon Passengers. I hear she intends visiting Paris to get a few frocks. My Friend Detective Julian was a Saloon Passenger on board on his way to Paris after another absconder. We became rather intimate and often conversed about various Matters. On my asking him if he had received the 10,000 Dollars for Kerr's apprehension he said no but he expected it would be ready for him on his return to New York. It appears Part of these rewards, a certain amount goes to a fund to make provision for use in their old age. The Saloon of the *Alaska* can accommodate 300 at dinner, this will give some idea of the extent of this ship. 120 would fill the *City of Sydney* Saloon and she is a ship of 3500 Tons. The *Alaska* appears large enough to receive two Vessels like the *City of Sydney*. The table was liberally provided and accommodation was very good. The smoking Room was large with a refreshment Bar in it but the gambling carried on was terrific. I believe many travel back and forward for gambling Purposes only. During this short trip it was carried on very extensively and a large amount of money must have been won and lost. On several occasions the Stakes were rather high. Sometimes you could not get into the smoking Room it being so crowded with Gamblers playing different Games and all for money. On July 28 a Grand Concert was performed during the Evening. The Singing was first Class, Mrs Langtry giving Recitation in the Yorkshire Dialogue [i.e. dialect] which she rendered in first class style. We were crossing the Banks of Newfoundland, a great Place for fishing I believe.

On July 31 arrived at Queenstown Ireland. Landed Mails sent Telegram to Leicester to let my Parents know I should be in Leicester next day if all went well. The *Alaska* made the trip from New York to Queenstown in 6 days 20 hours 21 minutes. The trip along the coast of Ireland is very nice the various landscapes on your left and as you proceed towards Liverpool lots of Ships appear in sight some going and others coming from Liverpool. As we worked towards Liverpool being very dark the Light on various Points on the Welsh Coast and Holyhead looked very pretty. Several light ships showing the Channel looked very nice. About 2 o'clock a.m. we came to anchor to wait the flow of the tide the entrance to Liverpool being too shallow for the *Alaska*. As daylight appeared the water rose and about 8 o'clock we were inside the entrance to the River Mersey and a Steam Tender came alongside and took all Saloon Passengers and their Luggage off and landed us in front of the Custom house. Here I was after an absence of nearly 36 years on about the very spot I went on board a Ship in the Year 1847 and never set foot on England since. When I left Birkenhead docks were being excavated and Birkenhead Park was a Brickfield. I certainly thanked God that he had landed me safe in England. Many a time I often thought I should never see England again. In 1856 I paid Part of my Passage Money to go home in the *Ocean Chief* but the Victorian Gold fields had too much attraction for me and I bought an Hotel on the Simpson Ranges (Maryborough) and forfeited my £25 deposited as Part of myself and Wife's Passage money.

On landing we had to Wait for the Custom House officers so I took a walk about a Portion of Liverpool. How greatly altered everything about the docks appeared. There was the old Church with four Clock faces on its Exchange Square and Nelson Monument the same as I seen it 40 years before, but by going towards St Georges Hall vast improvements were perceptible, wonderful and costly Buildings. The Colonials would find something to look at by coming to Liverpool. What a difference. I felt enchanted but had to return to the Quay and get my things through the Customs and depart on my way to Leicester. About 11 o'clock I succeeded to get my Portmanteau through the Customs. I had a box of 100 cigars in my Portmanteau. I forgot to take any out and directly I seen them I opened the lid and took a handful out and put them into my Pocket and offered the officer some. I smiled and passed on. Mrs Langtry had fully three Tons of Cargo with her and none of them were taken to the Custom house. The largest cases I had seen with anyone travelling to call it Luggage. Some of them measured nearly a Ton of 40 feet.

On board the *Alaska* I got acquainted with a Gent from one of the Southern States of America. He was an Orange Farmer, and he told me he done very well at that business. He was on a Visit to England after many years absence. He was a very good companion. At 12.15 I took Train for Leicester, and from the Liverpool Station for about 5 Miles it was a Succession of short Tunnels but as we rattled along in the open Country it was delightful the appearance of the Fields Woods Villages rivers and small streams, the beautiful green of the foliage and Meadows was enchanting. In all my 36 years rambles I had not seen anything to compare to this delightful scenery on this 1st day of August 1883 passing through that Portion of Derbyshire, Nottinghamshire and Leicestershire. I believe there is nothing to surpass it in England.

At last I arrived at Leicester Railway Station. I hardly knew myself. I was rather bewildered and was not many yards from the Railway Carriage before I was accosted by a Stranger. 'I beg your Pardon Sir but are you Mr Bodell?' I stood and looked at the individual and said that is my name. He made himself known to me as my Brother-in-Law the Husband of my Sister Ellen. This Sister was not born when I left Home. However my Brother-in-Law Fredrick Mann soon proved himself a jolly companion. We [took a] Cab at once and proceeded to my eldest Sister's house. I did not care to go straight to my Parents' Residence as I considered it might be too much for them they being so old. We soon arrived at Sister Elizabeth's and I could tell her at once. I could hear her say as I was alighting from the Cab, 'I am sure that's him.' Meeting over I was introduced to her Husband and Family. I became very fond of her Husband and of course every Member of the Family also.

In a few minutes we started to my Parents' Dwelling and here there was a fine embracing Tears etc. Suffice it to say during that day I had many pleasant Meetings with my fine Sisters their Husbands and Families and I am glad to say they were in very fair circumstances. My Mother was hale and hearty for her age, but my poor Father a few years before had partly lost the use of his right Side. The right arm hung helpless by his side. He could just manage with help of Mother to get from one room to the other. When I left home in 1847 he was as hale and as hearty a man as was in Leicester. My eldest and only Brother had been dead about two years and I ascertained his Wife and Family were living in Lancashire. My eldest Sister's eldest Son was living in Lancashire also, he having charge of a Church at Over Darwen. This was the Rev[r] Harry Bodell Smith['s] first charge since he left College.

My first few days in Leicester was occupied by visiting and being visited by my sisters their Husbands and Families and other family friends. On the third day after arrival I was off to London to see George Vesey Stewart[3] who had come to England to float a Railway and also to send Farmers and others out to Tauranga, Bay of Plenty New Zealand he having been successful in forming three Settlements of Farmers before in the Tauranga District. I found him up to his eyes in business about Railway matters and making contracts to charter a large ship to take Settlers out to New Zealand. He was very glad to see me and said I should make a good Representative for the Bay of Plenty New Zealand being a good specimen to represent any country. I soon had a specimen of this. Two Parties called on him about going out to New Zealand, when I was introduced as the Specimen. When they had departed I told him I should certainly object to be exhibited in that style. We waited on one of the large Firms in Fenchurch Avenue. G. V. Stewart introduced me to Anderson and Anderson Railway matters. One of these Gentlemen had visited the Bay of Plenty and Tauranga in particular and he praised the Place very much in a letter that was shown us. He was still on his travels. The interview was very satisfactory. On this occasion the extension of the Tauranga Rotorua and East Coast Railway to the Town of Opotiki in Bay of Plenty was the principal Topic and was received very favourably and as I write these lines the company formed to make the Railway from Tauranga to Rotorua have increased the capital of the Company from £250,000 to £420,000 to extend the Railway to Opotiki if the New Zealand Government will deal liberally with them under the

---

[3] G. V. Stewart established several New Zealand settlements, including that at Katikati. The settlers were recruited through the Orange Lodges in Northern Ireland.

Railway Construction Act. The principal members of this Firm
were very courteous and invited us to call on them again, that
during my Stay in England they would always be glad to see me and
to give them a call as often as I could.

I returned to Leicester. On Bank Holiday I took 28 members of
my Family including my Parents, accompanied by a Photographer
to Bradgate Park. This is the ancient spot where Lady Jane Grey
was born, to have a Photo taken of all in one Group. The Drive to
Bradgate Park is one of the most delightful in all Leicestershire.
The last time I was here was in 1844. The old ruins of the ancient
castle was very much reduced since my former Visit. By the kind
Permission of the Park Keeper we were allowed to enter the
Chapel. Here is a monument of the Count & Countess [in fact the
Duke and Duchess] of Suffolk the parents of Lady Jane Grey.
Interior of this Chapel is very damp. We also visited Old John.
This Place was a former Keeper's Lodge or Place, standing on a
high hill as a look out Place in former years. Deer and Stags are
very numerous in the Park. In fact all kinds of Game are plentiful.
We visited the Keeper's and Servant's dwelling Place. Here was a
fine buck Stag with large Antlers just been killed. We had a very
enjoyable Picnic on the Grass. Several schools were here enjoying
themselves and we had a most enjoyable dance on the Green. We
returned to Leicester through Anstey and Grooby, arriving about
8 p.m. after passing a very enjoyable day. The Group was photo-
graphed very well. The following Monday I took my five Sisters to
Bradgate Park and went to Swithland Wood and collected some
nuts. On this occasion I purchased the antlers of the Stag and got
them mounted and have them hung in the entrance Hall to Belle
Vue House Tauranga. They look very nice. After enjoying
ourselves very much returned to Leicester. In a day or two I was off
to London in company with my Brother-in-Law Mr James Smith. I
was determined to see some of those ancient Buildings I had read so
much about. The first place we visited was the Tower of
London. . .[4]

I came to the conclusion to see the Sights of London and do it
Justice would take three months. I returned to Leicester and I got

---

[4] Several pages which are largely copied from tourist brochures have been
deleted here.

large Posters issued in the principal Towns of Central Counties of England to induce and assist Mr G. V. Stewart to get Settlers of the farming class to go out in the fine Ship *Northumberland* to sail for Auckland and Tauranga in November 1883. In a day or two I was off to Liverpool to find out and visit a Cousin, a young Girl when I left Home, of 18 years. After some difficulty I found her but very much altered. There she was an old woman with Specs on very stout, and looking much older than her age with a Family of Sons and daughters some of them married with families. My companion on these trips was my Brother-in-Law Mr James Smith of Leicester my eldest Sister's Husband. After leaving Liverpool we went by train to Over Darwen to visit Mr Smith's eldest Son, Rev Harry Bodell Smith and his good Wife. We found them very comfortable living in a fine House and my Nephew was the pastor of a nice little Church, his first Charge in that line. We also visited my Brother's Widow and Family at Great Harwood and one of her sons with five children of a Family at Langho. He was an Engineer. This was her second son, the eldest son was Engineer at Great Harwood. They appeared to be getting along very well. On my entering the House the two Girls after a little while commenced to cry. They said as I represented their lost Father. On Sunday attended Nephew Harry's Church. I was very pleased with his Sermon. He is blessed with a good dear Creature for a Wife. They made us very comfortable. On the Monday we visited several Factories, a Wall Paper making factory. This was not at work unfortunately. Stopped for a few days. Another Paper Factory was at full swing. Here we seen the Process from the coarse material of old dirty Rags and Grass to a Sheet of fine white Paper for the London Standard. We also visited a Calico making Factory. Here were 400 Looms in full work in one room, the operatives principally Girls and Women. Every Manufacturing Town I visited the operatives were principally Females and I was told they can earn more money per week than men in these Factories. It is a grand Sight every day at the dinner time to see the tens of thousands of these operatives principally Females turn out for Dinner.

On Monday we with Harry his Wife and Servant took train for Manchester. On arriving at this City (not been here since 1846) I noticed vast improvements. We took tram to Gorton and arrived at Beech House, the Residence of Harry's Wife's Parents, M^r & Mrs Woodhouse, and the various members of the Family gave us a hearty Welcome and made us very comfortable. In the Evening we visited the celebrated Belle Vue Gardens, showery weather. The Gardens are the best in England for Sights and Amusements. On this occasion there was a Band Competition. I heard there was 20 different Bands competing. The various Birds, monkeys and Wild Animals were worth seeing and to finish up a representation of the Battle of Tel el Kebir and the fireworks was very grand. One time about one hundred Couples were dancing in the open and the Steam Boats on the lake were well patronized. I should estimate the numbers in attendance were fully 30,000. About 10 p.m. we returned to Gorton.

Next morning went to Manchester and went through that magnificent Building the Grand Town Hall. We were showed round the vast Building by a man in Livery. During our Visit the Chimes connected with the Clock played very nicely. In the afternoon myself and Mr Smith Father of Harry returned to Leicester. Mr & Mrs Woodhouse pressed us very much to make our Stay longer, but I was compelled to make our Stay in Manchester brief on account of other business. A delightful country to travel between Manchester & Leicester.

In a few days off to London to visit G. V. Stewart re Railway and other Matters. Here I found that the Valuation per acre of the Land the company were to get for making the Railway in New Zealand had been telegraphed from New Zealand. The Valuation was satisfactory and all matters concerning the Railway were going on very satisfactory. The Ship *Northumberland* by the energetic excursions of Mr Stewart was nearly a full ship. I executed several commissions and had the Goods shipped on board the SS *Triumph* bound to Auckland New Zealand. Have business at Weybridge. I proceeded there and the Person I interviewed, having a little leisure time we proceeded to Windsor and visited the Great Castle. . .

In a day or two I was off to Cheltenham via Hinckley, Coventry, Birmingham, Leamington. Here I called on Mrs Shaw and Family recently arrived from New Zealand, very comfortable. I then proceeded to Cheltenham on the invitation of Mr Joseph Shaw. Here I found him in possession of palatial Residence and large Grounds with Gardens Conservatories, orchards all denoting wealth. Here I remained two days and on my departure Mrs Shaw &

Daughter requested me in a very pressing manner to renew my
Visit before leaving for New Zealand. From this I proceeded to
London and as I heard the Orient SS *Liguria* was leaving for
Melbourne and Sydney on October the 19th I booked myself for a
Saloon Passage. These Steamers fill with Passengers very quick, so
I booked four weeks previous to sailing. I also called on G. V.
Stewart and Railway Matters were going on satisfactory.

I left for Leicester and on my return I found the Posters about
the Ship *Northumberland* which had been distributed in various
Towns were taking effect and several letters were waiting my
arrival. During the next week many more arrived all wishing to go
out to New Zealand and asking for information. I found this more
troublesome than I expected as my time in England was drawing to
a close and I have many Visits to make to various Parts of England I
directed applicants to correspond with G. V. Stewart Esqr 34
Leadenhall Street London E.C. who would attend to their require-
ments. We, two of my sisters and self returned to Manchester and
as usual no sooner than we got into the Vicinity of this cotton
Metropolis it was raining as usual. The remark in reference to
Manchester was the—Pot of England, always raining. Visited M^r
& Mrs Woodhouse at Beech House Gorton and visited Belle Vue
Gardens. In the Evening, went to Birmingham in company with
my Brother-in-Law Mr Smith and delivered a small Parcel brought
from New Zealand. Went out to Bradgate Park the Band playing. I
heard this Park was the gift of a young Lady. . . Early in October
went to Nottingham Goose fair. The Show fair in the Market Place
was the Largest I ever seen crowded. I visited Arnold 3 Miles from
Nottingham the place of my birth. All Places visited had improved
most wonderful and the conditions of the Working Classes had
improved in a wonderful manner, better housed better clothed and
had more money than in my day. Visited Nottingham Castle. This
Building has been restored and made into a Museum. A capital
Place to pass a few hours. Now I had to make my final arrangements to leave my Parents Sisters their Husbands and Families and
all Friends. I had passed a very pleasant time in Leicester. The Rev
Harry Bodell Smith with his amiable Wife had visited us and
Friends from Burton-on-Trent had been on a Visit. What with
attending Bicycling Racing for the Championship of England, Tea
Parties, Theatres, Visits to Bradgate Park, Mountsorrel, Quorn,
Cropston, Loughborough and other Places and not forgetting

Leicester Races, I had enjoyed my time very much. The Parting from my Relatives & Friends was more touching than the Meeting. I left Leicester on 18 Octr for Plymouth to catch the Magnificent Steamer SS *Liguria*. . .

By 4 p.m. on 12 December 1883 we arrived at Auckland wharf. Here I was after going around the world, carried fine weather from Start to finish, had eleven Weeks and five days in England, 15 days in America and only absent six Months to a day or so. I was thankful to the Almighty for landing me safe and sound. The only Vessel for Tauranga was the small Steamer *Argyle*. Several Passengers for the Lake district preferred to take the Waikato route and pay much more than go to Tauranga in such a small Steamer. Our regular trader the *Wellington* was laid up, having new Machinery and Boilers put into her. About 5.30 on the 13th we left for Tauranga and on our way we called into Mercury Bay and tarried this latter Place just to land a Parson to go on Shore to make several Couples one. About 10 o.c. a.m. on the 14th Decr we were going round Mount Maunganui. I remarked the little Steamer was too near the Mount. As we approached the beacon the tide being at ebb, the tide caught the Steamer Bow and drove us astern. If we had gone another 30 feet the *Argyle* would have been in the same Place as the *Taupo* was wrecked and through sheer Carelessness on behalf of the Captain. We stopped here some 20 Minutes before the Vessel got out of her difficulties and about 12 noon we were alongside Tauranga Town Wharf. On my appearance I received a cheer, and on landing I met my Wife and Family all well, and myself well, pleased with my trip and everything else. In fact it had been a wonderful trip. Captain Dearborn of the *City of Sydney* said he had an unusual fine trip to Frisco. I had a very pleasant trip across the Continent of America a pleasant time in England and a splendid fine Passage out.

Tauranga Again,
1883–92

When James Bodell returned to New Zealand he noted that Tauranga was experiencing an economic decline; in fact, New Zealand's long depression had arrived. But this brought no setback to his own fortunes; indeed, he thrived as never before, throwing himself into fresh enterprises with unflagging vigour. By now he was a leading merchant. His advertisements in the Bay of Plenty Times show that he was a real estate agent, buying and selling farms, and a general merchant, selling farming equipment, seeds and a wide range of goods. He had a cattleyard. He collected rents and debts. He was the agent for some Auckland lawyers. After his return he set up a sawmill in the Oropi bush, concentrating on milling mangeao, a timber in demand from the coach builders. He also opened up land on the edge of the bush for sale under the Government's Village Settlement Scheme. He was praised in the local newspaper as 'one of the most energetic settlers in Tauranga'.[1] Bodell also began to take an interest in coastal shipping, and acquired two small vessels. As a member of the Borough Council, in 1885 he was one of a deputation negotiating with the Government in Wellington for a subsidy towards the cost of dredging Tauranga Harbour. The citizens had raised £500 by subscription for this purpose.[2] These activities were of considerable importance to Tauranga. In those days, when the only roads were those in or near the main towns, communication between settlements was almost entirely by sea. There were by the late eighteen-sixties over a hundred ports in operation and there was great competition between them to attract trade. So far Tauranga had not been very successful as a port. One of its problems was that it was cut off from its interior by the almost impassable Kaimai range of mountains. In 1881 the Government closed Tauranga as a port of entry and withdrew the Collector of Customs, only to relent a year later, when ships carrying

---

[1] *Bay of Plenty Times*, 1 June 1887. There are several references to his sawmill.
[2] *Ibid.*, 28 May 1885.

new settlers arrived, but in 1887 it lost its status as a port again, and for the rest of the century. *James Bodell did not, however, despair. In 1891, when he finished his memoirs, and near his death, he forwarded a petition of citizens to the Union Steamship Company asking that it should make Tauranga a regular port of call.*[3] *It should be added, in conclusion, that nearly a century later Tauranga was to become a major port.*

Late in 1888 Bodell was elected unopposed as Mayor. In his reminiscences he does not refer to his service on the Council or his mayoralty, possibly because he was disillusioned with local politics, as indeed he was, but more likely because he had lost interest in his reminiscences. His comment on his later life is very sketchy. The minutes of the Borough Council and the local newspaper, however, give a fairly detailed picture of the work of the Council. In a small settlement, only fifteen years after the Hauhau campaigns, almost everything remained to be done. There were a series of committees, which indicate something of the scope of the work: notably Finance, Streets, Wharves, and Fire Brigade. The Council was always discussing fencing cuttings, widening tracks, the collection of 'night soil'. Various officials were appointed — an Inspector of Nuisances, and a Registrar of Dogs, for instance.

The Borough was heavily in debt, to the extent of some £3000. £1415 of this was inherited from the earlier Town Board, which had owed that sum to the Bank of New Zealand. The main event of Bodell's mayoralty was the raising of a £3000 loan with the help of the Government (in fact, the Auditor-General) to pay this off. The Council passed a vote of thanks to Bodell for his success in raising a loan to pay in full the liabilities which had been hampering the operations of the Borough.[4]

There was a good deal of petty faction-fighting. J. H. McCaw, the Town Clerk, was a friend of Bodell — they were called 'the McCaw faction' by a correspondent of the Bay of Plenty Times. Bodell came into some hot political fire over complaints by citizens that their names had been left off the Burghers' Roll. He was disappointed over his failure to secure a lease on the foreshore, an episode which he mentions. In 1889 Bodell said that he would not stand again. R. P. Galbraith, the proprietor of the local newspaper, announced his candidacy, and

---

[3] *Ibid.*, 6 March 1891.
[4] Tauranga Borough Council minute book, 1 July 1889. Bodell was Mayor-elect from 3 December 1888, and was installed on 19 December.

Bodell's friends prevailed on him to accept nomination.[5] *He was invited, as Mayor, to chair a meeting of ratepayers. He declined and his opponent took the chair. The Mayor and Council came into a great deal of criticism. Bodell's two step-sons, Peter and James, tried to answer his critics and an obstreperous priest defended him, but the meeting passed a vote of thanks to his opponent.*[6] *Bodell obviously lacked political skills: he was not a man to equivocate. He was beaten 60:46 — there were only 260 on the roll. He did not stand for office again, though he continued to be active in the town's affairs.*

Bodell died in September 1892 of 'serious apoplexy'. He was sixty-one. He died on his way to choir practice at Trinity Church. He left his property to his Wife (providing that she did not re-marry), to two step-children and to his sisters in England.

———

About 7 days after my return I had noticed business did not appear so brisk as when I left for England the previous June,[7] that one of my tenants had flown and another in his Place at 10/- per week less rent. Christmas 1883 came, very little festivities but glorious Weather. I invited my married son with his Wife and Child for Christmas Dinner. We dined all together. At mid night of the Old Year Church service as usual was held the old year out and new year in. I rather enjoy this service. The Church members have carried on this mid night Service for some years.

Early in 1884 I was consulted in reference to erecting a Saw Mill. One man had a new Steam Engine another owned the Land with plenty of good Mangeao Timber, large Rimu Trees also in plenty. After consultation I consented to erect a Jigger Saw for breaking down purposes and I commenced operation and in about 10 weeks had the Machine in working order, and we commenced operations. I was to be the Agent to sell the timber get orders etc., etc. In about one month I had a good few orders, but the sawn timber did not come down as I expected so I went up to ascertain the Cause and I

[5] *Bay of Plenty Times*, 18 November 1889, letter from 'Mrs Caesar'.
[6] *Bay of Plenty Times*, 25 November 1889, report of meeting.
[7] The 'long depression' lasted from late 1879 to 1895. It was at first worse in the South Island and spread to the Auckland Province two or three years later.

soon found out several other articles were required. Another expenditure of about £20 and then the timber commenced to be delivered on the Wharf for Shipment to fill orders on hand. I despatched a few small orders but I could not get sufficient for orders. Then the Bullock driver would not cart the Timber less than 2/6 per 100 super feet. This I gave, then the saws was not in going order and the Mill Manager was not able or understood the working of the Mill to keep the saw in good order. Now before I took any move to erect Sawing Plant the Manager told me and Corby the owner of the Engine that he could work a Saw Mill and had done so for years. Knowing that he had worked at the Saw Mills at Port Charles I certainly expected he was perfect[ly] able to take Charge of a Mill in Tauranga. There was always something and I could not get the sawn timber down to the Wharf to execute orders on hand. Things went on so unsatisfactorily at last I removed the Manager and engaged a thorough good man from Auckland, Wages to be £3 per week. This man did know his work and worked well for a week or two. The sawn timber came to the Wharf and orders were executed. Then something was wrong at the Mill. Went up several times. At last started again. In a short time no sawn timber came down. This Manager had a Wife and Family living in one of my cottages and bits of Furniture and other necessaries required soon brought a good round sum in my Books. I ascertained this man went to the half way House with native Women to drink about 10 miles away on the Rotorua Road and neglected his work. I had plenty of business to look after besides this. Then the Bullock driver was too busy to draw Logs out of the bush and cart the sawn timber to the Wharf. What with the Bullock driver being too busy and the Manager too lazy or drinking I was in a bad fix so I bought a team of Bullocks dray and yokes and commenced drawing logs. Things appeared improved and I delivered several orders. Then the Bullock driver was little good to drive bullocks in the bush removing logs, very good on a Road. Two mornings I caught the Bullock driver in the Hut at 11 o'clock a.m. had not harnessed the Bullocks the Manager telling me he had no logs. I was giving the driver 50/- per week a very good wage. I gave him the Sack and the Manager also. He owed me 30 Weeks' rent of Cottage and about £30 besides. Good Spec this. Put another Manager on Wages 9/6 per 100 feet super for each 100 feet. This man went to work with a good will and in 5 Weeks I paid him

£47.18.6. It was now Christmas 1886 and he went for his Holidays to his Wife and Family (Native) at Rotorua.

I must relate another speculation at this time. I bought a small steam Launch to carry 10 Passengers and 8 Tons of Cargo for the Maketu and Kati Kati Trade nothing but small sailing boats on this trade so we commenced Steam. This I carried on successfully for several years. The little Steamer paid very well.

In 1887 in January my Mill Manager came to me after his Christmas Holidays and I heard he lost all his money the third day, got drunk and was robbed, sold his little Home for £20 and drank that also. So he came to me hard up his wife and Family living on her Friends. I let him go to work gave him about £3 worth of Provisions. He worked at the Mill about 3 Weeks when not having sawn timber come down I went up to the Mill and found no one there. It appeared a contract for 2 Bridges had been let by Government and my Manager had took the Contract to hand saw the Timber. These Bridges were about 15 miles from the Mill. This man had taken my 2 timber Jacks and cooking Utensils from the Mill and I wrote to him if he did not send them back I would give him in charge. Back come my things. The 3 Weeks he had worked at the Mill he had been cutting timber for other People. I ascertained that he had received about £15 on my account and had cleared away with this money. I did not see him for 5 months when one day he passed my store and I stuck him up and asked for my money, when he said it is not yours till you get it. Here was an Answer. I immediately went and got a Summons for him, the Case was heard and I got a Verdict but the man had nothing and so it remains.

During this time I bought Mr Corby's Engine and all the interest of Mr C. Kensington. At last all the Mill Plant became my Property with a lease of the bush. During this time the Great Eruption of June 10th 1886 took Place.[8] This changed the aspect of everything. Business got bad. I bought another 30 ton Steamer expecting our Railway to Rotorua to be made but it was all smoke. Unfortunately the Steamer could not get sufficient Work. A fine little Steamer carry[ing] 50 Passengers and 30 Tons of Cargo. In the month of Augt I earned £70 with this steamer. The little one was working

[8] The eruption of Mt Tarawera. Bodell quotes a long newspaper report, which has been deleted.

away. At last she had a leak and I had her put on the stocks and while there a storm arose and swamped her off the blocks and broke her back. This cost about £42 to repair. Here I was with two Steamers and not sufficient work for them. The Steamer *Waitoa* was a nice little Steamer, go loaded in 3 feet of Water, had twin Screws. In fact a nice handy little Steamer. She cost about £1000. The Eruption destroyed all chance of any work for her, so the following Novr I sold her in Auckland at £500 loss. If I had her now she would pay well. Another small steamer is doing the work.

Referring to the Eruption. On the Morning of 10 June 1886 about 3 a.m. my bed was rocking like a cradle. One heavy roll nearly rolled me out of Bed so I jumped up and dressed, lit the fire and put the Kettle on then went on to the Verandah to have a look at the Weather. All was jet black. In a few seconds Balls of fire went up in the Air, a rumbling noise like heavy Artillery at a distance. The quakes repeating and the fire shooting up and the dismal darkness, it was something awful. I did not know what to think of it. I could see the fire was in the direction of Rotorua and hot Lake Country. I thought it might be Mount Tongariro at Lake Taupo in Eruption. It being near Midwinter day light was late. 8 o'clock came, 9 o'clock very little daylight and the brown Ashes falling very fast. About 9.30 I went down to the Store and then to the Telegraph Office. A wire came, Part of Rotorua disappeared send relief Women and Children on Tauranga Road in night dresses no boots no shoes on. Here was bad news. We got all Coaches and Buggies we could put Provisions and clothing in them ready to start, when about 11.30 a.m. a Wire came to the Magistrate. We are are all right don't send relief. What did this mean. This was good news but could not understand. Then we ascertained that the Telegraph wires were not workable between here and Rotorua, all messages had to go via Auckland.

Then word came that Mount Tarawera had busted up and destroyed all Buildings and many lives at the Wairoa. An English Tourist had been killed named Mr Bainbridge, that Mr Haggard the School Master was killed and other members of his Family. Several Maori Villages had been smothered. In fact Consternation everywhere. About 4 p.m. 3 Women and several children walked into Tauranga, had come all the way from Rotorua 42 miles. These we housed and fed. At intervals rumours was circulated. However it turned out bad enough. We in Tauranga only got scared with plenty dust all over Buildings. We had to carry Lanterns up to about 12 o'clock noon.

Down the Coast the dust had dropped pretty thick covered up all feed. At the Neigh Farm it covered everything. This is near 9 Miles from Rotorua. All down Coast no feed for the Cattle and horses. The SS *Wellington* was chartered to come from Auckland to take all Tauranga People to Auckland. We expected the whole District to be engulfed. This Steamer did come but was not required. Next day several Messengers came in from Rotorua and reported all well at Rotorua. The Lake Rotorua had received a large quantity of Debris from Mount Tarawera and the water had risen considerably. Mr J. McRae of the Wairoa Hotel with all his Family and servants had left the Wairoa Hotel to its fate. The Te Ketapu bush on the way to the Wairoa had been crushed down and destroyed, one of the finest bushes in the district. The Eruption had caused Consternation all over the District. The White and Pink Terraces of Lake Rotomahana were all destroyed and all the grand Sights about Lake Rotomahana. It had done the District a great Injury. Two native Villages on Lake Tarawera was completely buried. A European was in one Village and all were smothered, 18 feet of debris over them. For weeks after some one would turn up. At the Wairoa 6 days after the Eruption a old Maori Chief worked his way out of his Whare or house. His house had been smothered several feet thick and he worked himself out.

About a fortnight after the Eruption I myself visited Te Wairoa and such a fearful alteration. The old church was demolished, the School House, the Teacher's Residence, the Residence of Captain Way were all destroyed and the orchard was levelled down. Opposite was the Te Wairoa Hotel. This was partly demolished. The roof was broken in with the heavy weight of Mullock. Parlour Furniture, Bedroom furniture, all barrels and Glasses were there. Bedclothing the family linen and clothing also the Servants' clothing all mixed up together. Thorough destruction. The part of Balcony that fell and killed Mr Bainbridge a Yorkshire man was there. The Bridge on the Road was filled up to the Rail with Mullock. I believe M^r McRae lost fully £2000. It nearly ruined him. I have known the said Mr Joseph McRae for many years and he was a very hard working industrious man. When he first settled at Te Wairoa he opened a Store and baked Bread. He used to be storekeeper and do the baking as well. After he commenced to sell

Grog, and as he was commencing to get paid for his years of Toil, this Eruption took place and ruined him. I am glad to say at present he is in a fair way to put a little money together he having both the Palace and Lake House Hotels at Rotorua.

This Eruption has altered the whole District. Now in place of thousands of Tourists there is only a few comes for the wonderful Baths and it destroyed any chance we may have had to get our Railway. By 1888 Rents in Tauranga had gone down 100 per cent. Shops that I rented at 30/- per week at present I only get 5/- per week. Dwelling Houses are not lettable. What I formerly got 12/- per week [for] I am glad to get 2/- & 3/- per week. Again Mortgaged Property is not worth above one half that has been advanced on it. It is awful how everything, Business, Property and Tourists all have gone bad. Very few Ships come into this fine Harbour except the usual two Steamers per week. Land and Property is nearly valueless. A few years ago I sold Land about one chain from my store for £16 per foot, £400 for 25 feet frontage in Wharf Street, and now the same Land would not fetch £100. I consider my Property has reduced in Value £3000.

Now I must go back to the Saw Mill. This I worked on for about 4 years when on account of the dishonesty of the employees and that fine Timber Mangeao got scarce, I closed the Mill. I may state this Mangeao Timber is a fine close grained tough Timber and I supplied various Coach and Carriage Firms also the New Zealand Government. This Timber was the finest in New Zealand to build Railway Carriages, Buses, Tram Cars, all kind of carriages and fancy work. It is very thinly scattered through the Bush at Oropi about 12 miles from Tauranga, never over 30 inch diameter and often the tree would be not sound. The Rimu Timber is a red Pine good for building and Furniture but the carpenters don't like it so long as they can get Kauri Timber. Kauri Timber does not grow south of Tauranga, very little south of Auckland.

After the Mill had been closed a few months I conceived the Idea if I could get a Lease of about half acre of Land on the foreshore of the Harbour in the Town of Tauranga I would shift my Mill. I applied to the Borough Council for a 14 years Lease of this said piece of Land and the Lease was granted at £5 Per Annum rent. I put men on to remove the Engine and Plant to Tauranga and re-erected it on the foreshore. By having it on the foreshore I could have Mangeao delivered from all parts of the district by Water as well as by Road also get Kauri logs to cut up for building and other Purposes, but to my great Consternation rumours got about that a certain Lawyer (Mr Moss) was objecting to have the Mill on the foreshore as his Yacht was moored near the Site and the logs would damage his Yacht and so it turned out. The next Meeting of the Borough Council I received Notice that the Lease for the Land was cancelled because certain Parties objected.[9] This confounded me to think the Councillors could be so foolish as to listen to any one Party. I went and seen this Mr Moss and he told me there would be no Mill on that foreshore. I came away and was determined not to erect the Mill but sell it and I advertised it and after 18 months I sold it at a great loss, determined not to speculate any more. No wonder the Place is getting worse off when we have such numb-skulls as Councillors to prevent local industry. In a short time I should have paid £10 to £20 per week in Wages. What has made Places like Auckland and County Towns also but these industries? At the Towns north of Auckland and in the City of Auckland to this day there are Saw Mills employing hundreds of men and boys, but it was beneath Councillors of the Borough of Tauranga to have local industries. Some of these Councillors are at present suffering from such short sightedness, no wonder we in Tauranga are complaining of bad times when such old Fossils rule us. I had the Mill Plant removed to Tauranga and put into a small Paddock behind my Residence and built a Shed for the Engine. At last I sold the lot, at a great Loss.

All this time I was running the Steam Launch and it was paying fairly well. As business was not so brisk with the little Steamer I suggested that the Captain and Engineer's wages should be reduced to £11 per month each. This was the wages they had when they commenced with me, business turned out good and I volunteered and gave them £13 each Per Month. No they would not consent to the reduction so I gave them the Sack, went to Auckland and engaged Captain and Engineer to work on Shares. This suited me much better. We were getting along very well when I got Notice that the Steamer was not to go to Maketu, and outside Port. I got this notice on account of the late Captain going to the Customs

---

[9] The Council approved the lease on 1 July 1889. The Borough Solicitor, E. G. B. Moss, protested and the Council reversed its decision on 16 September. Bodell absented himself from this meeting.

house officer and complained that the Steam Launch *Result* was running to Maketu when she was not qualified. This Maketu trade was a great assistance towards making the Steamer pay. After this the Captain and Engineer got dissatisfied and they left. The Kati Kati Trade would not pay itself so I laid the Launch up and at last sold the steamer.

Here I was with nothing to look after but my business as a storekeeper. I bought a small Cutter and commenced to run her to Kati Kati, Maketu, Matau, Whangamata and Tairua Saw Mills. I got plenty of Trade for her. Things went on very well for some time when on one trip the Cutter was making a trip to Whangamata when she got into a heavy Gale and was driven ashore. The cargo was damaged about £20. I chartered another cutter and removed cargo and had it took to Whangamata. Then I found the bottom of the cutter was opened and had her removed to Tauranga. Had her repaired cost about £40. I ran her for some time when I sold her and took part cash and part Prom. Note. I left for England in April and on arrival in Sydney the first I noticed in the Papers was the Wreck of the Cutter outside Tauranga Harbour and the Crew of 2 drowned. I lost amount of the Prom. Note . . .[10]

I am of opinion 'The Reminiscences' I have wrote of my life from 1847 to 1891 if properly compiled and arranged should make a good sized Book. It is a strange life as I sit writing this beautiful morning in September, incidents that occurred 44 years ago, come as vividly to my mind as if they took place last month. I thank my God for all his mercies bestowed upon me when I recollect the time in China in 1850 and 1851 when my Comrades were dying by the scores around me and only 62 of us left out of the Regiment 630 strong that left the City of Cork 8th June 1849. I should thank the Great Almighty God for all his mercies.

James Bodell

25/9/91

---

[10] A newspaper account of the Tarawera eruption and some repetitive remarks on Tauranga have been deleted.